Firmly I Believe

Raymond Chapman is Emeritus Professor of English in the University of London and former Deputy Chairman of the Prayer Book Society. He is a non-stipendiary priest in the Diocese of Southwark and is the author of numerous literary and religious books, including *Leading Intercessions*, *Stations of the Nativity*, *Stations of the Resurrection* and *Godly and Righteous, Peevish and Perverse: Clergy and Religious in Literature and Letters*.

D0907299

CANTERBURY STUDIES IN SPIRITUAL THEOLOGY

Firmly I Believe

An Oxford Movement Reader

Raymond Chapman

CANTERBURY PRESS

Norwich

First published in 2006 by the Canterbury Press Norwich
(a publishing imprint of Hymns Ancient & Modern Limited,
a registered charity)
9–17 St Alban's Place, London N1 0NX

www.scm-canterburypress.co.uk

British Library Cataloguing in Publication data

A catalogue record for this book is available
from the British Library

ISBN 1-85311-722-6/978-1-85311-722-0

Typeset by Regent Typesetting
Printed and bound in Great Britain by
William Clowes Ltd, Beccles, Suffolk

Contents

Editorial Notes

The usage of authors in spelling and punctuation has been treated liberally rather than with absolute consistency. It has mostly been accepted, but changed wherever it was likely to cause difficulty or misunderstanding to the modern reader. The original use of capital letters within sentences, which may give a distinctive emphasis, has generally been retained.

The Oxford Movement writers often put the divine names, GOD, CHRIST, LORD, into full capitals as well as using capital letters for the divine pronouns. In this matter I have maintained the usage of the early editions; although it is not always consistent, it represents the reverent spirit which went into the work.

[ ] denotes editorial additions or comments within extracts.
[...] denotes editorial omissions from the original text.
⟨ ⟩ denotes expansion of initials or abbreviations in the text.

In the list of Sources, the date of first publication of a text is given in parentheses after the title, where it differs from that of the edition used. Extracts from well-known poems and novels that have appeared in many editions are usually referenced only by title and chapter or lines.

I

The Oxford Movement:
1833–45

The sermon which John Keble preached at the opening of the Oxford
Assize on 14 July 1833 stands to the Oxford Movement as the display
of Luther's theses does to the Reformation. It was not the cause of all
that was to follow, but it was the occasion, which focused many existing concerns. Years later, Newman wrote, 'I have ever considered
and kept the day as the start of the religious movement of 1833.'
Keble spoke for many in the Church of England who were troubled
by increasing Government control over Church affairs. The particular issue which Keble addressed was the proposed suppression of ten
bishoprics in Ireland, an action which seemed to him and to others an
attack on Church rights and a treatment of bishops as state officials,
not as men ordained in a succession going back to the Apostles and
holding their order within the Holy Catholic Church.

As Luther's protest was a focus of many preceding influences,
Keble's sermon said much that was already in people's minds. The
Church of England at that time was still entrenched, but was seriously embattled. Its long reign of Establishment, after the controversies
and divisions of the seventeenth century, was being challenged. In
1828, repeal of the Test and Corporation Acts freed Protestant dissenters from most of their civil disabilities, which in practice had not
been recently imposed. More threatening to most Anglicans was the
Act for the emancipation of Roman Catholics in 1829, more a political than a doctrinal concession, intended to assuage the growing discontent in Ireland. The Reform Act of 1832 produced a new House of
Commons, less reformed indeed than some had hoped, but certainly
in a mood for widespread change. No longer composed entirely of
men who gave at least official allegiance to the Church of England,
it turned attention to the privileged position of that Church. It was
an Evangelical Anglican who made the first formal proposals. Lord
Henley, brother-in law of Robert Peel, issued his *Plan of Church*

Reform, which among other things suggested radical changes in cathedral and collegiate establishments, and a Commission to manage church income and property. The Ecclesiastical Commission was in fact set up in 1835. In the summer of 1833 there was already enough to make the slogan 'Church in danger' heard on many sides.

Keble spoke of this sense of a crisis in church affairs as an urgent need to stop the erosion of its ecclesiastical status and restore its recognition as a divine society. Yet his words from the pulpit of the University Church might have disappeared into the sleepiness of Oxford in the Long Vacation had not four clergymen met ten days later at the rectory of Hadleigh in Suffolk. They were H. J. Rose, the Rector of Hadleigh; William Palmer, Fellow of Worcester College, Oxford, a leading liturgical scholar; Arthur Perceval, son of a peer, a royal chaplain and a former pupil of Keble's; and a young Fellow of Oriel College, once Keble's pupil and now his colleague.

This last, Richard Hurrell Froude, was a man of ebullient temper and personal charm, and impatient of the moderation of the others. While they honoured the Elizabethan and Caroline divines, Froude looked back before the Reformation to the undivided Catholic Church of the West. The current cult of medievalism showed him an age of faith and Christian living when the Church was greater than the State. In his search for continuing catholicity he was willing to deny assumptions that the others took for granted; he broadened the cause and also endangered it. He drove himself with manic recklessness and left a troublesome legacy after his death. Beneath the show of vigour he was a tormented character, and as he fought with himself, he fought with the outward enemy as well, rejoicing in the clash of battle between Church and State.

The four who met at Hadleigh considered forming an association to resist state encroachments of the kind which Keble's sermon had attacked. It came to nothing beyond an address to the Archbishop of Canterbury, which supported those principles with a number of clerical and lay signatures. Whatever encouragement it may have given to Archbishop Howley, this indication of loyalty did not suggest that anything new and exciting was afoot. What lay behind the Assize Sermon and the Hadleigh Conference found its full expression in a different way.

Oxford in 1833 was a reassuring place for loyal or timid members of the Church of England, embodying those powers and privileges towards which jealous eyes were turning at Westminster. Matriculation, graduation and fellowships were limited to Anglicans, or at least to those who would subscribe to the Articles of the Church of England.

Each college had its chapel at which a certain number of attendances were compulsory for undergraduates. The great moments of the academic year had religious orientation with their special formularies, bidding prayers or sermons. The less satisfactory side of the national Church was seen in the light pressure of these duties on the majority. Yet out of the conformism, the sinecures, the amassed revenues from old endowments, a new spirit was growing. There were Fellows to whom faith was true and serious.

Oriel College had led the way towards elected fellowships by examination. Keble was an Oriel Fellow, already a respected figure in Oxford at the time of the Assize Sermon. He had a brilliant academic record, and a national reputation as a religious poet with the publication of *The Christian Year* in 1827. Like Froude he was a High Churchman by upbringing, suspicious of the current liberal morality which could accept a show of religious duties to the neglect of those eternal values which should govern conduct. He was the product of a quiet country parsonage, his knowledge of England limited to Oxford and the rural south, a priest who had little patience with speculation and for whom doubt was sin. Yet he had gifts which were significant for the Movement: a deeply sacramental sense, and a sanctified Romanticism which found the presence of God in all material creation. He had experience of parish work and carried Tractarian ideas back into parish life when he married in 1835 and became a parish priest. His quality was recognized when he was elected Professor of Poetry in 1831. The Assize Sermon was the work of a man known to have strong views about the question of state power over the Church. He was out of Oxford when the Movement was at its height, but he had helped to start something which outran his expectations and even his desires.

For men like Keble, the rights and dignity of the Church were axioms to be defended rather than proved. For others, however, they were revelations, and it was they who took the Movement away from the old High Church tradition. Neither 'High' nor 'Low' in regard to churchmanship had the connotations of doctrine and practice which were later associated with them. And the Oxford Movement itself would help to change their popular meanings. A brief description may help to explain the background to the Movement, although the groupings were not so precise or clearly defined as it may suggest.

The High Church party included those whose main concern was the Tory resistance to Whig encroachments on ecclesiastical privileges but who were otherwise content with the Establishment. The more theologically minded of them held that their priesthood was

within the Apostolic Succession to which Newman appealed in the
first Tract. But a High doctrine of the Church as a divine society
rather than a department of state was held by Evangelicals and even
some Liberals.

To regard the Church as a part of the national system, a profession
within which both the privileges and the obligations of the national
law operated, was to take a 'Low' view. The generally conformist
view of the Church of England was Low; its opponents sometimes
called it Erastian. Belief that the Church should be subject to the
ordinances of the State went with a pragmatic general desire for law-
ful order and a distrust of sects. High Churchmen counted themselves
equally loyal citizens but were more inclined to stress the rights of the
Church as an abiding institution which the State had not created,
and to look with some favour on the example of the non-jurors who
had been deprived for refusing the Oath of Allegiance to William III.
They found strength in the Caroline divines who had promulgated a
theory of the Church within which Anglicanism had an honourable
identity and had held their ministry as something more than a Crown
licence to preach.

High or Low, the clergy may have received some deference in their
parishes, but they were not well placed in public esteem. The wealth
and temporal assets of the higher dignitaries were contrasted with
the poverty not only of the lay working class but also of many parish
priests. The bishops were members of the House of Lords, where
their presence seemed to symbolize the radical view that clergy in
general were state hirelings, oppressive allies of the governing class.
The fact that all but two of them voted against the Reform Bill in
1832 was another black mark.

The Evangelical Movement, which had begun in the eighteenth
century, had a strong influence on some members of both the Church
of England and the nonconformist churches; its greatest leader, John
Wesley, had been lost to the Established Church and become the
founder of Methodism. The Evangelical emphasis was on personal
salvation by acceptance of Christ's saving power. After conviction of
sin there should be repentance, a humble acknowledgement of justification in Christ, followed by assurance of pardon and of perseverance
to final salvation. The encounter between Christ and the individual
soul could be mediated by no person or institution, though preaching
could open the heart to conversion. Sacraments were effective not for
the power inherent in them or in their minister but as tokens of what
Christ had done and commanded. This would be a point of division between the Movement and those Evangelicals who at first welcomed it.

The man who would lead and eventually leave the new movement had already experienced the Evangelical sense of conversion and assurance. John Henry Newman, elected to an Oriel Fellowship in 1821, had grown up not in a country parsonage but in a London family where business worries and failures were discussed more than theology. Oxford nourished his appetite for religious inquiry, and gave a home to a man who drove himself hard in the quest for absolute authority, and who would follow through a problem at whatever cost to himself or to others. In July 1833 Newman had just returned from a journey abroad, which had begun with Froude for the sake of the latter's health. What Newman saw in Italy confirmed his prejudice against Roman Catholicism but gave him an uneasy sense that there was more to this foreign Church than Englishmen generally supposed. While he was recovering from a serious illness, he became convinced that he had work to do at home. Keble's warnings and Froude's enthusiasm were a confirmation rather than a sudden epiphany. His early Evangelical years enabled him to understand the strongest force in English Protestantism. Whately, the Provost of Oriel, taught him the principles of logic and how to apply them to such matters as Church Establishment. Hawkins, the next Provost, guided his Evangelical individualism towards regard for tradition, handed on through the continuing Church and not dependent on subjective experience. In his private self, the darkness and tragedy in the life of faith were realities. His sermons and writings stressed the cost of believing and the probability that faithfulness would bring suffering. Through all his changes he never shed the sense of personal encounter, the self-examination that sometimes verged on introspection, the sense of numinous awe, the thirst for holiness. These were aspects of faith not peculiar to the Evangelical temper, but it was in Evangelical circles that they were most highly valued. Newman's gift was to take them from the realm of loose, unstructured piety and subject them to the discipline of a great intellect.

For a man who distrusted the comfortable way in religion, the easy association of Church and State was irksome. He opposed the complex political and religious attitudes known as Liberalism, disliked the assumption that all things were well and tending to become better. Many in the Church of England seemed arrogant in their reliance on individual interpretation of the Bible, and a minimal submission to ecclesiastical duties. A Church that put so much weight on the essential goodness of individuals and allowed them to find their own way to truth must be lacking in sanctity. Yet the Church of Rome seemed to crush the individual by a weight of organizational and doctrinal compulsions. To work through seemingly insoluble dilemmas was Newman's gift to the Church which he later joined, and his legacy to the Church which he left.

The Fellow elected to Oriel in the year after Newman was Edward Bouverie Pusey. He shared the High Church tradition in which Froude and Keble had grown up, but from a different background: not the country parsonage but a rich lay family with aristocratic connections. He had secular as well as religious reasons for disliking the political erosion of traditional privileges. Newman, admiring his goodness and devotion, at first distrusted him as an opponent of the Evangelical party. Pusey was one of the outstanding scholars in Oxford, the Professor of Hebrew. To learn more of that language, as yet little studied in England, he had travelled to Germany, where the new biblical criticism had excited rather than dismayed him. He was destined to become the leader of the Oxford Movement after Newman went; his name to become its name, revered or execrated. He would be suspended from preaching for putting forward doctrines deemed contrary to his Church; he would retract many of his views about German theology. All of which seemed in 1833 to be an unlikely future for the brilliant, shy, devout young don who played no part in the first months after Hadleigh.

Those months were active largely because Hurrell Froude did not have the temperament to wait for loyal addresses and associations. He wanted to do something at once, and in a way that would bring maximum publicity. The printed word was gaining more importance as literacy and leisure increased; book production became cheaper and more efficient; better communications carried books to all parts of the kingdom. The serious-minded in both secular and religious thought were seeking to win over the new army of readers. The Society for the Diffusion of Useful Knowledge was as zealous in disseminating secular learning as was the Religious Tract Society for the theological. Therefore, men like Froude concluded, why not use these resources to influence the minds of the learned as others tried to influence the minds of the poor? The Church of England could be aroused in these dangerous times by a series of tracts: let them be called *Tracts for the Times*.

The first of the Tracts, written by Newman, appeared in September 1833 under the title, *Thoughts on the Ministerial Commission, Respectfully Addressed to the Clergy*. It had only four pages, but with a concentrated intellectual power expressed in lucid prose that only Newman of the Anglican party could have written. He published it anonymously – 'I am but one of yourselves – a Presbyter' – and warned his fellow clergy of the dangers threatening the Church. He told them that they were in the Apostolic Succession, with sacerdotal power, derived from ordination by bishops in an unbroken line back to Apostolic times, not simply ministers commissioned to preach and perform other services within an established Church. In rousing the clergy to their perilous state, Newman was forcing them to look at the nature of their office and authority.

More tracts followed rapidly; Newman was joined in their production by Keble, Froude and his lay friend, John Bowden. The tracts were distributed to country incumbents who found themselves called to accept a status which some had never fully understood. Bishops were reminded that they had a power greater than any conferred by a legislative assembly. Pusey was persuaded to write the eighteenth Tract, on the practice of fasting. Not yet fully committed to the Movement, he insisted that it should be signed with his initials to distinguish it as an individual production. The departure from anonymity, combined with his immense learning and his reputation as a sound and pious man, gave the Tracts new status: from clever squibs they were becoming mines that would disturb the whole Church. Ancient questions of dogma and practice were brought out of the study and into the daily life of Anglicans. The writers were being called Tractarians, a name which spread from them to their supporters and their principles.

In Oxford the power of the Tracts was enhanced by the preaching of Newman as vicar of the University Church. Few talents are more fleeting, few more potent at the time, than those of the great preacher; but the evidence of both friends and enemies agrees on Newman's quality in the pulpit. Softly but with penetrating power, rapidly but with long pauses between his sentences, he made his listeners think about neglected truths. With his dogmatic appeals to the clergy and his pastoral power over undergraduates, Newman was now one of the most influential men in Oxford. But he did not convince all, even in his own college. Newman, Keble, Pusey and Froude were a formidable quartet; but the Liberalism which they challenged found some of its most intelligent expression in the Oriel Senior Common Room. Other Fellows who had applied their critical and logical minds to Church affairs came to be known as Noetics. They were loyal to their Church, but prepared to look at awkward challenges, to accept that questioning was not forbidden, to look critically at the Bible. An undergraduate who went to Keble with doubts about such things as the chronological inconsistencies of the Old Testament might be told that he was in danger of sin; if he went to one of the Noetics he was more likely to be soothed and told not to worry.

Similar views were held by Thomas Arnold, the headmaster of Rugby, to whose place at Oriel Newman had succeeded. His ecumenical outlook and his broad theological views made him unsympathetic to the Tractarians. In 1836 he openly attacked them in an article headed 'The Oxford Malignants', expressing the fears of those who thought that the Tracts were going beyond Anglican loyalty. The occasion for his article was the affair of the new Regius Professor of Divinity, Richard Hampden, whose Bampton Lectures in 1832 had been critical of Church traditions. They aroused little comment at the time, but now the Tractarians felt strong enough to oppose his appointment. It was an ill-timed move, with the suspicion of personal motives since Hawkins had sent pupils to Hampden after a quarrel with Newman about the functions of a tutor. The Regius Chair was a Crown appointment, not vulnerable to attack from within Oxford, but an underhand blow could be struck by depriving the Professor of his voice in the selection of University preachers. A motion to this effect was introduced to a Convocation packed with supporters of both sides and failed when the proctors gave their seldom-used veto. It was reintroduced successfully under new proctors a month or two later.

While Liberals opposed the Tracts, Evangelicals were at first more sympathetic. The sense of a supernatural order, threatened by laws passed by men who might have no Christian conviction, was equally dear to them. The early Tracts contained little to upset them, until there came increasing emphasis on the sacerdotal priesthood and on the sacraments as means of salvation rather than continuing obedience to the individual conversion experience. The Tracts were becoming longer, more detailed, and more insistent on particular beliefs. Pusey's three tracts on baptism made a whole treatise, adducing views, which set him squarely within the new movement and against the tenets of popular Protestantism. The series which had started in defence of a threatened Church was now making claims for the power of that Church which not all her members could accept. A new periodical, the *British Magazine*, was publishing Tractarian ideas to an even larger circle of readers. The *British Critic*, founded in 1793, became an important organ under Newman's editorship from 1838 to 1841.

Opponents began to accuse the Tractarians of Romeward leanings. Their strict orthodoxy, their sacramentalism, their apostolical view of the priesthood, all seemed manifestations of what English Protestants had been taught to fear. The men of the Oxford Movement, in that generation and in the next, suffered from the common fear of

Rome. Although Nicholas Wiseman, later the head of the restored Roman hierarchy, had spoken against them, some saw the Tractarians not as reformers of the Church from within but as dangerous separatists who would drive people to Rome, or spread popish ideas within the English fold. Newman still saw himself as defending his Church against the corruptions of Rome as much as against the onslaughts of Liberalism. In 1837 he wrote 'Romanism and Popular Protestantism' asking for more care and scruple in controversy, and in the same year he opened the appeal to antiquity which was to lead him and others into unexpected paths. With Pusey and Keble he began the *Library of the Fathers,* editions of patristic writings, products of an undivided Church to support claims to catholicity that did not depend on acknowledging the Bishop of Rome as Universal Pontiff. But although many Anglican divines had respected patristic thought, others held that the Fathers were popish and that pre-Reformation theology was inconsistent with sound Protestant doctrine.

Then a reverent attempt to honour a friend's memory brought more condemnation than anything they had yet published. Hurrell Froude died in 1836, worn out by the controversy which he had loved but which had been too much for his diseased lungs and weakened frame. His papers were entrusted to Newman and Keble for publication. The appearance in 1838 of *The Remains of the Late Reverend Richard Hurrell Froude* brought a violent reaction. In Froude's letters and journals many things of which the Tractarians were already suspected were set out in print: the inordinate scruples, the practice of mortification, and the hints of secret temptations. Even more damaging were letters which contained remarks like, 'I am becoming less and less a son of the Reformation' or 'the Reformation was a limb badly set; it must be broken again to be righted'. Such sentiments from a clergyman of the Established Church, doubly committed by his order and his Fellowship, seemed unacceptable, and although in their preface Newman and Keble emphasized Froude's Anglican loyalty, his own words seemed to make them liars as well as traitors. Those who had known him, and could recall his laughing tone in the outrageous epigrams, had sadly misjudged.

The opponents of the Movement in Oxford itself thought that the time for a test of loyalty had come. A public demonstration of support for Reformation principles would compel the leaders either to recant or to stand revealed as enemies to their own Church. When a proposal was made for a memorial to the Marian martyrs who had suffered in Oxford, Newman, Keble and Pusey refused to subscribe. The Martyrs' Memorial was erected, ironically in the neo-Gothic style that was popular in current Catholic architecture, and there it remains today in token not of one religious controversy but of two.

The Tractarians lost some supporters but gained others. Newman was now the unquestioned leader of a movement which was no longer a purely Oxford affair as the Tracts reached lay as well as clerical readers across the country. Even the august pages of *The Times*, hostile to all things savouring of Romanism, tended to be friendly – admittedly influenced by the fact that the editor's brother was a Tractarian sympathizer. Keble had returned to life as a parish priest and there were many less famous but equally dedicated men who had gone down from Oxford with a new sense of pastoral duties, to become parish clergy or private tutors, spreading the opinions, which they had come to admire.

The Movement which had started as an extension of the High doctrine of the rightful claims of the Church against the State had raised deeper questions of ecclesiology. When Anglicans made the credal assent to a Catholic and Apostolic Church, the Tracts told them that they were claiming membership of a Church going back to the Apostles, from whom power to celebrate valid sacraments had been passed in unbroken line to the modern clergy. The English parson celebrated Holy Communion not as a memorial only but as bringing the Real Presence to those who knelt to receive. It was this confidence, more precious than incomes and endowments, which made Parliamentary control seem sacrilegious. The Tractarians urged the laity to recognize that true authority lay not in Parliament but in the episcopate, and that their duty was not solely to go to church to join in the psalms and responses and listen to the sermon: Holy Communion was the most important service and private confession, permitted and indeed enjoined by the Prayer Book for unquiet consciences or in sickness, could be used more widely.

Some of the new disciples did little to alleviate fears. Their loyalty to the Church of England was less firmly rooted than that of the first Tractarians, their suspicion of Rome was less strong, and they did not share the scholarly reticence of their elders. The most forceful among them was W. G. Ward; young, lively, eager to be liked, equally ready to shock, he was in some ways a successor to Hurrell Froude, seeking like him for the home of true catholicity as proved by marks of holiness. He had been a follower of Arnold until Froude's *Remains* led him into the new movement, with the convert's zeal that he later brought to the Roman Church. His quest was taking him away from parallels with the undivided patristic Church and closer to the modern Roman Catholics.

Meanwhile Newman was facing his own problems. His studies of patristic theology aroused the uncomfortable idea that the Anglican Church might be in the position of the early heretics against whom Rome had maintained the orthodox truth. An article by Wiseman openly comparing the Anglicans to the Donatists quoted St Augustine, '*Securus judicat orbis terrarum*' [the judgement of the world is assured]. 'By those great words of the ancient Father', Newman wrote years later, 'the theory of the *Via Media* was absolutely pulverized.' Struggling with his inner doubts and his outward opponents, he began to withdraw from the centre of controversy. His charge of St Mary's gave him also the small parish of Littlemore, where he had built a new church in 1836, and he retired there in the hope of finding peace to work out his true position.

He had 'received three blows which broke me . . . from the end of 1841, I was on my death bed as regards my membership with the Anglican Church'. One blow came from his study of the Arian controversy, which suggested to him that the Arians were like the more extreme Protestants of his own time, the Anglicans were like the semi-Arians, and Rome was in the position of sole authority and orthodoxy which she still claimed. His gift for analogy now threatened his own security: he had appealed to history, and history had returned an unexpected and unwelcome answer. The second blow was a proposal to establish a bishopric in Jerusalem in collaboration with the Lutheran Church of Prussia, for the pastoral care of all Protestants in Palestine. The State was taking on ecclesiastical privilege, establishing sees as freely as they had been suppressed in Ireland, and ignoring the unique claims of the Church of England.

The third blow, more damaging to the whole movement, came with the ninetieth and last of the Tracts. To justify Anglican claims to catholicity, Newman turned his attention to the Thirty-nine Articles to which all clergy had to assent. With the whole force of his intellect he claimed that the Articles were directed against abuses in popular Romanism and not against the orthodoxy of the undivided Church. He hoped to strengthen the waverers, to show men like Ward that their search for catholicity need not drive them out of the Church of England. Justification of purgatory and saintly intercessions, even though set out in the sweet reasonableness of Newman's prose, was bound to arouse Protestant fury. Four Oxford tutors delated the Tract and the heads of colleges followed with an almost unanimous condemnation. Newman offered to conclude the Tract series provided the last one was not withdrawn, putting upon it his reputation in the Anglican Church. But Oxford and the nation did not want to be persuaded that the Articles 'may be subscribed by those who aim at being Catholic in heart and doctrine'.

Ward, increasingly critical of Anglicanism, in 1844 produced a long and aggressive volume entitled *The Ideal of a Christian Church, considered in comparison with Existing Practice*. Not content to assert that the Roman Catholic Church alone had kept true catholicity, he declared that he and others remained in the Church of England while holding and promulgating Roman doctrine. It was a severe blow to the whole Tractarian principle, admitting and even rejoicing in the charges which opponents were making. Froude had been beyond reprisal when his *Remains* were published: Ward was a ready sacrifice for the opposition. When Convocation assembled on a bleak day of frost and snow in February 1845 it was not Ward's book alone that was on trial; there was a further motion of censure on Tract 90. Ward spoke eloquently in his own defence; the *Ideal* was condemned by a large majority and his own deprivation was passed by a smaller one. When the motion was put for the condemnation of Tract 90, the Hampden affair was ironically repeated and the proctors exercised their veto before a vote was taken.

The great twelve years of the Oxford Movement were drawing to their close. What had begun partly from fear of the newly emancipated Roman Catholics was now embroiled in disputes about whether or not they were the sole heirs of Apostolic tradition. The phrase 'Church in danger' was acquiring a new significance. Secessions to Rome were increasing and the Established Church was fighting back with more severe reprisals. Pusey had already suffered two years of suspension from preaching for a sermon censured as heretical, although he had been allowed to make no defence.

Ward was received into the Roman Catholic Church soon after his condemnation and others followed him. Still Newman remained, but his ties with the Anglican Church were loosening one by one. At Littlemore he had found neither the physical solitude nor the spiritual peace for which he had hoped. Rumours that he was setting up a monastery brought everyone, from heads of colleges to undergraduates, to spy on him. His last sermon before the University was preached in February 1843, a month after he published an article retracting some of his strongest words against Romanism. In the following September he resigned from St Mary's, and he preached for the last time as an Anglican at Littlemore that month, in a sermon which took his formal leave of the Church which he had tried to defend and which was slowly driving him away. Two years later he resigned his Oriel Fellowship. The suspense with which his final act of withdrawal was expected, in Oxford and throughout the country, was remarkable even for that time when a change of religious allegiance was more than a private decision. The years following Keble's Assize sermon had brought problems of Church authority into greater prominence. Out of the suffering and the triumph, the hope and the despair, a point of departure had been reached. On the night of 8 October 1845 the Passionist Father Dominic received John Henry Newman into the Roman Catholic Church.

It was over: Newman was gone, Froude dead, Keble obscure in a rural parsonage. Only Pusey of the first Tractarians remained active, and he now emerged as the leader of the loyalists, to gain new stature and respect as well as new obloquy. Others at Oxford developed what the Tractarians had begun: Charles Marriott, Richard Church and James Mozley took their principles forward in the University, while Keble and others carried them into the parishes. There was no one with Newman's great intellect or charismatic power, though there were many with holiness and devotion from whose writings and examples the Church of England would benefit in the years to come.

The voices of the Tractarians are lost for ever; we cannot listen to the distinctive style of Newman's preaching, which enchanted even his opponents. The written word is their only record, more personal than it is in an age of fleeting visual images and electronic communication. We cannot hear the sermons, but we can read them, as well as the Tracts themselves and the other thoughts which they set down in books and journals. They wrote copiously, and what follows here is a small sample drawn from the principal concerns and suppositions of the Movement. The Tractarians had a vision for their Church, but it was not always coherent or consistent. Some of them, particularly Newman, changed their ideas in the process of developing them and meeting the arguments of opponents, so that they may seem sometimes to contradict themselves or each other, and the headings under which the extracts are placed may overlap. Yet there is a cumulative statement of belief and intent, an ethos as they would have called it, and a general agreement on the means of achieving it.

Underlying all that they wrote was a resolve to prove that the Church of England was a full member of the Holy, Catholic and Apostolic Church, a firmly rooted branch, a middle way between Rome and Protestant Dissent: this is the subject of Chapter 2. It followed that the Anglican clergy were sacerdotal priests, ordained in the Apostolic Succession, and this is illustrated in Chapter 3. Therefore the sacraments which they celebrated were valid, the Holy Communion was more than a memorial but was central to corporate worship, and baptism was not a mere sign of faith but an effective act of regeneration, and these are the themes of Chapter 4. Such claims raised questions about the sources of authority: appeals to Scripture, tradition and reason are quoted in Chapter 5. Every member of the Church, ordained or lay, should accept the traditional disciplines of regular prayer and worship, frequent communions, fasting and sacramental confession as means to holiness, as set out in Chapter 6. Chapter 7 addresses the questions of Establishment, Church rights and state control which were the genesis of the Movement, were soon subordinated to more specific matters of ecclesiology, but never went away and brought increasing concern for a social gospel. Chapter 8 considers an aspect of the Movement which has been often noticed but seldom given the attention it deserves: the teaching of Reserve or moderation and restraint in preaching and in personal affirmations of faith. Chapter 9 looks at the subsequent influence of the Movement on parish worship and church building, the foundation of Anglican religious orders, the quest for personal holiness, and some of the later judgements passed upon it. Finally Chapter 10 attempts briefly to assess the main characteristics of the Oxford Movement, and its lasting effect on the Church of England.

2

The Church of England: Holy, Catholic and Apostolic

A basic aim of the Oxford Movement was to prove the continuing catholicity of the Church of England, against Roman Catholic claims that it was schismatic and heretical, and Protestant objections to anything 'Catholic'. It was not an innovative defence: Jewel, Hooker and others had firmly maintained the continuity of the reformed Church of England in an unbroken Catholic line, but the Tractarians needed to assert it afresh. They also wished to give warning of the threats to the integrity of the Church and of the likely cost of maintaining that integrity.

In his Assize Sermon Keble called on church people to honour their profession and obligations.

Under the guise of charity and tolerance we are come almost to this pass, that no difference, in matters of faith, is to disqualify for our approbation and confidence, whether in public or domestic life. Can we conceal it from ourselves, that every year the practice is becoming more common, of trusting men unreservedly in the most delicate and important matters, without one serious inquiry, whether they do not hold principles which make it impossible for them to be loyal to their Creator, Redeemer, and Sanctifier? Are not offices conferred, partnerships formed, intimacies courted – nay, (what is almost too painful to think of) do not parents commit their children to be educated, do they not encourage them to intermarry, in houses, on which Apostolical Authority would rather teach them to set a mark, as unfit to be entered by a faithful servant of Christ?

I do not now speak of public measures only or chiefly; many things of that kind may be thought, whether wisely or no, to become from time to time necessary, which are in reality as little desired by those who lend them a seeming, concurrence, as they are, in themselves, undesirable. But I speak of the spirit which leads men to exult in every step of that kind to congratulate one another on the supposed decay of what they call an exclusive system.

Very different are the feelings with which it seems natural for a true Churchman to regard such a state of things, from those which would arise in his mind on witnessing the mere triumph of any given set of adverse opinions, exaggerated or even heretical as he might deem them, he might feel as melancholy, he could hardly feel so indignant.

But this is not a becoming place, nor are these safe topics, for the indulgence of mere feeling. The point really to be considered is, whether, according to the coolest estimate, the fashionable liberality of this generation be not ascribable, in a great measure, to the same temper which led the Jews voluntarily to set about degrading themselves to a level with the idolatrous Gentiles? And, if it be true anywhere, that such enactments are forced on the Legislature by public opinion, is APOSTASY too hard a word to describe the temper of that nation?

The same tendency is still more apparent, because the fair gloss of candour and forbearance is wanting, in the surly or scornful impatience often exhibited, by persons who would regret passing for unbelievers, when Christian motives are suggested, and checks from Christian principles attempted to be enforced on their public conduct. I say, 'their public conduct', more especially; because in that, I know not how, persons are apt to be more shameless, and readier to avow the irreligion that is in them; amongst other reasons, probably, from each feeling that he is one of a multitude, and fancying, therefore, that his responsibility is divided.

For example: whatever be the cause, in this country of late years, (though we are lavish in professions of piety,) there has been observable a growing disinclination, on the part of those bound by VOLUNTARY oaths to whatever reminds them of their obligation; a growing disposition to explain it all away. We know what, some years ago, would have been thought of such uneasiness, if betrayed by persons officially sworn, in private, legal, or commercial life. If there be any subjects or occasions, now, on which men are inclined to judge of it more lightly, it concerns them deeply to be quite sure, that they are not indulging or encouraging a profane dislike of God's awful Presence; a general tendency, as a people, to leave Him out of all their thoughts.

They will have the more reason to suspect themselves, in proportion as they see and feel more of that impatience under pastoral authority, which our Saviour Himself has taught us to consider as a never-failing symptom of an unchristian temper. 'He that heareth you, heareth Me; and he that despiseth you, despiseth Me'. Those words of divine truth put beyond all sophistical exception, what common sense would lead us to infer, and what daily experience teaches; that disrespect to the Successors of the Apostles, as such, is an unquestionable symptom of enmity to Him, Who gave them their commission at first, and has pledged Himself to be with them for ever. Suppose such disrespect general and national, suppose it also avowedly grounded not on any fancied tenet of religion, but on mere human reasons of popularity and expediency, either there is no meaning at all in these emphatic declarations of our Lord, or that nation, how highly soever she may think of her own religion and morality, stands convicted in His sight of a direct disavowal of His Sovereignty.

John Keble, 'National Apostasy', Sermons Academical and Occasional,
Parker, 1848, pages 136–40

Although Newman took Keble's Assize Sermon as the beginning of the Movement, the importance of the Hadleigh Conference is not to be forgotten. A. P. Perceval (1799–1853), in a sermon preached at the time of that conference though not specifically designed for it, struck the same note as Keble's sermon and the Tracts that followed. He refers to Rowland Taylor, a rector of Hadleigh martyred in the Marian persecution.

You will perceive, that I have spoken of times of trouble, as if they were certainly coming. When things are plainly written, he may run that readeth; and, in truth, a man must needs shut his eyes who does not, in the signs of the times, see much reason to fear that troubles are at hand. Are not all men's minds unsettled, and ill at ease, men betraying one another, and hating one another? All the signs and tokens of evil which marked the days when good King Charles was put to death, are gathering around, and showing themselves again. God keep our nation from a repetition of such sin and misery! But, brethren, it behoves us to prepare for it. Already, indeed, as far as words go, the persecution is begun and, as in all times of trouble, the first mark at which evil men aim, has always been the ministers of religion, so it is now. The ministers of religion are openly reviled and abused, for no other reason but because they are the ministers of religion and endeavour, in the discharge of their duty by the ministry of God's Word, to stem the torrent of infidelity and confusion, which is bringing misery upon all around them. The property which the piety of former days gave to support the clergy, and by means of which the poor have the Gospel preached to them without charge, is the object of men's covetousness. Nor let it be supposed that this hatred of order will long be confined to words. Too soon, I fear, many of us may be called upon to put in practice those lessons which the Scriptures teach, of how to suffer persecution. God's will be done in all things! and if it be His will that we suffer affliction and evil treatment, for our steadfast adherence to His cause, may He give us grace to bear it as His servants should do; 'not rendering evil for evil, nor railing for railing; but contrariwise blessing'; forgiving, and praying for, those who injure us. Then, though iniquity may abound though the love of many may wax cold, may we be enabled, by God's grace, to hold the beginning of our confidence firm unto the end.

And in the midst of all this, what shall be our consolation? Why, brethren, what higher consolation and encouragement can we look for, than that which our text affords – 'He that shall endure unto the end, the same shall be saved'? Let this encourage all whom it shall please God to call upon to suffer, to suffer in meekness, patience, and constancy. 'He that shall endure unto the end'. Yes, brethren, remember these words; and whether it be God's will that we should serve Him, as heretofore, in peace and quietness, or whether it seem good to Him to try us in the fiery trial of suffering and of evil, let us remember, that in neither case will it be enough to have begun our course well; we must, by His help, be enabled to continue it to the end, that we may be saved in the day of our Lord Jesus Christ.

I stand where the martyr, Rowland Taylor, stood. May God in His mercy give grace to the clergy of this day to follow his example, and, if need be, to testify for the truth, even unto the death! And how shall we continue aright? Why, only by His help, who suffers the evil, or the temptation, to come upon us. That help will not fail us, if we seek for it aright; and, with it, we may become 'more than conquerors through Him who loved us, and gave Himself for us'. For so are the words of promise: 'God is faithful, who will not suffer you to be tempted above what ye are able, but will with the temptation also make a way to escape, that ye may be able to bear it'. And I believe God's promise, that it shall be even as He hath said, through Jesus Christ our Lord.

A. P. Perceval, *A Collection of Papers Connected with the Theological Movement of 1833*, Rivington, 1842, pages 42–3

In an early Tract, Newman asserted the status and rights of the Church; after condemning the interference with Irish bishoprics, he continued:

Bear with me, while I express my fear that we do not, as much as we ought, consider the force of that article of our belief, 'The One Catholic and Apostolic Church'. This is a tenet so important as to have been in the Creed from the beginning. It is mentioned there as a *fact,* and a fact *to be believed,* and therefore practical. Now what do we conceive is meant by it? As people vaguely take it in the present day, it seems only an assertion that there is a number of sincere Christians scattered through the world. But is not this a truism? who doubts it? who can deny that there are people in various places who are sincere believers? what comes of this? how is it important? why should it be placed as an article of faith, after the belief in the Holy Ghost? Doubtless the only true and satisfactory meaning is that which our Divines have ever taken, that there is on earth an existing Society, Apostolic as founded by the Apostles, Catholic because it spreads its branches in every place; i.e., the Church Visible with its Bishops, Priests, and Deacons. And this surely *is* a most important doctrine; for what can be better news to the bulk of mankind than to be told that Christ when He ascended did not leave us orphans, but appointed representatives of Himself to the end of time? [...]

If then we express our belief in the existence of One Church on earth from Christ's coming to the end of all things, if there is a promise it shall continue, and if it is our duty to do our part in our generation towards its continuance, how can we with a safe conscience countenance the interference of the Nation in its concerns? Does not such interference tend to destroy it? Would it not destroy it if consistently followed up? Now, may we sit still and keep silence, when efforts are making to break up, or at least materially to weaken that Ecclesiastical Body which we know is intended to last while the world endures, and the safety of which is committed to our keeping in our day? How shall we answer for it, if we transmit that Ordinance of God less entire than it came to us?

Now what am I calling on you to do? You cannot help what has been done in Ireland; but you may protest against it. You may as a duty protest against it in public and private; you may keep a jealous watch on the proceedings of the Nation, lest a second act of the same kind be attempted. You may keep it before you as a desirable object that the Irish Church should at some future day meet in Synod and protest herself against what has been done; and then proceed to establish or rescind the state injunction, as may be thought expedient.

I know it is too much the fashion of the times to think any earnestness for ecclesiastical rights unseasonable and absurd, as if it were the feeling of those who live among books and not in the world. But it is our *duty* to live among books, especially to live by one book, and a very old one; and therein we are enjoined to 'keep that good thing which is committed unto us', to 'neglect not our gift'. And when men talk, as they sometimes do, as if in opposing them we were standing on technical difficulties instead of welcoming great and extensive benefits which would be the result of their measures, I would ask them (letting alone the question of their beneficial nature, which *is* a question) whether this is not being wise above that is written, whether it is not doing evil that good may come? We cannot know the effects which will follow certain alterations; but we can decide that the means by which it is proposed to attain them are unprecedented and disrespectful to the Church.

And when men say, 'the day is past for stickling about ecclesiastical rights', let them see to it, lest they use substantially the same arguments to maintain their position as those who say, 'The day is past for being a Christian'.

J. H. Newman, Tract 2, 'The Catholic Church', pages 2, 4

A few Tracts later, Newman insisted that there must be one visible, structured and undivided Church.

You are in the practice of distinguishing between the Visible and Invisible Church. Of course I have no wish to maintain that those who shall be saved hereafter are exactly the same company that are under the means of grace here; still I must insist on it, that Scripture makes the existence of a Visible Church a condition of the existence of the Invisible. I mean, the *Sacraments* are evidently in the hands of the Church Visible; and these, we know, are generally necessary, to salvation, as the Catechism says. Thus it is an undeniable fact, as true as that souls will be saved, that a Visible Church must exist as a means towards that end. The Sacraments are in the hands of the Clergy; this few will deny, or that their efficacy is independent of the personal character of the administrator. What then shall be thought of any attempts to weaken or exterminate that Community, or that Ministry, which is an appointed condition of the salvation of the elect? But everyone who makes or encourages a schism, must weaken it. Thus it is plain, schism must be wrong in itself, even if Scripture did not in express terms forbid it, as it does.

But further than this: it is plain this Visible Church is a *standing* body. Every one who is baptised, is baptised *into* an existing community. Our Service expresses this when it speaks of baptised infants being *incorporated* into God's holy Church. Thus the Visible Church is not a voluntary association of the day, but a continuation of one which existed in the age before us, and then again in the age before that; and so back till we come to the age of the Apostles. In the same sense, in which Corporations of the state's creating are perpetual, is this which Christ has founded. This is a matter of fact hitherto: and it necessarily will be so always, for is not the notion absurd of an unbaptised person baptising others? which is the only way in which the Christian community can have a new beginning.

Moreover, Scripture directly *insists* upon the doctrine of the Visible Church, as being of importance. E.g. St. Paul says, 'There is *one body*, and one Spirit even as ye are called in one hope of your calling; one Lord, one faith, one baptism, one God and Father of all' (Ephes. iv. 5, 6). Thus, as far as the Apostle's words go, it is false and unchristian (I do not mean in degree of guilt, but in its intrinsic sinfulness) to make more bodies than one, as to have many Lords, many Gods, many Creeds. Now, I wish to know, how it is possible for anyone to fall into this sin, if Dissenters are clear of it? What *is* the sin, if separation from the Existing Church is not it?

J. H. Newman, Tract 11, 'The Visible Church', pages 2–3

A. P. Perceval did not take a major part in the Movement after Hadleigh, but he wrote a Tract defending the integrity of the Church of England and warning against its enemies.

The Rock, then, upon which the Church is built, is the confession that Jesus is the Christ, the Son of the Living God; a truth set forth and shadowed by the Prophets, but only and plainly taught by the Apostles [...]

Our very spiritual existence depends upon our adhering to this great and fundamental truth; and this I said not of us as individuals only, but as members of the Church of Christ, and of that portion of Christ's Church in this kingdom which is usually called the Church of England. It is true of us individually, as appears by the words of St. John: 'He that hath the Son, hath life; and he that hath not the Son of God, hath not life' (i John v. 12); by which we learn that as long as

we slight or disbelieve or deny this sacred truth, we have no spiritual
life in us. It is also true of us, as Members of the Church of Christ,
and of that portion of Christ's Church in this kingdom which is usually called the Church of England, as appears from the passage before
us: 'Upon this rock' (i.e. upon this firm confession of faith in Jesus as
the Christ, the Son of the Living God) 'I will build My Church; and
the gates of hell shall not prevail against it'. For from this we learn
that the Church, and any given portion of that Church, is only then
able to defy the assaults of the Devil, that she can only then look
forward with confidence to get the victory, so long as she adheres
firmly to this faith and belief in Christ. When she departs from that
foundation, then she ceases to have a claim for the continuance of
the promised aid. This is a matter which it behoves Christians at all
times to place before their eyes, and to keep in remembrance; but
especially, at the present time, does it behove us, who are Members of
the Church of Christ in England, to do so; because of the unceasing
endeavours which are being made by men who are either careless of
religion altogether, or who have embraced false views of it, to overthrow our Church: endeavours which we have reason to regard either
with fear, or not, according as we have reason, or not, to suppose that
the Members of the Church have departed from the true faith and
fear of God, and of the Lord Jesus Christ. If there is reason to believe
that many or most of the Members of our Church are regardless of
that true faith, and of the honour of Him in whom we believe, that
by their lips, or by their lives, they set at nought His Majesty, neglect
His Sacraments, despise His Word, forsake His Worship, obey not
His Voice, or look for redemption and salvation by any other means
than by His Cross and Blood, then we have every reason to fear that
these endeavours of our enemies will be successful; that the light of
God's presence will be withheld from us; and that, as He withdrew
from the Jews when they neglected Christ, the Lord of Glory, so He
will withdraw from our Nation also, and leave it to the wretchedness
of its own chosen ways; to the enjoyment of those idols, the world,
the flesh, and the Devil, for which it will have forsaken the Holy One
of Israel, and refused to hearken to the Voice of the Lamb of God,
who died to take away the sins of the world. But if not, if we have
reason to hope that there are many true servants of God still to be
found; that there are many who, not with their lips only, but in their
hearts and with their lives, acknowledge Him the only true God,
and Jesus Christ whom He has sent; acknowledge Him so as to obey
His voice, and keep and do what He has commanded; then may we
regard the attempts of our enemies without dismay; then may we

have firm and steadfast hope that the gates of Hell shall not prevail against us, that though it may please God that we should suffer for a while; as we suffered, together with good King Charles, at the hands of the Dissenters; as we suffered in the days of bloody Queen Mary, at the hands of the Roman Catholics; as we suffered during the first three hundred years after Christ, at the hands of the Heathens and the Jews; yet that eventually triumph will await us; that He will bring our Church out of the trial, like gold out of the fire, more pure and of greater worth ('I will purely purge away thy dross, and take away all thy sin' (Isa. i. 25), that 'all things will work together for good' to us; and that the purpose, aimed at by the affliction is, that He 'may present our Church to Himself as a glorious Church, not having spot, or wrinkle, or any such thing; but that it should be holy and without blemish' (Ephes. v. 27).

It will hence appear that it is in the power of every individual, by a holy and religious life in the true faith and fear of God and our Lord Jesus Christ, to promote not only his own salvation, but the welfare and stability of the Church of Christ; or by an unholy, careless, and irreligious life, not only to secure his own damnation, but to assist the enemies of God and Man, who are purposed to overthrow that Church.

> A. P. Perceval, Tract 23, 'The Faith and Obedience of Churchmen
> the Strength of the Church', 1, 3–4

Newman defended the claim of the Church of England to catholicity

The remark may seem paradoxical at first sight, yet surely it is just, that the English Church is, for certain, deficient in particulars, because it does not profess itself infallible. I mean as follows. Every thoughtful mind must at times have been beset by the following doubt '*How is it* that the particular Christian body to which I belong *happens* to be the right one? I hear every one about me saying *his own* society is alone right, and others wrong; is not each one of us as much justified in saying so as every one else? is not any one as much justified as I am? In other words, the truth is surely nowhere to be found pure, unadulterated and entire, but is shared through the world, each Christian body having a portion of it, none the whole of it'. A certain liberalism is commonly the fruit of this perplexity. Men are led on to gratify the pride of human nature, by standing aloof from all systems, forming a truth for themselves, and countenancing, this or that body of Christians according as each maintains portions of that which they themselves have already assumed to be the truth. Now the primitive Church answered this question, by appealing to the simple fact, that all the Apostolic Churches all over the world did agree together. True, there were sects in every country, but they bore their own refutation on their forehead, in that they were of recent origin; whereas all those societies in every country, which the Apostles had founded, did agree together in one, and no time short of the Apostles' could be assigned, with any show of argument, for the rise of their existing doctrine. This doctrine in which they agreed was accordingly called *Catholic* truth, and there was plainly no room at all for asking, 'Why should my own Church be more true than another's?' But at this day, it need not he said, such an evidence is lost, except as regards the articles of the Creed. It is a very great mercy that the Church Catholic all over the world, as descended from the Apostles, does at this day speak one and the same doctrine about the Trinity and Incarnation, as it has always spoken it, excepting in one single point, which rather *probat regulam* [proves the rule] than interferes with it, viz. as to the procession of the HOLY GHOST from the Son. With this solitary exception, we have the certainty of possessing the entire truth as regards the high theological doctrines, by an argument which supersedes the necessity of arguing from Scripture against those who oppose them. It is quite impossible that all countries should have agreed to that which was not Apostolic. They are a number of concordant witnesses to certain definite truths, and while their testimony is one and the same from the very first moment they publicly utter it, so, on the other hand, if there be bodies which speak otherwise, we can show historically that they rose later than the Apostles.

> J. H. Newman, 'On the Mode of Conducting the Controversy with Rome',
> *The Via Media of the Anglican Church* (1835), Longmans, Green,
> 1838, vol. 2, pages 131–3

Isaac Williams (1802–65) asserted the claims of the Church of England, citing the preservation of its liturgy as evidence of catholicity. The Convocations of Canterbury and York had been suspended since 1717 and were not restored until later in the nineteenth century.

The necessity of obedience to our own Church, and consequently the security to be found therein, are to be set higher than they usually are, even by her friends; such obedience extending to her spirit and intention (when not opposed to Scripture and the Church Catholic) as much as to points of positive command. For we are bound to obey the Church by CHRIST appointed. (St. Matt xviii. 19.) And how does this obedience come before us individually, but by our own, while she is neither heretical nor schismatical? We cannot help ourselves, we have no choice. Obedience, therefore, to her is obedience to GOD in the highest sense, as to His appointment. And therefore such obedience contains within itself somehow its own protection, has within it safety, and more than safety. When we quit her guidance in pursuit of any apparent good, we lose this security; it is in this manner that our Church becomes to us the seat of 'quietness and confidence' [...]

Or, to put the argument more particularly, we have the promise of our SAVIOUR's guidance in His Church to the end; where are we to obtain that guidance so as to regulate our course? In the universal agreement of a general Council. But these have been found impracticable, from the very necessity of the case; therefore such suspension, or cessation, is the work of GOD, not of man. Where, therefore, is the allegiance due to such to be transferred? GOD has supplied us with that which, though not even a Council, perhaps, of itself, yet, in our state of necessity, stands in the nearest place to claim that allegiance, in a Convocation. But these Convocations have been now suspended by the same Power. General Councils have been found unworthy to preserve the deposit, from the unfaithfulness or divisions of Christendom; Convocation, from those of our own. To what, therefore, is our allegiance due? As in the former case to the last general Councils, which were Catholic, so is it also now in our own case due to the last Convocation, and to that order of things which it has bequeathed to us in our own Liturgy. The very suspension of Convocation seems to rivet and fix the necessity of our obedience the more, for the Divine Lesson imparted thereby is, that since we are not in a state fit to regulate ourselves, we must abide by the fixed regulations of a better age. In this also are indications of the same fatherly Hand.

And, with respect to that teaching which GOD has supplied us with, in the very matter and structure of our forms of worship, it must be remembered that, in this Treatise, our Liturgy has been considered with respect to its weak points, its modern changes, wherein it has been our object to show, that the strength of GOD has been evinced even in this our weakness, that even those changes have been regulated by a Divine control. Much more, then, may it be concluded to be the case, that our strength and guidance consists in those ancient and Catholic forms themselves. To take one single instance; the appointment of select passages from Scripture in the Epistle and Gospel. Consider how valuable this is; to say nothing of the harmonious union it supports with other Churches, consider how it prevents any popular religion of the day, and its peculiar doctrines, from taking up their abode in our sanctuary; or again, how it counteracts the very evils arising, from a reaction against them; how, in short, it preserves the Catholicity of the Church. If any new Gospel were to prevail, it would endeavour to speak with the voice of Scripture, by selecting passages to suit its own purpose. But permanency and continuance is one of the chief attributes of the Church. of whom, as of her Divine Founder and Ruler, it may in some sense be said that she is 'the same yesterday, and to-day, and for ever'.

I. Williams, Tract 86, 'Indications of a Superintending Providence and the Preservation of the Prayer Book', pages 90–1

Newman saw his Church as part of the Catholic Church, which is a unity made effective in different branches

Now we may form a clearer notion than is commonly taken of the one Church Catholic which is in all lands. Properly it is not on earth, except so far as heaven can be said to be on earth, or as the dead are still with us. It is not on earth, except in such sense as Christ or His Spirit are on the earth. I mean it is not locally or visibly on earth. The Church is not in time or place, but in the region of spirits; it is in the Holy Ghost; and as the soul of man is in every part of his body, yet in no part, not here nor there, yet everywhere; not in any one part, head or heart, hands or feet, so as not to be in every other; so also the heavenly Jerusalem, the mother of our new birth, is in all lands at once, fully and entirely, as a spirit; in the East and in the West, in the North and in the South – that is, wherever her outward instruments are to be found. The Ministry and Sacraments, the bodily presence of bishop and people, are given us as keys and spells, by which we bring ourselves into the presence of the great company of saints; they are but the outskirts of it; they are but porches to the pool of Bethesda, entrances into that which is indivisible and one. Baptism admits, not into a mere visible society, varying with the country in which it is administered, Roman here, and Greek there, and English there, but through the English or the Greek or the Roman porch into the one invisible company of elect souls, which is independent of time and place, and untinctured with the imperfections or errors of that visible porch by which entrance is made. And its efficacy lies in the flowing upon the soul of the grace of God lodged in that unseen body into which it opens, not, in any respect, in the personal character of those who administer or assist in it. When a child is brought for Baptism, the Church invisible claims it, begs it of God, receives it, and extends to it, as God's instrument, her own sanctity. When we praise God in Holy Communion, we praise Him with the Angels and Archangels, who are the guards, and with the Saints, who are the citizens of the City of God. When we offer our Sacrifice of praise and thanksgiving, or partake in the sacred elements so offered, we solemnly eat and drink of the powers of the world to come. When we read the Psalms, we use before many witnesses the very words on which those witnesses themselves – I mean, all successive generations of that holy company – have sustained themselves in their own day, for thousands of years past, during their pilgrimage heavenward. When we profess the Creed, it is in no self-willed, arbitrary sense, but in the presence of those innumerable Saints who well remember what its words mean, and are witnesses of it before God, in spite of the heresy or indifference of this or that day. When we stand over their graves, we are in the very vestibule of that dwelling which is 'all-glorious within', full of light and purity, and of voices crying, 'Lord, how long?' When we pray in private, we are not solitary; others 'are gathered together' with us 'in Christ's Name' though we see them not, with Christ in the midst of them. When we approach the Ministry He has ordained, we approach the steps of His throne. When we approach the bishops, who are the centres of that Ministry, what have we before us but the Twelve Apostles, present but invisible? When we use the sacred Name of Jesus, or the Sign given us in Baptism, what do we but bid defiance to devils and evil men, and gain strength to resist them? When we protest, or confess, or suffer in the Name of Christ, what are we but ourselves types and symbols of the Cross of Christ, and of the strength of Him who died on it? When we are called to battle for the Lord, what are we who are seen but mere outposts, the advanced guard of a mighty host, ourselves few in number and despicable, but bold beyond our numbers, because supported by chariots of fire and horses of fire round about the Mountain of the Lord of Hosts under which we stand?

Such is the City of God, the Holy Church Catholic throughout the world, manifested in and acting through what is called in each country the Church visible; which visible Church really depends solely on it, on the invisible – not on civil power, not on princes or any child of man, not on endowments, not on its numbers, not on any thing that is seen, unless indeed heaven can depend on earth, eternity on time, angels on men, the dead on the living. The unseen world through God's secret power and mercy encroaches upon this; and the Church that is seen is just that portion of it by which it encroaches; and thus, though the visible Churches of the Saints in this world seem rare, and scattered to and fro, like islands in the sea, they are in truth the tops of the everlasting hills, high and vast and deeply rooted, which a deluge covers.

J. H. Newman, *Parochial Sermons*, iv, pages 198–201

A robust defence of the Church of England by a layman, Newman's friend John Bowden. The Rector, Dr Spencer, convinces John Evans who has been led by a friend who belongs to a 'dissenting congregation' to go to a 'meeting-house'.

D⟨octo⟩r As the eternal truth of God is contained in His revealed word in the Bible, no Church, whatever may be the errors of her individual members, can be said, as a Church, to have fallen away, and consequently to have lost her claim to the obedience of Christ's true disciples, while she still reverences that Bible; while she puts it into the hand of each of her followers, and bids him read it, and seek there, and there only, the proofs of the doctrine which she inculcates; and while she declares, as the Church of England does in her sixth Article, that 'Holy Scripture containeth all things necessary to salvation; so that whatsoever is not read therein, nor may be proved thereby, is not to be required of any man that it should be believed as an article of the Faith, or be thought requisite or necessary to salvation'.

J⟨ohn⟩ Then according to you, sir, the Church of England is not only the true, but the original Church of Christ established in this kingdom. Now, Sam Jones, the Catholic, who attends the Popish Chapel in the next parish, tells me that his is the original Church, and that the Church of England is a new one.

D⟨octo⟩r That which is truly the Catholic Church is indeed the oldest; but though we in a common way call the Papists, or followers of the Pope, Catholics, yet it is we who are the true Catholics; for the term only means members of Christ's universal Church. The history of the Papists is this. Many centuries ago, strange and corrupt notions and practices prevailed in many of the Churches in Europe. Among others, people thought the Pope or Bishop of Rome was gifted with authority from Heaven to control all the branches of the Church on earth, and that his word was to be of more weight than even the Holy Scriptures themselves. But about three hundred years ago, the Bishops of the Church of England saw these errors in their true light;

they saw that the Pope's authority was not founded on Scripture, and they consequently refused to acknowledge it, while they at the same time corrected, upon Scriptural principles, the other errors and evil practices which I have alluded to. These changes did not make the Church of England a new Church, nor prevent that body which was Christ's true and original Church before from being Christ's true and original Church still. Some Bishops of that day, it is true, disapproved of these changes, and refused to accede to them; but as, when they died, they providentially appointed no successors, there has never since been any real ground for doubt which was the true Church of Christ in this favoured land. The Bishops of the Church of England, and they only, are the representatives by succession of those who, more than a thousand years ago, planted the Gospel on our shores.

J⟨ohn⟩ But there are persons whom the Papists call their Bishops – whence do they come?

D⟨octo⟩r They derive what they call their right from their appointment by foreign Bishops in an unauthorised manner. The Pope and his followers would by no means acknowledge the changes which had taken place in England; they declared that our Church had apostatised from the faith, and refused to communicate with us, till we should return to all our ancient errors. They have since, upon the alleged ground that our line of Bishops was extinct, given commission from time to time to different persons to exercise episcopal authority here; but as the ground was false, the commission was of course void. We acknowledge the Pope and his Bishops in foreign countries to be, by station, ministers of the Church, though we admit and lament the fact that they have led the branches of it over which they preside into apostasy and shame; yet we feel that in sending their representatives hither, to act in defiance of the Church already established, they are exceeding the limits of their authority. We feel that God, who is not the author of confusion, but of peace, in all churches of the saints (1 Cor. xiv. 33), cannot sanction the intrusion of one Bishop, however duly consecrated, into the See of another, with a view to the usurpation of his name and office, and to the organising a systematic opposition to his authority. We are compelled therefore to regard those who are ordained, as Popish Priests by these intruding Bishops, as unauthorised and schismatical ministers of religion, and as violators, like the other dissenters around them, of the laws of Christ's Church, and of the unity of His fold.

J. W. Bowden, Tract 30, 'Christian Liberty: or Why should we Belong to the Church of England?', Part II, 1834

Newman speaking as 'Clericus' argues about the catholicity of the Church of England with 'Laicus', who is not convinced that there is really any difference between this view of the Church and the Roman Catholic. Clericus replies:

Be assured of this – no party will be more opposed to our doctrine, if it ever prospers and makes noise, than the Roman party. This has been proved before now. In the seventeenth century the theology of the divines of the English Church was substantially the same as ours is; and it experienced the full hostility of the Papacy. It was the true *Via Media*; Rome sought to block up that way as fiercely as the Puritans. History tells us this. Did I not fear to incur the guilt of railing against other branches of Christ's Church, I would, before we separated, attempt a few words in explanation of my irreconcilable differences with the system of Rome, as it is; but, on the whole, I feel it better to stop at the point to which we have come.

J. H. Newman, Tract 38, 'Via Media', part 1, 11

He also claims that the Church of England is 'more Protestant than our Reformers'.

A number of distinct doctrines are included in the notion of Protestantism and as to all these, our Church has taken the *Via Media* between it and Popery. At present I will use it in the sense most apposite to the topics we have been discussing – viz, as the religion of so-called freedom and independence, as hating superstition, suspicious of forms, jealous of priestcraft, advocating heart-worship; characteristics which admit of a good or a bad interpretation, but which, understood as they are instanced in the majority of persons who are zealous for what is called Protestant doctrine, are (I maintain) very inconsistent with the Liturgy of our Church.

J. H. Newman, Tract 41, 'Via Media', part 2, 6

William Gresley (1801–76), a Prebendary of Lichfield, wrote both in both treatise and fiction to support the ideals of the Oxford Movement and assert the special quality of the Church of England.

There is a peculiarity in the Anglican Church which distinguishes it from all other Protestant communities. When God opened men's eyes to discern the errors of Romanism, the English reformers did not, like their continental brethren, cast aside the authority of ages, and reconstruct a Church for themselves; they simply repaired and cleansed their ancient temples: for, though neglected and dilapidated, the framework was entire, the plan was perfect. They subjected her doctrine and discipline to the test of Scripture. What was contrary to Scripture, they at once discarded; what was agreeable to it, they retained and reverenced as a sacred legacy from the Apostolic ages. Her outward form and structure, her threefold ministry, her dioceses and parishes, her Apostolic ordination, her creeds, her very services, which had been handed down from age to age – all these they retained; only they removed from them whatsoever was contrary to the word of God; and the Church stood forth to the world fresh in the beauty of her intrinsic holiness, the exact model, nay, rather the continued identification, of the one Catholic and Apostolic Church.

On the same principle of deference to authority, but of appeal to Scripture as the sole standard of divine truth, our Church freely opens the Bible to all her children; not bidding them carve out of it a religion for themselves, but requiring them to reverence her ordinances and her ministers, and compare her doctrines with those of Scripture; being confident that Scripture will confirm them in her communion. Thus she encourages free inquiry, but at the same time represses rash enthusiasm; and unites a perfect liberty of thought with a due regard for authority. These are the principles which have formed the English character; and have trained a race of men faithful but not bigoted, reverential but not superstitious. And these religious principles, descending to the thoughts and actions of common life, and elevating and sanctifying, as they could not fail, the habitual tenor of our lives, have rendered us, as a nation, independent yet not licentious, intellectual yet not arrogant, manly yet humble, loyal yet free.

William Gresley, *Portrait of an English Churchman*, Rivington, 1840,
pages 75–6

Through many years of questioning, Newman maintained his confidence in the Church of England.

Now if there ever were a Church on whom the experiment has been tried whether it had life in it or not, the English is that one. For three centuries it has endured all vicissitudes of fortune. It has endured in trouble and prosperity, under seduction and under oppression. It has been practised upon by theorists, browbeaten by sophists, intimidated by princes, betrayed by false sons, laid waste by tyranny, corrupted by wealth, torn by schism, and persecuted by fanaticism. Revolutions have come upon it sharply and suddenly, to and fro, hot and cold, as if to try what it was made of. It has been a sort of battlefield on which opposite principles have been tried. No opinion, however extreme any way, but may be found, as the Romanists are not slow to reproach us, among its bishops and divines. Yet what has been its career upon the whole? Which way has it been moving through three hundred years? Where does it find itself at the end? Lutherans have tended to Rationalism; Calvinists have become Socinians; but what has it become? As far as its formularies are concerned, it may be said all along to have grown towards a more perfect Catholicism than that with which it started at the time of its estrangement; every act, every crisis, which marks its course, has been upward.

J. H. Newman, *The Via Media of the Anglican Church* (1835),
Longmans, 1845, page 155

But W. G. Ward, moving more rapidly towards his change of ecclesiastical allegiance, wrote condescendingly about 'high churchmen' and denigrated the English Reformation as Froude had done.

The points at issue between 'high churchmen' though not at this moment *externally* practical, must be at all times, as I have hinted above, *internally* so in a very high degree. Take, merely as instances, those particular opinions just now mentioned; the admiration of monastic institutions, of celibacy, of voluntary poverty. Is it not plain, on being once stated, that these opinions spring from real and important peculiarities of mind; from a far deeper sense than is now common among us of the supernatural character of Christian obedience, of the corrupting tendency of this world's goods, of the extreme arduousness of the path to heaven, of the peculiar beauty of virgin purity, of the inestimable value of habitual and abstracted spiritual contemplation? It cannot be of little moment, were it only for their own sakes, whether individuals do or do not entertain opinions such as these. For without them the Christian character is in a fair way to lose all that is most heavenly and most peculiar to itself. And believing, as we do most firmly, that in proportion as the Christian walks more steadily and consistently in the path of ordinary conscientiousness, he is likely to be attracted the more forcibly to these opinions, provided only they be fairly placed before him; it would be impossible to reconcile our conduct with the most obvious principles of duty, were we parties to any compromise, which might tend to withhold the knowledge of them, from any who may be prepared to receive them. And the same considerations render it equally impossible to refrain from the most earnest and almost indignant disavowals of the language, adopted by many 'high churchmen' towards Rome. A small, very small, knot of individuals, in using such language, intend only to attack certain modern developments of doctrine, which they consider corruptions; but with the general body the case is very far different. 'High churchmen' of the present day are not in general (nor have any need to be) subtle and accurate theologians: in attacking Rome, they attack not this or that particular, but a certain general spirit, to which Rome has ever most prominently and honourably witnessed; that very spirit of which I spoke above. It is a mere theory, refuted by the smallest practical experience, to suppose that these peculiarly Christian tempers of mind can ever be held in due honour and reverence, I do not say by a very few individuals, but by any numerous class, while such language towards Rome, as that to which I allude, receives encouragement or indeed tolerance. Nor in like manner can the all-important principles of dutifulness and faith be apprehended in their true colours, so long as it is supposed to be an acknowledged fact, that the English Reformation (which to me appears the very embodiment of the sins most opposed to those principles) is to be regarded with respect.

Ward made an emotional and highly imaginative appeal to the Roman Catholic Church for recognition of the catholicity of the Church of England.

Taking these respective considerations into account, and observing what evidence of strict and holy fear of God is presented by various Christians who remain in this Church, surely Roman Catholics are fully at liberty, if they will, without violating any necessary part of their system, to hold that those who are 'in invincible ignorance' (to use the technical term) and enjoy sacramental grace, who on the one hand, are diligent in self-examination and prayer, and on the other hand are allowed by God to retain that peace of mind which St. Alphonsus considers so sure a mark of His favour. Or again – supposing that some Apostle had been carried by the Spirit to America, and there founded a Church: would not that be a truly Christian Church, though it had never heard the name of Rome? or at the first discovery of America, supposing that it was not ripe for an immediate and corporate union, would Roman Catholics have summoned its members summarily and singly to quit its Communion? or would they not rather have allowed every possible time and opportunity, that misunderstandings might be removed, and Christian love perform its full work? The same principles which would allow them, in such a case to delay rather than precipitate a crisis and formal rupture, might enable them to extend, in our case a similar forbearance. And surely the Roman Catholic Church would far more suitably fulfil the character she claims, by showing herself full of love and sympathy for holiness of life and orthodoxy of creed wherever found, and exhorting those, in whom she finds those essential characteristics, to persevere in their noble course, than by appearing deficient in all regard for them, until they have developed into their very last stage, into a craving, for union with herself, and into what have frequently been considered her distinctive doctrines.

Nor should there be any misgiving, lest such principles as those I have attempted to advocate should tend to justify a permanent state of schism. It should be taken as first principles by all Catholic-minded men that the true Catholic character *exists,* is irresistibly attracted towards the image of itself. If then holy living and orthodox faith actively flourish in the Roman Church (which I have no disposition at all to deny), it is plain that to implant it in our Church is to take the merest possible means of *effecting* a real, and lasting union; and if a Catholic minded individual is not attracted at once towards Rome, it is because he is retained by an attraction nearer home; or, in other words, a leaven is working, not in himself only, but in a certain mass of which he is part, a leaven which will assuredly cause it to gravitate speedily, as a whole, in that very direction. And so far from the separated Greek Church being a difficulty in the way of this obvious view, all the facts I am able to gather concerning the existing condition of that Church, seem to me forcibly to *confirm* the view.

W.G. Ward, *The Idea of a Christian Church*, Toovey, 1844,
pages 98–9, 584–6

As his doubts increased, Newman tried to prove that the Thirty-nine Articles were capable of a Catholic interpretation.

It is often urged, and sometimes felt and granted, that there are in the Articles propositions or terms inconsistent with the Catholic faith; or, at least, when persons do not go so far as to feel the objection as of force, they are perplexed how best to reply to it, or how most simply to explain the passages on which it is made to rest. The following Tract is drawn up with the view of showing how groundless

the objection is, and further of approximating towards the argumentative answer to it, of which most men have an implicit apprehension,
though they may have nothing more. That there are real difficulties
to a Catholic Christian in the Ecclesiastical position of our Church at
this day, no one can deny; but the statements of the Articles are not
in the number; and it may be right at the present moment to insist
upon this. If in any quarter it is supposed that persons who profess
to be disciples of the early Church will silently concur with those of
very opposite sentiments in furthering a relaxation of subscriptions
which, it is imagined, are galling to both parties, though for different reasons, and that they will do this against the wish of the great
body of the Church, the writer of the following pages would raise
one voice, at least, in protest against any such anticipation. Even in
such points as he may think the English Church deficient, never can
he, without a great alteration of sentiment, be party to forcing the
opinion or project of one school upon another. Religious changes,
to be beneficial, should be the act of the whole body; they are worth
little if they are the mere act of a majority. No good can come of any
change which is not heartfelt, a development of feelings springing up
freely and calmly within the bosom of the whole body itself. Moreover, a change in theological teaching involves either the commission
or the confession of sin; it is either the profession or renunciation
of erroneous doctrine, and if it does not succeed in proving the fact
of past guilt, it, *ipso facto,* implies present. In other words, every
change in religion carries with it its own condemnation, which is not
attended by deep repentance. Even supposing then that any changes
in contemplation, whatever they were, were good in themselves, they
would cease to be good to a Church in which they were the fruits
not of the quiet conviction of all, but of the agitation, or tyranny, or
intrigue of a few; nurtured not in mutual love, but in strife and envy-
ing; perfected not in humiliation and grief, but in pride, elation, and
triumph. Moreover it is a very serious truth, that persons and bodies who put themselves into a disadvantageous state, cannot at their
pleasure extricate themselves from it. They are unworthy of it; they
are in prison, and Christ is the keeper. There is but one way towards
a real reformation – a return to Him in heart and spirit, whose sacred
truth they have betrayed; all other methods, however fair they may
promise, will prove to be but shadows and failures. [...] But these
remarks are beyond our present scope, which is merely to show that,
while our Prayer Book is acknowledged on all hands to be of Catholic origin, our Articles also, the offspring of an uncatholic age, are,
through God's good providence, to say the least, not uncatholic, and

may be subscribed by those who aim at being catholic in heart and doctrine.

J. H. Newman, Tract 90, 'Remarks on Certain Passages in the
Thirty-Nine Articles', pages 1, 4

By 1843 Newman was turning away from the Church of England, which he felt had failed to support his hopes and his early assurance. In his last sermon as an Anglican, preached at Littlemore, he movingly expressed his disappointment and showed the way which he and some of the other members of the Movement would follow.

O my mother, whence is this unto thee, that thou hast good things poured upon thee and canst not keep them, and bearest children, yet darest not own them? Why hast thou not the skill to use their services, nor the heart to rejoice in their love? How is it that whatever is generous in purpose, and tender or deep in devotion, thy flower and thy promise, falls from thy bosom and finds no home within thine arms? Who hath put this note upon thee, to have 'a miscarrying womb and dry breasts', to be strange to thine own flesh, and thine eye cruel towards thy little ones? Thine own offspring, the fruit of thy womb, who love thee and would toil for thee, thou dost gaze upon with fear, as though a portent, or thou dost loath as an offence; at best thou dost but endure, as if they had no claim but on thy patience, self-possession, and vigilance, to be rid of them as easily as thou mayest. Thou makest them 'stand all the day idle' as the very condition of thy bearing with them; or thou biddest them be gone, where they will be more welcome; or thou sellest them for nought to the stranger that passes by. And what wilt thou do in the end thereof? Scripture is a refuge in any trouble; only let us be on our guard against seeming to use it further than is fitting, or doing more than sheltering ourselves under its shadow. Let us use it according to our measure. It is far higher and wider than our need; and it conceals our feelings while it gives expression to them. It is sacred and heavenly; and it restrains and purifies, while it sanctions them.

And O, my brethren, O kind and affectionate hearts, O loving friends, should you know any one whose lot it has been, by writing or by word of mouth, in some degree to help you thus to act; if he has ever told you what you knew about yourselves, or what you did not know; has read to you your wants or feelings, and comforted you by the very reading: has made you feel that there was a higher life than this daily one, and a brighter world than that you see; or encouraged you, or sobered you, or opened a way to the inquiring, or soothed the perplexed; if what he has said or done has ever made you take interest in him, and feel well inclined towards him; remember such a one in time to come, though you hear him not, and pray for him, that in all things he may know God's will, and at all times he may be ready to fulfil it.

J. H. Newman, 'The Parting of Friends', *Sermons Bearing on Subjects of the Day*, Rivington, 1843, pages 461–4

3

Continuity in the Apostolic Succession

In order to maintain the full catholicity of the Church of England it was necessary to prove that her clergy were sacerdotal priests in the Apostolic Succession: which they usually called 'Apostolical'. Denial of this claim was, then and later, a principal part of Roman Catholic polemic.

Newman wrote the first Tract to call his fellow-priests to recognize their sacred office.

I am but one of yourselves, a Presbyter; and therefore I conceal my name, lest I should take too much on myself by speaking in my own person. Yet speak I must; for the times are very evil, yet no one speaks against them.

Is not this so? Do not we 'look upon one another', yet perform nothing? Do we not all confess the peril into which the Church is come, yet sit still each in his own retirement, as if mountains and seas cut off brother from brother? Therefore suffer me, while I try to draw you forth from those pleasant retreats which it has been our blessedness hitherto to enjoy, to contemplate the condition and prospects of our Holy Mother in a practical way; so that one and all may unlearn that idle habit, which has grown upon us, of owning the state of things to be bad, yet doing nothing to remedy it.

Consider a moment. Is it fair, is it dutiful, to suffer our Bishops to stand the brunt of the battle without doing our part to support them? Upon them comes 'the care of all the Churches'. This cannot be helped: indeed it is their glory. Not one of us would wish in the least to deprive them of the duties, the toils, the responsibilities of their high Office. And, black event as it would be for the country, yet (as far as they are concerned) we could not wish them a more blessed termination of their course than the spoiling of their goods, and martyrdom.

To them then we willingly and affectionately relinquish their high privileges and honours; we encroach not upon the rights of the successors of the Apostles; we touch not their sword and crosier. Yet surely we may be their shield-bearers in the battle without offence; and by our voice and deeds be to them what Luke and Timothy were to St. Paul.

Now then let me come at once to the subject which leads me to address you. Should the Government and Country so far forget their God as to cast off the Church, to deprive it of its temporal honours and substance, *on what* will you rest the claim of respect and attention which you make upon your flocks? Hitherto you have been upheld by your birth, your education, your wealth, your connections; should these secular advantages cease, on what must Christ's Ministers depend? Is not this a serious practical question? We know how miserable is the state of religious bodies not supported by the state. Look at the Dissenters on all sides of you, and you will see at once that their Ministers, depending simply upon the people, become the *creatures* of the people. Are you content that this should be your case? Alas! can a greater evil befall Christians than for their teachers to be guided by them, instead of guiding? How can we 'hold fast the form of sound words', and 'keep that which is committed to our trust', if our influence is to depend simply on our popularity? Is it not our very office to *oppose* the world? can we then allow ourselves to *court* it? to preach smooth things and prophesy deceits? to make the way of life easy to the rich and indolent, and to bribe the humbler classes by excitements and strong intoxicating doctrine? Surely it must not be so; and the question recurs, on *what* are we to rest our authority when the state deserts us?

Christ has not left His Church without claim of its own upon the attention of men. Surely not. Hard Master He cannot be, to bid us oppose the world, yet give us no credentials for so doing. There are some who rest their divine mission on their own unsupported assertion; others, who rest it upon their popularity; others, on their success; and others, who rest it upon their temporal distinctions. This last case has, perhaps, been too much our own; I fear we have neglected the real ground on which our authority is built, our apostolical descent.

We have been born, not of blood, nor of the will of the flesh, nor of the will of man, but of God. The Lord Jesus Christ gave His Spirit to His Apostles; they in turn laid their hands on those who should succeed them; and these again on others; and so the sacred gift has been handed down to our present Bishops, who have appointed us as their assistants, and in some sense representatives.

Now every one of us believes this. I know that some will at first deny they do; still they do believe it. Only, it is not sufficiently practically impressed on their minds. They do believe it; for it is the doctrine of the Ordination Service, which they have recognised as truth in the most solemn season of their lives. In order, then, not to prove, but to remind and impress, I entreat your attention to the words used when you were made Ministers of Christ's Church.

The office of Deacon was thus committed to you: 'Take thou authority to execute the office of a Deacon in the Church of God committed unto thee: In the name', etc.

And the priesthood thus: 'Receive the Holy Ghost for the office and work of a Priest in the Church of God, now committed unto thee by the imposition of our hands. Whose sins thou dost forgive, they are forgiven; and whose sins thou dost retain, they are retained. And be thou a faithful dispenser of the Word of God, and of His Holy Sacraments: In the name', etc.

These, I say, were words spoken to us, and received by us, when we were brought nearer to God than at any other time of our lives. I know the grace of ordination is contained in the laying on of hands, not in any form of words; yet in our own case (as has ever been usual in the Church) words of blessing have accompanied the act. Thus we have confessed before God our belief that through the Bishop who ordained us, we received the Holy Ghost, the power to bind and to loose, to administer the Sacraments, and to preach. Now *how* is he able to give these great gifts? *Whence* is his right? Are these words idle (which would be taking God's name in vain), or do they express merely a wish (which surely is very far below their meaning), or do they not rather indicate that the speaker is conveying a gift? Surely they can mean nothing short of this. But whence, I ask, his right to do so? Has he any right, except as having received the power from those who consecrated him to be a Bishop? He could not give what he had never received. It is plain then that he but *transmits*; and that the Christian Ministry is a *succession*. And if we trace back the power of ordination from hand to hand, of course we shall come to the Apostles at last. We know we do, as a plain historical fact. And therefore all we, who have been ordained Clergy, in the very form of our ordination acknowledged the doctrine of the Apostolical Succession.

And for the same reason, we must necessarily consider none to be *really* ordained who have not *thus* been ordained. For if ordination is a divine ordinance, it must be necessary; and if it is not a divine ordinance, how dare we use it? Therefore all who use it, all of *us*, must consider it necessary. As well might we pretend the Sacraments are not necessary to Salvation, while we make use of the offices of the Liturgy; for when God appoints means of grace, they are *the* means.

I do not see how any one can escape from this plain view of the subject, except (as I have already hinted) by declaring that the words do not mean all that they say. But only reflect what a most unseemly time for random words is that in which Ministers are set apart for their office. Do we not adopt a Liturgy, *in order to* hinder inconsiderate idle language, and shall we, in the most sacred of all services, write down, subscribe, and use again and again forms of speech, which have not been weighed, and cannot be taken strictly?

Therefore, my dear Brethren, act up to your professions. Let it not be said that you have neglected a gift; for if you have the Spirit of the Apostles on you, surely this *is* a great gift. 'Stir up the gift of God which is in you.' Make much of it. Show your value of it. Keep it before your minds as an honourable badge, far higher than that secular respectability, or cultivation, or polish, or learning, or rank, which gives you a hearing with the many. Tell *them* of your gift. The times will soon drive you to do this, if you mean to be still any thing. But wait not for the times. Do not be compelled, by the world's forsaking you, to recur as if unwillingly to the high source of your authority. Speak out now, before you are forced, both as glorying in your privilege, and to ensure your rightful honour from your people. A notion has gone abroad that they can take away your power. They think they have given and can take it away. They think it lies in the Church property, and they know that they have politically the power to confiscate that property. They have been deluded into a notion that present palpable usefulness, produceable results, acceptableness to your flocks, that these and such-like are the tests of your Divine commission. Enlighten them in this matter. Exalt our Holy Fathers, the Bishops, as the Representatives of the Apostles, and the Angels of the Churches; and magnify your office, as being ordained by them to take part in their Ministry.

But if you will not adopt my view of the subject, which I offer to you, not doubtingly, yet (I hope) respectfully, at all events, choose your side. To remain neuter much longer will be itself to take a part. *Choose* your side; since side you shortly must with one or other party, even though you do nothing. Fear to be of those whose line is decided for them by chance circumstances, and who may perchance find themselves with the enemies of Christ, while they think but to remove themselves from worldly politics. Such abstinence is impossible

in troubled times. 'He that is not with Me is against Me, and he that
gathereth not with Me scattereth abroad.'

J. H. Newman, Tract 1, 'Thoughts on the Ministerial Commission
Respectfully Addressed to the Clergy'

*In a later Tract Newman took the argument further, declaring the
necessity of the Apostolic Succession.*

As to the *fact* of the Apostolical Succession, i.e. that our present
Bishops are the heirs and representatives of the Apostles by successive transmission of the prerogative of being so, this is too notorious
to require proof. Every link in the chain is known, from St Peter to
our present Metropolitans. Here then I only ask, looking at this plain
fact by itself, is there not something of a divine providence in it?
Can we conceive that this Succession has been preserved all over the
world, amid many revolutions, through many centuries, *for nothing*?
Is it wise or pious to despise or neglect a gift thus transmitted to us in
matter of fact, even if Scripture did not touch upon the subject?

Next, consider how *natural* is the doctrine of a succession. When
an individual comes to me, claiming to speak in the name of the
Most High, it is natural to ask him for his authority. If he replies,
that we are all bound to instruct each other, this reply is intelligible,
but in the very form of it excludes the notion of a ministerial order,
i.e. a class of persons set apart from others for religious offices. If he
appeals to some miraculous gift, this too is intelligible, and only unsatisfactory when the alleged gift is proved to be a fiction. No other
answer can be given except a reference to some person, who has given
him license to exercise ministerial functions; then follows the question, *how* that individual obtained his authority to do so. In the case
of the Catholic the person referred to, i.e. the Bishop, has received it
from a predecessor, and he from another, and so on, till we arrive at
the Apostles themselves, and thence our LORD and SAVIOUR. It is
superfluous to dwell on so plain a principle, which in matters of this
world we act upon daily.

Lastly, the argument *from Scripture* is surely quite clear to those
who honestly wish direction for *practice*. CHRIST promised He
would be with His Apostles always, as ministers of His religion, even
unto the end of the world. In one sense the Apostles were to be alive
till He came again; but they all died at the natural time. Does it
not follow, that there are those now alive who represent them? Now
who were the most probable representatives of them in the generation

next their death? They surely, whom they had ordained to succeed them in the ministerial work. If any persons could be said to have Christ's power and presence, and the gifts of ruling and ordaining, of teaching, of binding and loosing (and comparing together the various Scriptures on the subject, all these seem included in the promise to be with the Church always) surely those, on whom the Apostles laid their hands, were they. And so in the next age, if any were representatives of the first representatives, they must be the next generation of Bishops, and so on. Nor does it materially alter the argument, though we suppose the blessing upon Ministerial Offices made not to the Apostles, but to the whole body of Disciples; i.e. the Church. For, even if it be the Church that has the power of ordination committed to it, still it exercises it through the Bishops as its organs; and the question recurs, how has the Presbytery in this or that country obtained the power? The Church certainly has from the first committed it to the Bishops, and has never resumed it; and the Bishops have nowhere committed it to the Presbytery, who therefore cannot be in possession of it.

However, it is merely for argument sake that I make this allowance, as to the meaning of the text in Matt. xxviii; for our LORD's promise of His presence 'unto the end of the world', was made to the Apostles, *by themselves*. At the same time, let it be observed what force is added to the argument for the Apostolical Succession, by the acknowledged existence in Scripture of the doctrine of a standing Church, or permanent Body Corporate for spiritual purposes. For, if Scripture has formed all Christians into one continuous community through all ages, (which I do not here prove,) it is but according to the same analogy, that the Ministerial Office should be vested in an order, propagated from age to age, on the principle of Succession. And, if we proceed to considerations of utility and expedience, it is plain that, according to our notions, it is more necessary that a Minister should be perpetuated by a fixed law, than that the community of Christians should be, which can scarcely be considered to be vested with any powers such as to require the visible authority which a Succession supplies.

J. H. Newman, Tract 17, 'The Episcopal Church Apostolical', pages 2–4

J. W. Bowden (1798–1844), a lay friend and admirer of Newman, joined the writers of the Tracts with a powerful defence of the Apostolic Succession and its continuation in the Church of England. He alludes to the safeguard against unworthy ministers in number 26

*of the Thirty-nine Articles, and to the Branch theory of the Church.
He does not reckon ordination to be one of the 'seven sacraments'
as it would be regarded by Roman Catholics and by later Anglo-
Catholics.*

Since the Apostolic age seventeen centuries have rolled away: exactly
eighteen hundred years have elapsed since the delivery of CHRIST'S
recorded promise; and, blessed be GOD, the Church is with us still.
Amid all the political storms and vicissitudes, amid all the religious
errors and corruptions which have chequered, during that long
period, the world's eventful history, a regular unbroken succession
has preserved among us Ministers of GOD, whose authority to con-
fer the gifts of His SPIRIT is derived originally from the laying on
of the hands of the Apostles themselves. Many intermediate posses-
sors of that authority have, it is true, intervened between them and
these, their hallowed predecessors, but 'the gifts of GOD are without
repentance'; the same Spirit rules over the Church now who presided
at the consecration of St. Paul, and the eighteen centuries that are
past can have had no power to invalidate the promise of our GOD.
Nor, even though we may admit that many of those who formed the
connecting links of this holy chain were themselves unworthy of the
bishop's charge reposed in them, can this furnish us with any solid
ground for doubting or denying their power to exercise that legiti-
mate authority with which they were duly invested, of transmitting
the sacred gift to worthier followers.

Ordination, or, as it is called in the case of Bishops, Consecration,
though it does not precisely come within our definition of a sacrament,
is nevertheless a rite partaking, in a high degree, of the sacramental character, and it is by reference to the proper sacraments that its
nature can be most satisfactorily illustrated. And with respect to these,
it would lead us into endless difficulties were we to admit that, when
administered by a minister duly authorised according to the outward
forms of the Church, either Baptism or the LORD's Supper depended
for its validity either on the moral and spiritual attainments of that
minister, or on the frame of mind in which he might have received,
at his ordination, the outward and visible sign of his authority. Did
the Sacraments indeed rest on such circumstances as these for their
efficacy in each case of their ministration, who would there be of us,
or of any Christian congregation, who could possibly say whether he
had been baptized or not; or what preparation or self-examination
could give to a penitent the confidence that he had truly partaken of
the Body and Blood of CHRIST, were the reality of that partaking

to depend upon something of which he had no knowledge, and over which he could exercise no control; upon the spiritual state not only of the officiating minister himself, but of every individual Bishop through whom that minister had received his authority, through the long lapse of eighteen hundred years? He who receives unworthily, or in an improper state of mind, either ordination or consecration, may probably receive to his own soul no saving health from the hallowed rite; but while we admit, as we do, the validity of sacraments administered by a Priest thus unworthily ordained, we cannot consistently deny that of ordination, in any of its grades, when bestowed by a Bishop as unworthily consecrated.

The very question of worth indeed, with relation to such matters, is absurd. Who is worthy? Who is a fit and meet dispenser of the gifts of the Holy SPIRIT? What are, after all, the petty differences between sinner and sinner, when viewed in relation to Him whose eyes are too pure to behold iniquity, and who charges His very angels with folly? And be it remembered that the Apostolic powers, if not transmitted through these, in some instances corrupt, channels, have not been transmitted to our times at all. Unless then we acknowledge the reality of such transmission, we must admit that the Church which CHRIST founded is no longer to be found upon the earth, and that the promise of His protection, far from being available to the end of the world, is forgotten and out of date already.

The unworthiness of man, then, cannot prevent the goodness of GOD from flowing in those channels in which He has destined it to flow, and the Christian congregations of the present day, who sit at the feet of Ministers duly ordained, have the same reason for reverencing in them the successors of the Apostles, as the Primitive Churches of Ephesus and of Crete had for honouring in Timothy and in Titus the Apostolical authority of him who had appointed them.

A branch of this holy Catholic (or universal) Church has been, through GOD's blessing, established for ages in our island; a branch which, as has been already stated, we denominate the Church of England. Its officiating ministers are divided into the three original orders of Bishops, Priests, and Deacons, and into no other. In the exercise of that authority which is inherent in every society, of making salutary laws and regulations for its own guidance, it has been found expedient to vest in two of the principal members of the episcopal order in England a certain authority over the rest, and to style them Archbishops, but this is not by any means to be understood as constituting them another order in the Church. They are but, in strictness of language, the first and leading Bishops of our land.

The Priests and Deacons, (whom we usually class together under the common name of Clergymen), who officiate in the Churches and Chapels of our Establishment, have each received ordination to the discharge of their holy office by the laying on of hands of a Bishop, assisted, in the case of Priests, by members already admitted into the presbytery or priesthood, as St Paul was assisted in the ordination of Timothy (1 Tim. iv. 14.)

And each Bishop of our Church has, at the hands of another Bishop, (himself similarly called to the office), received in the most solemn manner the gift of the HOLY GHOST, and that Apostolical power over the Church, for the support of which the Redeemer pledged Himself that His assistance should never be wanting to the end of time.

Wonderful indeed is the providence of GOD, which has so long preserved the unbroken line, and thus brought it to pass that our Bishops should, even at this distance of time, stand before their flocks as the authorised successors of the Apostles.

J. W. Bowden, Tract 5, 'On the Nature and Constitution of the
Church of Christ', pages 10–12

Keble exhorted his clerical brethren to magnify their office and claim their apostolic authority.

I fear it must be owned that much of the evil is owing to the comparatively low ground which we ourselves, the Ministers of God, have chosen to occupy in defence of our commission. For many years, we have been much in the habit of resting our claim on the general duties of submission to authority, of decency and order, of respecting precedents long established; instead of appealing to that warrant, which marks us, *exclusively,* for God's Ambassadors. We have spoken much in the same tone, as we might, had we been mere Laymen, acting for ecclesiastical purposes by a commission under the Great Seal. Waiving the question, 'Was this wise? was it right, in higher respects?' I ask, was it not obviously certain, in some degree, to damp and deaden the interest with which men of devout minds would naturally regard the Christian Ministry? Would not more than half the reverential feeling, with which we look on a Church or Cathedral, be gone, if we ceased to contemplate it as the house of God, and learned to esteem it merely as a place set apart by the state for moral and religious instruction?

It would be going too deep into history, were one now to enter on any statement of the causes which have led, silently and insensibly, almost to the abandonment of the high ground which our Fathers of the Primitive Church – i.e. the Bishops and Presbyters of the first five centuries, invariably took, in preferring their claim to canonical obedience. For the present, it is rather wished to urge, on plain positive considerations, the wisdom and duty of keeping in view the simple principle on which they relied.

Their principle, in short, was this: That the Holy Feast on our Saviour's sacrifice, which all confess to be 'generally necessary to salvation', was intended by Him to be constantly conveyed through the hands of commissioned persons. Except therefore we can show such a warrant, we cannot be sure that our hands convey the sacrifice; we cannot be sure that souls worthily prepared, receiving the bread which we break, and the cup of blessing which we bless, are partakers of the Body and Blood of Christ. Piety, then, and Christian Reverence, and sincere devout Love of our Redeemer, nay, and Charity to the souls of our brethren, not good order and expediency only, would prompt us, at all earthly risks, to preserve and transmit the seal and warrant of Christ.

If the rules of Christian conduct were founded merely on visible expediency, the zeal with which those holy men were used to maintain the Apostolical Succession might appear a strange unaccountable thing. Not so, if our duties to our Saviour be like our duties to a parent or a brother, the unalterable result of certain known relations, previous to all consideration of consequences. Reflect on this, and you will presently feel what a difference it makes in a pious mind, whether ministerial prerogatives be traced to our Lord's own institution, or to mere voluntary ecclesiastical arrangement. Let two plans of Government, as far as we can see, be equally good and expedient in themselves, yet if there be but a fair probability of the one rather than the other proceeding from our Blessed Lord Himself, those who love Him in sincerity will know at once which to prefer. They will not demand that every point be made out by inevitable demonstration, or promulgated in form, like a state decree. According to the beautiful expression of the Psalmist, they will consent to be 'guided by our Lord's eye'; the *indications* of His pleasure will be enough for them. They will state the matter thus to themselves: 'Jesus Christ's own commission is the best external security I can have, that in receiving this bread and wine, I verily receive His Body and Blood. Either the Bishops have that commission, or there is no such thing in the world. For at least Bishops have it with as much evidence, as Presbyters without them. In proportion, then, to my Christian anxiety for keeping as near my Saviour as I can, I shall, of course, be very unwilling

to separate myself from Episcopal communion. And in proportion
to my charitable care for others, will be my industry to preserve and
extend the like consolation and security to them'.

J. Keble, Tract 4, 'Adherence to the Apostolical Succession
the Safest Course', pages 1–3

*Benjamin Harrison (1808–67), chaplain to Archbishop Howley
and later Archdeacon of Maidstone, wrote about the status and
authority of the priestly order, citing the Book of Common Prayer
in evidence.*

It is to be feared, that there are many of our brethren, in the present
day, who allow the thought of present and past transgressions, of
our own sins, and those of our fathers, to banish entirely the remembrance of the glorious promises and privileges which belong to us.
They see so much neglected, and so much to be done, that they think
it were better for us each to work apart in lonely humiliation, 'in fear
and in much trembling', than to endeavour to magnify our office, and
cheer one another with the songs of Zion. Now, I would ask, if this
notion exists in any of our brethren, whether, under the semblance
of good, it does not argue something of mistaken feeling, and that in
more than one essential point?

Does not this opinion seem to imply the supposition, that the dignity conferred on the Ministerial Office is something given for the
exaltation of the Clergy, and not for the benefit of the people? as if
there were a different interest in the two orders, and, in maintaining
their Divine appointment, the Clergy would make themselves 'lords
over GOD'S heritage'? I do not now enter upon the point, that to
magnify the *office* is not necessarily to exalt the *individual* who bears
it; nay, that the thought which will most deeply humble the individual, most oppress him with the overwhelming sense of his own
insufficiency, is the consciousness 'into how high a dignity, and to
how weighty an office and charge' he has been called; an office 'of
such excellency, and of so great difficulty'. I would now rather ask,
for whose benefit this high and sacred office has been instituted? For
the Clergy, or for the people? The Apostle will decide this point: 'He
gave some, Apostles; and some, Prophets; and some Evangelists; and
some, Pastors and Teachers; for the perfecting of the saints, for the
work of the ministry, for *the edifying of the body of* CHRIST' (Eph.
iv. 11, 12). 'All things' are *yours*, whether Paul, or Apollos, or Cephas
(1 Cor. iii. 21). And this, it should be well observed, the Apostle says

on purpose to put an end to that *exaltation* of individuals, which the
Church of Corinth had fallen into, from forgetting that their pastors
and teachers were all *'Ministers of Christ'*, Ministers by whom they
believed *'even as the* LORD *gave to every man'*. And so again to the
same Church, and in reference to the same subject, St Paul says, 'All
things are for *your sakes,* that the abundant grace might, through
the thanksgiving of many, redound to the glory of GOD'. (2 Cor. iv.
15.) Scripture then is express upon this point, that whatever power
and grace Christ has given to His Ministers, He has given them for
the good of His people, and the glory of His heavenly FATHER.
And do not our own understandings and consciences bear witness
to the same truth? For what is our commission? Is it not a 'Ministry
of reconciliation'? – to wit, that 'GOD was in CHRIST, reconciling
the world unto Himself'; and hath committed to us the proclamation
of the pardon? Let us put the case on which the Apostle's language
is founded; the case, I mean, of a people in rebellion against their
sovereign, visited with the news that their king is willing, nay, even
anxiously desirous to grant them forgiveness and favour. In such a
case, would not the first question be, what authority does this report
go upon? who are the persons who bring it? is it merely a matter of
their individual belief, or are they duly *authorised* and *commissioned*
from the court; are they come as volunteers, or have they been *sent* by
their master? 'Now then we are *Ambassadors for* CHRIST'; we are
sent to 'bring good tidings and to publish peace', 'to preach deliver-
ance to the captives, and the opening of the prison to them that are
bound'; and if we allow our commission to be questioned, nay, if we
do not most unequivocally and prominently assert it, whom are we
robbing? not ourselves of honour, but the people, to whom we are
sent, of the blessedness and joy of knowing, that GOD 'desireth not
the death of a sinner, but rather that he should turn from his wicked-
ness and live'; and that, in token of this desire, He 'hath given power
and commandment to His Ministers to declare and pronounce to His
people, being penitent, the absolution and remission of their sins.'
We are sent to preach good tidings unto the meek, to bind up the
broken-hearted, to comfort all that mourn; and it is the meek, and
the broken-hearted, and the mourners, that will feel the loss, if our
blessed Office be set at nought, or disregarded. Let us well consider
this point. There is a humble and fearful member of CHRIST's flock,
who desires to strengthen and refresh his soul by the Body and Blood
of CHRIST; but he cannot quiet his own conscience; he requires
further comfort and counsel. Surely it is to *his* comfort, that there
is a duly commissioned Minister of GOD's Word at hand; to whom

he may come and open his grief, and receive the benefit of the sentence of GOD's pardon, and so prepare himself to approach the holy Table 'with a full trust in GOD's mercy, and with a quiet conscience'; and thus draw near with faith, and take that holy Sacrament to his comfort. And then, again, when he lieth sick upon his bed, does not his SAVIOUR 'make all his bed in his sickness', when his Minister comes to him, to receive the confession of his sins, and to relieve his conscience of the 'weighty' things which press it down and then, ('if he humbly and heartily desire it') by virtue of CHRIST's authority committed to him, assures him 'the pardon of all his sins', that so, as his sufferings abound, his consolation also may abound through CHRIST; and as his outward man perisheth, the inward man may be renewed day by day. How then ought we to look upon the power which has been given us by CHRIST, but as a sacred treasure, of which we are Ministers and Stewards; and which it is our duty to guard for the sake of those little ones, for whose edification (2 Cor. xiii. 10) it was that our LORD left power with His Church? And if we suffer it to be lost to our Christian brethren, how shall we answer it, not only to those that might now rejoice in its holy comfort, but to those also who are to come after us? 'For the promise is unto you and to your children, and unto all that are afar off, even as many as the LORD our GOD shall call'.

B. Harrison, Tract 17, 'The Ministerial Commission a Trust from
Christ for the Benefit of His People', pages 2–4

A further defence of the Apostolic Succession in the Church of England was made in a Tract first drafted by William Palmer, one of the Hadleigh four, and completed by Newman.

When Churchmen in England maintain the Apostolical Commission of their Ministers, they are sometimes met with the objection that they cannot prove it without tracing their orders back to the Church of Rome; a position, indeed, which in a certain sense is true. And hence it is argued that they are reduced to the dilemma, either of acknowledging they had no right to separate from the Pope, or, on the other hand, of giving up the Ministerial Succession altogether, and resting the claims of their pastors on some other ground; in other words, that they are *inconsistent* in reprobating Popery, while they draw a line between their Ministers and those of Dissenting Communions.

It is intended, in the pages that follow, to reply to this supposed difficulty; but first a few words shall be said, by way of preface, on the doctrine itself, which we Churchmen advocate.

The Christian Church is a body consisting of Clergy and Laity: this is generally agreed upon, and may here be assumed. Now, what we say is, that these two classes are distinguished from each other, and united to each other, by the commandment of God Himself; that the clergy have a commission from God Almighty, through regular succession from the Apostles, to preach the Gospel, administer the Sacraments, and guide the Church; and again, that in consequence the people are bound to hear them with attention, receive the Sacrament from their hands, and pay them all dutiful obedience. [...]

But here we are met by the objection, on which I propose to make a few remarks, that, though it is true there was a continual Succession of pastors and teachers in the early Church who had a Divine commission, yet that no Protestants can have it; that we gave it up when our communion ceased with Rome, in which Church it still remains; or, at least, that no Protestant can plead it without condemning the Reformation itself, for that our own predecessors then revolted and separated from those spiritual pastors, who, according to our principles, then had the commission of Jesus Christ.

Our reply to this is a flat denial of the alleged facts on which it rests. The English Church did *not* revolt from those who in that day had authority by succession from the Apostles. On the contrary, it is certain that the Bishops and Clergy in England and Ireland remained the same as before the separation, and that it was these, with the aid of the civil power, who delivered the Church of those kingdoms from the yoke of Papal tyranny and usurpation, while at the same time they gradually removed from the minds of the people various superstitious opinions and practices which had grown up during the middle ages, and which, though never formally received by the judgement of the whole Church, were yet very prevalent. I do not say the case might never arise, when it might become the duty of private individuals to take upon themselves the office of protesting against and abjuring the heresies of a corrupt Church. But such an extreme case it is unpleasant and unhealthy to contemplate. All I say here is, that this was not the state of things at the time of the Reformation. The Church then by its proper rulers and officers reformed itself. There was no new Church founded among us, but the rights and the true doctrines of the ancient existing Church were asserted and established. [...]

The people of England, then, in casting off the Pope, but obeyed and concurred in the acts of their own spiritual Superiors, and committed no schism. Queen Mary, it is true, drove out after many years the orthodox Bishops, and reduced our Church again under the Bishop of Rome; but this submission was only exacted by force, and in itself null and void; and, moreover, in matter of fact it lasted but a little while, for on the succession of Queen Elizabeth, the true Successors of the Apostles in the English Church were reinstated in their ancient rights. So, I repeat, there was no revolt, in any part of these transactions, against those who had a commission from God; for it was the Bishops and Clergy themselves who maintained the just rights of their Church.

> J. H. Newman and William Palmer, Tract 15, 'On the Apostolical
> Succession in the English Church', pages 1, 4

Newman kept up the exhortation made in the first Tract.

If a Clergyman is quite convinced that the Apostolical Succession is lost, then of course he is at liberty to turn his mind from the subject. But if he is not quite sure of this, it surely is his duty seriously to examine the question, and to make up his mind carefully and deliberately. For if there be a chance of its being preserved to us, there is a chance of his having had a momentous talent committed to him, which he is burying in the earth.

It cannot be supposed that any serious man would treat the subject scoffingly. If any one is tempted to do so, let him remember the fearful words of the Apostle: 'Esau, a *profane person, who* for one morsel of meat, sold his birthright'.

If any are afraid that to insist on their commission will bring upon them ridicule, and diminish their usefulness, let them ask themselves whether it be not cowardice to refuse to leave the event to God. It was the reproach of the men of Ephraim that, though they were 'harnessed and carried bows', they 'turned themselves back in the day of battle.'

> J. H. Newman, Tract 19, 'On Arguing Concerning the
> Apostolical Succession', page 4

Keble had a more poetic vision of priestly authority.

> A mortal youth I saw
> Nigh to God's Altar draw
> And lowly kneel, while o'er him pastoral hands
> Were spread with many a prayer,
> And when he rose up there,
> He could undo or bind the dread celestial bands.

When bread and wine he takes,
And of Christ's Passion makes
Memorial high before the mercy throne,
Faith speaks, and we are sure
That offering good and pure
Is more than angels' bread to all whom Christ will own.

J. Keble, 'Church Rites', *Lyra Innocentium* (1846),
Methuen, 1903, 26 January 1843

Newman reminded the clergy of their duty not only to celebrate Holy Communion but also to say the daily offices.

If a Christian Minister might suitably offer up common prayer by himself three centuries ago, surely he may do so now. If he then was the spokesman of the saints far and near, gathering together their holy and concordant suffrages, and presenting them by virtue of his priesthood, he is so now. The revival of this usage is merely a matter of place and time; and though neither our Lord nor His Church would have us make sudden alterations, even though for the better, yet certainly we ought never to forget what is abstractedly our duty, what is in itself best, what it is we have to aim at and labour towards. If authority were needed, besides our Church's own, for the propriety of Christian Ministers praying even by themselves in places of worship, we have it in the life of our great pattern of Christian faith and wisdom, Hooker. 'To what he persuaded others', says his biographer, 'he added his own example of fasting and prayer; and did usually every Ember week take from the parish clerk the key of the church-door, into which place he retired every day, and locked himself up for many hours; and did the like most Fridays, and other days of fasting.'

That holy man, in this instance, kept his prayers to himself. He was not offering up the Daily Service; but I adduce his instance to show that there is nothing strange or unseemly in a Christian Minister praying in Church by himself, and if so, much less when he gives his people the opportunity of coming if they will. *This*, then, is what I felt and feel: it is commonly said, when week-day prayers are spoken of, 'you will not get a congregation, or you will get but a few'; but they whom Christ has brought near to Himself to be the Stewards of His Mysteries, depend on no man; rather, after His pattern, they are to draw men after them. He prayed alone on the mountain; He prays alone (for who is there to join with Him?), before His Father's throne. He is the one effectual Intercessor for sinners at the right hand of God. And what He is really, such are we in figure; what He is meritoriously, such are we instrumentally. Such are we, by His grace, allowed to occupy His place visibly, however unworthily, in His absence till He come; allowed to depend on Him, and not on our people; allowed to draw our commission from Him, not from them; allowed to be a centre, about which the Church may grow, and about which it really exists, be it great or little.

J. H. Newman, *Parochial Sermons*, Rivington, 1834–42, III, pages 341–2

Later in the Tract series Isaac Williams still rebuked Anglican clergy for failing to 'magnify their office' and thinking more of social status than apostolic ministry. After the familiar complaints about state interference with the Church, he turns to the parish priests.

Consider the many circumstances in which the clergy feel themselves not free to act, on account of that weight of deference which the world claims of them; as, e.g. in omitting to baptize before the congregation, and to read the Prayer for the Church Militant. But the more subtle influence of the same principle may be seen in this, that clergymen, individually, do not like to rest their influence and authority on their spiritual station, as such; they consider that their respectability depends on their liberal education, their talents, their rank in society, their worldly connections and property, which afford the whole body, and each member of it, a high respectability in the eyes of the world. But, on the contrary, there is a secret contempt entertained for their Ministerial profession as such, which they are aware is only warded off by their external advantages. Notwithstanding all that can be said of their inherent right to Spiritual authority, and indeed claims to honour and veneration, as stewards of GOD, the highest which man can bestow, these are not met with any responsive feelings in others, nor supported in themselves by a sense of responsibility compatible with such claims, merely on account of their intimate connection with things of an opposite character, the worldly benefits which are attached to it. The bonds of Laud, the sufferings of Ken and Wilson, not only were to themselves the means of spiritual succour, but the remembrance of them throws a hallowing light over their Order, as being thus recognized occasionally in the appropriate dress of that Master whose ambassadors they are.

Isaac Williams, Tract 86, 'Indications of a Superintending Providence and the Preservation of the Prayer Book', pages 74–5

4

Sacramental Doctrine

One of the fundamental tenets of the Tractarians was that, since the Church of England had maintained the Apostolic Succession, her sacraments were valid in the Catholic tradition. They also claimed to have kept the purity of primitive doctrine. Innovation, whether Roman or Protestant, was seen as a departure from the faith once delivered, though Newman would later reflect at length on the development of doctrine and find in it some justification for his secession.

Preaching in 1836, Keble made the point strongly, taking a centrally Anglican position about the nature of the Eucharist. The whole sermon is an example of the conservative tendency of the early years of the Movement.

The sacred building is so divinely, though invisibly cemented, that, for aught we know, it is impossible to remove any portion, either of scriptural or traditionary truth without weakening the whole arch. We to whom the whole is committed, under the most solemn of all pledges, and with the actual gift of the all-sufficient Spirit to aid us in redeeming that Pledge; let us, above all things, beware of the presumption of selecting for ourselves among the truths and laws of the Most High, which we will retain, and which we may venture to dispense with.

In the next place, let us beware of novelty: novelty, I mean, as compared with the apostolic age; not the mere appearance of novelty as compared with the current notions of our time. For it is self-evident, that if in any age or country any portion of apostolical truth be lost, whenever it is revived it must for the time look new; and its maintainers will have to contend with the prejudice which constantly waits on the disturbers of things established. Not novelty, therefore, relative to us, but novelty relative to the primitive and original standard, is the thing above all to be deprecated in the whole of theology, by whatever plausible air of originality, ingenuity, completeness, it may seem to recommend itself.

Observe under what a fearful penalty, in a warning parallel to that of the text, St. Paul, writing to the Thessalonians, discourages every intrusion of speculative doctrine. The apostasy, he tells them, will come; the wicked one shall be revealed, actuated by Satan to deceive them that perish; 'on whom God will send strong delusion, that they may believe a lie'. And then he proceeds, 'Wherefore, brethren, stand fast, and hold the traditions which ye have been taught, whether by word or our epistle'. Is not this equivalent to saying, that whoever is studious of novelty in religion is in a way to take part with Antichrist; that the only security against him, and the spirit which prepares the way for him, is to hold the apostolical doctrine, whether taught in word or in writing; and to exclude all additions, however tempting to human ingenuity and love of system, however acutely they may appear to be reasoned out, and to fall in with allowed principles?

Had this rule been faithfully kept, it would have preserved the Church just as effectually from the assertion of transubstantiation on the one hand, as from the denial of Christ's presence on the other hand. The two errors in the original are perhaps but rationalism in different forms; endeavours to explain away, and bring nearer to the human intellect that which had been left thoroughly mysterious both by Scripture and tradition. They would both turn the attention of men from the real life-giving miracle to mere metaphysical or grammatical subtleties, such as our fathers never knew.

Observe, again, the phraseology of the Apostle, how it is formed throughout upon the supposition, that in the substance of the faith there is no such thing as improvement, discovery, evolution of new truths; none of those processes, which are the pride of human reason and knowledge, find any place here. Here the one thing needful is to 'retain the mystery of the faith'; to 'abide in the good instruction whereto we have already attained'; to 'teach no other doctrine'; to be on our guard against those who resist the truth under pretence of 'proceeding further', assured that such, although they seem to be 'ever learning', shall never be able to 'come to the knowledge of the truth'; they will '*proceed*' indeed, but it will be from bad to worse. All these cautions, and others no less fearful, the Holy Spirit has left for our admonition, directed not against any positive wrong opinion, but in general against the fatal error of treating theology like any human science, as a subject in which every succeeding age might be expected to advance on the former.

J. Keble, 'Primitive Tradition Recognised in Holy Scripture', Sermons Academical and Occasional, Parker, 1848, pages 212–14

Newman was firm about the importance of the sacraments, as against those who denigrated them and the idea of a priestly order, and believed that the promises of Scripture did not extend to the later Church. The conviction that to question one aspect of received tradition was to threaten the rest was something that he held strongly.

Hence the lamentable spectacle, as commonly seen, of men who deny the Apostolic commission proceeding to degrade the Eucharist from Sacrament to a bare commemorative rite; or to make Baptism a mere outward form, one sign of profession, as it would be childish or fanciful to revere. And reasonably; for they who find it superstitious to believe that particular persons are channels of grace, are but consistent in denying virtue to particular ordinances. Nor do they stop even here; for denying the grace of baptism, they proceed to deny the doctrine of original sin, for which that grace is the remedy. Further, denying the doctrine of original sin, they necessarily impair the doctrine of the Atonement, and so prepare a way for the denial of our Lord's Divinity. Again, denying the power of the Sacraments on the ground of its *mysteriousness*, demanding from the very text of Scripture the fullest proof of it conceivable, and thinking little of the blessedness of 'not seeing, and yet believing', they naturally proceed to object to the doctrine of the Trinity as obstructing and obscuring the simplicity (as they consider it) of the Gospel and but indirectly deducible from the extant documents of inspiration. Lastly, after they have thus divested the divine remedies of sin, and the treatment necessary for the sinner, of their solemnity and awe, having made the whole scheme of salvation of as intelligible and ordinary a character as the repair of any accident in the works of man, having robbed Faith of its mysteries, the Sacraments of their virtue, the priesthood of its commission, no wonder that sin itself is soon considered a venial matter, moral evil as a mere imperfection, man as involved in no great peril or misery, his duties of no very arduous or anxious nature. In a word, religion, as such, is in the way to disappear from the mind altogether; and in its stead a mere cold worldly morality, a decent regard to the claims of society, a cultivation of the benevolent affections, and a gentleness and polish of external deportment, will be supposed to constitute the entire duties of that being, who is conceived in sin, and the child of wrath, is redeemed by the precious blood of the Son of God, is born again and sustained by the Spirit through the invisible strength of Sacraments, and called, through self-denial and sanctification of the

inward man, to the Eternal Presence of the Father, Son, and Holy
Ghost.

Such is the course and issue of unbelief, though beginning in what
the world calls trifles. Beware then, O my Brethren, of entering a
way which leads to death. Fear to question what Scripture says of the
Ministers of Christ, lest the same perverse spirit lead you on to question its doctrine about Himself and His Father. 'Little children, it is
the last time; and as ye have heard that Antichrist shall come, even
now are there many Antichrists ... They went out from us, but they
were not of us'. 'Ye shall know them by their fruits'. If any man come
to you, bringing any scoff against the power of Christ's Ministers,
ask him what he holds concerning the Sacraments, or concerning the
Blessed Trinity; look narrowly after his belief as regards the Atonement, or Original Sin. Ascertain whether he holds with the Church's
doctrine in these points; see to it whether at very best he does not try
to evade the question, has recourse to explanations, or professes to
have no opinion at all upon it.

J. H. Newman, *Parochial and Plain Sermons*, Rivington, 1877,
vol. 2, pages 316–18

*Robert Wilberforce (1802–57), second son of the leading Evangelical
William Wilberforce, was a Fellow of Oriel College with Newman
and Froude. He was a supporter of the Oxford Movement, became
an archdeacon and was later received into the Roman Catholic
Church. In the course of a long and learned work of Christology, he
wrote about the importance of the sacraments as the centre and seal
of Christian faith.*

The importance of sacraments rests on the Incarnation of Christ,
and on their being the means through which his man's nature is communicated to his brethren. Let this be apprehended, and what offends
men in their arbitrary appointment will pass away. For since this is
a wholly supernatural work, we could not expect to see it effected,
except through some means specifically provided by God's peculiar
appointment; and the visible means employed are so far from appearing to be less suitable than any other with which the wisdom of God
could have connected the secret working of his power, that in several
respects we can discern them to be singularly appropriate. If man's
connection with the Supreme Being were the mere natural intercourse
of mind with mind – if man were still, as Adam was before the Fall,

the perfect image of his Maker, then indeed, to introduce such media of communication at all would be superfluous. And on this account the sacramental system is inconsistent with that rationalistic theory which supposes that the divine principle of holiness and truth is sufficiently possessed by nature. But allow the scheme of mediation to be essential to man's recovery, let it depend on union with that personal Being in whom holiness and truth became incarnate, and the sacramental system follows of course. In the mere intercourse of mind with mind, sacraments would be an unnatural interruption: but they are exactly suited to effect that union whereby the Divine Head of man's race is bound to his fellows. Since this union is itself foreign to the course of nature, so must the media be by which it is effected; the work cannot depend on their natural influence, but on that influence with which they are supernaturally endowed. And that those outward means which we call sacraments are truly attended by an inward effect, that what is done on earth in holy mysteries effects a real change in the whole nature of those who are acted upon, is known to us by the distinct declarations of God's word. We are told in plain and indubitable terms that baptism and the Lord's Supper are the means by which men are joined to the body of Christ, and therefore by which Christ our Lord joins himself to that renewed race, of which he has become the Head. So that, as St Leo expresses it, 'He that is received by Christ, and that receives Christ, is not the same after the laver of baptism as he was before it, because the body of the regenerate person becomes the flesh of the crucified one'. Now, these facts we learn from the express statements of St. Paul. 'For by one Spirit are we all baptized into one body' (1 Cor. 12.13). And again, 'We being many are one bread and one body, for we are all partakers of that one bread' (1 Cor. 10.7). Herein it is expressly declared that the one and the other of these sacraments are the peculiar means by which union with the body of Christ is bestowed upon men. They are the 'joints and bands' (Col. 2.19) whereby the whole body in its dependence on its Head has nourishment ministered. So that it is in the Church that union takes place with Christ, the new Adam or representative of our race, and it is by this actual union with the new Adam that the whole family of renewed men have that collective being whereby is derived to them their spiritual life.

Robert Wilberforce, *The Doctrine of the Incarnation of Our Lord Jesus Christ in its Relation to Mankind and to the Church*, 3rd edn, John Murray, 1850, pages 408–10

Newman could also be simple as well as profound in his eucharistic belief, like Keble refusing both Transubstantiation and Receptionism.

> Whene'er I seek the Holy Altar's rail,
>   And kneel to take the grace there offered me,
> It is no time to task my reason frail,
>   To try Christ's words, and search how they may be;
> Enough, I eat His Flesh and drink His Blood,
> More is not told – to ask it is not good.
>
> I will not say with these, that bread and wine
>   Have vanished at the consecration prayer;
> Far less with those deny that aught divine
>   And of immortal seed is hidden there.
> Hence, disputants! The din, which ye admire,
> Keeps but ill measure with the Church's choir.

Lyra Apostolica (1836), Mozley, 1841, page 37

Even before the first of the Tracts William Palmer was writing about the Real Presence, defending the absence of an epiclesis – a prayer for the sending of the Holy Spirit upon the bread and wine – in the Book of Common Prayer liturgy.

I argue that it is not essential to pray expressly for the Holy Ghost to sanctify the elements; because it is not essential in prayer to mention to God the means by which he is to accomplish the end which we pray for. God is all-wise. He knows all the methods by which any thing can be accomplished. If we mention them to him, it is chiefly to testify our knowledge of and faith in a revelation which he has been pleased to make those methods that he employs. God needs not that we should mention the way by which certain objects are to be accomplished, even though he may require us to pray for those objects. If, for instance, we prayed to him for the Christian virtues of humility and charity through Jesus Christ, such prayer would be as valid, as if we also testified our knowledge, by praying that the Holy Ghost might be the means of communicating to us that charity and humility; because God knows that the influence of the Holy Ghost is essential to the existence and growth of these Christian virtues, and in praying for them, we pray in effect for the Holy Ghost. It is the same in any prayer for consecrating the elements into Christ's mystical body and blood. However true it be that God effects this consecration by means of the Holy Ghost, it is unnecessary to pray expressly for the Holy Ghost to consecrate the elements of bread and wine, because God knows perfectly all the means and methods of consecration, and because any prayer for consecration is in fact a prayer that it may be accomplished by all the means which are known to INFINITE WISDOM.

These remarks will tend to illustrate and confirm the English prayer for consecration, which I now proceed to examine. It is as follows: 'Hear us, O merciful Father, we most humbly beseech thee; and grant that we, receiving these thy creatures of bread and wine, according to thy Son our Saviour Jesus Christ's holy institution, in remembrance of his death and passion, may be partakers of his most blessed body and blood'. The petition of this prayer, that we 'may be partakers of Christ's most blessed body and blood', in 'receiving these God's creatures of bread and wine', although it be not in itself necessarily referred to the *sacramental* participation of Christ's body and blood, yet is made to refer directly to this sacramental participation, by the words of limitation which accompany the passage. It is not merely a request that in receiving the creatures of bread and wine, we may partake of Christ's body and blood, which would not necessarily infer that we hoped to receive it in a sacramental manner; but it is a request that we may be partakers of Christ's body and blood, by receiving the bread and wine, according to Christ's '*holy institution*', in '*remembrance of his death and passion*'. These expressions define precisely the sort of participation of Christ's body and blood which we pray for, namely, that which is peculiar to the sacrament of the eucharist. This prayer for the participation of Christ's body and blood in the sacramental manner, may be reduced to the following short formula, by divesting it of the introduction and the limitations: 'Grant that we receiving these thy creatures of bread and wine, may be partakers of Christ's body and blood'. Although this prayer does not expressly mention the consecration of the elements, it is nevertheless in effect a prayer for that consecration. For it is necessary that consecration should take place before the bread and wine are the communion of Christ's body and blood. If then we pray that we may partake of Christ's body and blood in a sacramental manner, by receiving the bread and wine, we in effect pray that the elements may first be consecrated. If we pray for the end, we pray for all the means which are to accomplish it. And it is unnecessary to mention expressly those means to a God of infinite wisdom.

In fact, the omission of a direct prayer for consecration, in this prayer of the English liturgy, is analogous to the omission of the

direct prayer for the Holy Ghost to consecrate the elements, in the
ancient Roman and Italian liturgies. And if it be granted that the
Roman form is a valid prayer for consecration though it does not
speak of the means of consecration; it must also be granted, that the
English form is a valid prayer for the partaking of Christ's body and
blood in a sacramental manner, and therefore for the consecration,
which alone renders this possible, although the consecration itself is
not spoken of.

William Palmer, *Origines Liturgicae* (1832), Rivington, 4th edn,
1845, vol. 2, pages 138–40

*Without entering into discussions of Transubstantiation and Con-
substantiation, Newman, Keble and Pusey all stated their belief in
the Real Presence. The three short extracts sum up the Tractarian
position, though Pusey took a more advanced line later in his life.*

What is it that is vouchsafed to us at the Holy Table, when we commemorate the Lord's death? It is 'Jesus Christ before our eyes evidently set forth, crucified among us'. Not before our bodily eyes; so far,
every thing remains at the end of that Heavenly Communion as it did
at the beginning. What was bread remains bread, and what was wine
remains wine. We need no carnal, earthly, visible miracle to convince
us of the Presence of the Lord Incarnate. We have, we trust, more
faith than to need to see the heavens open, or the Holy Ghost descend
in bodily shape – more faith than to attempt, in default of sight, to
indulge our reason, and to confine our notion of the Sacrament to
some clear assemblage of words of our own framing. We have faith
and love, in St Paul's words, to '*discern* the Lord's Body'. He who is
at the right hand of God, manifests Himself in that Holy Sacrament
as really and fully as if He were visibly there. We are allowed to draw
near, to 'give, take, and eat' His sacred Body and Blood, as truly as
though like Thomas we could touch His hands and thrust our hand
into His side. When He ascended into the Mount, 'His face did shine
as the sun, and His raiment was white as the light'. Such is the glorious presence which faith sees in the Holy Communion, though every
thing looks as usual to the natural man. Not gold or precious stones,
pearls of great price or gold of Ophir, are to the eye of faith so radi-
ant as those lowly elements which He the Highest is pleased to make
the means of conveying to our hearts and bodies His own gracious
self. Not the light of the sun sevenfold is so awfully bright and over-
powering, if we could see as the Angels do, as that seed of eternal

life, which by eating and drinking we lay up in our hearts against the day of His coming. In spite then of all recollections of the past or fear for the future, we have a present source of rejoicing; whatever comes, weal or woe, however stands our account as yet in the books against the Last Day, this we have and this we may glory in, the present power and grace of God in us and over us, and the good hope thence flowing of victory in the end.

> J. H. Newman, *Parochial Sermons*, Rivington, 1834–42, vol. 4,
> pages 167–9

The true oblation in the Christian Sacrifice is in no sense earthly or material. It is altogether spiritual, the chief of those spiritual sacrifices in the offering whereof consists the common priesthood of us all. The Eucharist comprehends them all in one, and has besides, peculiar to itself that which alone causes any of them to be acceptable. For the true oblation in the Eucharist is not the Bread and Wine – that is only as the vessel which contains or the garment which veils it; but that which our Lord by the hands of the priest offers to His Father in the Holy Eucharist, is His own Body and Blood, the very same which He offers and presents to Him – with which, as St Paul says, He appears before Him *now,* night and day continually – in heaven, in commemoration of His having offered it once for all in His Passion and Death on the Cross. It is the one great reality, summing up in itself all the memorial sacrifices of old. In the Christian scheme, it is 'proportionable' to them; and of course it stands in the same rank and relation to them, as the other antitypes in the Gospel to their several types and shadows in the law.

> J. Keble, *On Eucharistical Adoration*, Parker, 1857

This is (if we may reverently so speak) the order of the mystery of the Incarnation, that the Eternal Word so took our flesh into Himself, as to impart to it His own inherent life; so then we, partaking of It, that life is transmitted on to us also, and not to our souls only, but our bodies also, since we become flesh of His flesh, and bone of His bone, and He Who is wholly life is imparted to us wholly. The Life which He is, spreads around, first giving Its own vitality to that sinless Flesh which He united indissolubly with Himself and in It encircling and vivifying our whole nature, and then through that bread which is His Flesh, finding an entrance to us individually, penetrating us, soul and body and spirit, and irradiating and transforming into his own light and life.

E. B. Pusey, 'The Holy Eucharist a Comfort to the Penitent' (1843), in
Nine Sermons Preached Before the University of Oxford,
Parker, 1865, pages 11–12

The sacramental theology of the Tractarians soon influenced many outside their immediate circle. William Gresley described the force of their ideas on a young curate who is the fictional narrator of a novel of parish life.

About this time there were published several Tracts entitled 'Scriptural Views of Holy Baptism', in many respects the most important of the series. The former had called the attention of religious men to many neglected doctrines – as, the apostolic succession, the unity and visibility of the Church, the true use of ordinances; but the present entered more deeply and fully into the real practical differences between the Church system and that of the sectarians. Of the convincing argument, the deep learning, the impressive sincerity, the pure charity, with which the Tracts on Baptism are written, it is impossible to speak in terms of too high praise. Difficult, indeed, it is to conceive how any sincere person can withstand the joint influence of these various appeals. To me the views exhibited appeared of the deepest importance.

The argument turns on the vital necessity and efficacious influence of the sacraments, as means of salvation ordained by Christ. The problem which I had long endeavoured to solve was the true practical means of conveying the benefits of Christ's atonement to the souls of men. The present Tracts answered my inquiry, by pointing out the important place which the sacraments occupy for this purpose.

The main difference between the Church and the sectarians, as regards the sacraments, is this: The whole Church for fifteen hundred years, and the great body of professing Christians even since that time – including the Romish and Greek Churches, the Lutherans, and the reformed English Church, with its dependencies in different parts of the world – all agree in considering the sacraments as the principal channels, appointed by God, for conveying Divine grace to the faithful. The Swiss reformer Zuingle [Zwingli], and after him Calvin, and certain sects which have since sprung up, consider the sacraments as mere outward signs or symbols. The formularies of our own Church, in conformity with the doctrine of the Church Catholic, teach that a sacrament is an outward visible sign of *an inward spiritual grace given unto us*, ordained by Christ Himself, as a means whereby we receive the same (i.e. the spiritual grace), and a pledge to assure us thereof. Thus, in the Lord's Supper, the outward sign is, 'the bread and wine, which the Lord hath commanded to be received'. The inward grace given to us is, 'the body and blood of Christ, which are verily and indeed taken and received by the faithful in the Lord's Supper'. This doctrine the sectarians deny, and consider the Lord's Supper as nothing more than a memorial or representation of Christ's death, given to assist our faith, and not a communion of His blessed body and blood; whereby in a mysterious way 'we dwell in Christ, and Christ in us; we are one with Christ, and Christ with us'.

And so with regard to the other sacrament, on which the Tract principally dwells, the Church declares the inward grace given at baptism to be 'a death unto sin, and a new birth unto righteousness' – in one word, regeneration; 'for being by nature born in sin, the children of wrath, we are thereby (i.e. by baptism) made the children of grace'. And in explaining to her children their position before God, she teaches them that they were made at baptism 'children of God, members of Christ (i.e. one with Him, and He with them), and inheritors of the kingdom of heaven'. The sectarian utterly denies this doctrine of baptismal regeneration, held by the Church from the beginning, and considers it a popish error. The evangelical members of our own Church lean to the Zuinglian, or dissenting, view of the sacraments; thinks that the expressions in various parts of our Liturgy are exceptionable when taken literally, and seeing that they cannot receive them, they explain them away in a most unscrupulous manner.

William Gresley, *Bernard Leslie*, Burns, 1842, vol. 1, pages 137–40

Pusey wrote of the Tractarian belief not only in the sacred nature of the Eucharist but also in the need for more frequent celebrations.

Since this Divine Sacrament has, as its immediate and proper end, union with Him who hath taken our manhood into God, and the infusion into us of His Spirit and life and immortality, making us one with His glorified Humanity, as He is One in the Godhead with the Father, and, besides this, it is ulteriorly, the cleansing of our sins, the refining our corruptions, the repairing of our decays, what must be the loss of the Church of the latter days, in which Communions are so infrequent! How can we wonder that love should have waxed cold, corruptions so abound, grievous falls have been, among our youth, almost the rule, to stand upright the exception, heathen strict-ness reproach Christian laxity, the Divine life become so rare, all higher instances of it so few and faint, when 'the stay and the staff', the strength of that life is willingly forfeited? How should there be the fulness of the Divine life, amid all but a month-long fast from our 'daily Bread'? While in the largest portion of the Church, the people mostly gaze at the threshold of the Heaven where they do not enter, what do we? We seem, alas! even to have forgotten, in our very thoughts, that daily Communion, which once was the common privi-lege of the whole Church, which, when the Eastern Church relaxed in her first love, the Western continued, and which they from whom we have our Communion Service in its present form, at first hoped to restore. It implies a life, so different from this our common-place ordinary tenor, a life so above this world as knit with Him who hath overcome the world; so angelic as living on Him who is Angels' food; a union with God so close; that we cannot mostly, I suppose, imagine to ourselves how we could daily thus be in Heaven, and in our daily business here below, how sanctify our daily duties, thoughts, refresh-ment, so that they should be tinged with the hues reflected by our daily Heaven, not that heavenly gift be dimmed with our earthiness; how our souls should through the day shine with the glory of that ineffable Presence to which we had approached, not we approach to it with earth-dimmed souls. It must ever be so; we cannot know the gift of God, if we forfeit it; we must cease mostly even to long for what we forego. We lose the very sense to understand it.

> E. B. Pusey, 'The Holy Eucharist a Comfort to the Penitent', (1843), in
> *Nine Sermons Preached Before the University of Oxford*,
> Parker, 1865, pages 27–9

He wished that there should be regular and devout communion by all faithful laity.

There is danger in not receiving whenever a person by any means can, because it is despising God's gift, and provoking Him to withdraw it, and give you over to a cold, unloving, careless temper. There is danger in every way of receiving It unduly; and in not receiving It at all, there is starvation and death of the soul; There is danger in every way but *one*; and that is, keeping your hearts diligently; preparing yourselves, when you can, carefully; praying to God fervently, to give you that holy frame of mind, which He will accept; receiving His gifts, whenever they are offered to you, humbly and thankfully; and bringing forth fruit enduringly and increasingly.

God has set dangers on all sides, that we may not shrink back, but may go onward in the one path, which leadeth unto Him. The wilderness shutteth us in; the sea is before, and the enemy behind: but God will place His pillar of fire between the enemy and us, and the sea shall part, and that which was our enemy, shall be our safeguard; a narrow path it is, but the sea which would devour us, should be a wall on the right hand and on the left to fence us in from straying, and protect us against the enemy, so will He conduct us to the promised land. We might have shrunk (who would not have shrunk?) from coming to the all-holy mysteries, but that our Saviour saith, 'Except ye eat the Flesh of the Son of Man and drink His Blood, ye have no life in you'. Come then, we must; and so, thou with trembling hearts and faint steps, mistrusting ourselves, but trusting in God, we will come. We should mistrust our own weakness, but we should not mistrust God's strength. He invites, who willeth not the sinner's death, who warneth us that He may not strike, who correcteth that He may not destroy. He who hath appointed us this narrow path, will keep therein those who will be kept. He who has made this Heavenly food needful for life, is able to keep us, if we commit ourselves to Him. He who giveth us His Son to dwell in us, how shall He not cleanse us wholly, if we will be cleansed? He who by giving us that Heavenly Body, keepeth us members of that body whereof He is the Head, how shall He not keep those members of Himself? How should Satan have power over the members of Christ? He will make each communion a means to enable you to receive the next more devoutly and profitably. He will increase your longing after that heavenly feast; He will make you more and more members of Him of whom you partake, more fruitful branches of that Vine whose richness He pours into you, richer in faith, stronger amid temptation, more victorious against Satan and yourselves. He will carry you on from strength to strength, until you appear before Him, the God of gods, and He remove you from His table here to His glorious presence in Heaven, from faith to sight, from longing to bliss, from spiritual union to see Him eye to eye, from these broken and occasional refreshments to be for ever with Him your Lord. Only come hither with hearty repentance, with lively faith, with real charity, with thankful remembrance of His Death, with steadfast purpose to amend, and as thou drawest near, and art about to partake of the heavenly Food, cast thyself more wholly upon God, pray Him to deepen all that He would have in thee, and to take away all He would not have. Pray Him to increase thy longing, thy sense of need, of thy emptiness and His exceeding fullness, and He will fill thee, He will give thee all thou needest, He will give thee Himself.

E. B. Pusey, *Parochial Sermons*, Parker, 1864, pages 336–8

The other great sacramental controversy was about baptism: did it bring about actual spiritual regeneration or was it only a sign of faith and commitment? After discussing conversion as a deliberate turning towards God and away from sin, Pusey affirmed baptismal regeneration and its effect on the believer.

But, besides this, conversion may be taken in a narrower sense, for the first turning of the soul to God after it has been estranged from Him. This, had we been faithful, we never should have needed. In Holy Baptism, we were 'made children of God', and we never need have left our Father's house; we were made 'members of Christ', and if we would, His life, into Whom we were then engrafted, would have flowed more fully into us, according to our needs, filling us according to our capacities, hallowing our childhood, strengthening our youth, controlling us in the perils of opening manhood, mastering each wayward thought, subduing each rising appetite. It was pledged to us, had we been willing to receive it. Had we admitted it, it would have flowed on equably and gently through us, and we had never needed that sharp, though wholesome remedy, whereby the way must be again reopened to it, when once we have closed it. We were 'made inheritors of heaven'; we need never have stood in fear and alarm, lest we had forfeited it, nor had 'sought it carefully with tears'. We might have ever looked on humbly to it, not as our right, but as His Who purchased it for us and made it ours, and has given us the earnest of it, and gave us, day by day, the forgiveness of the trespasses we prayed for, that we might not forfeit it. This is the happy lot of those, who, though more or less slowly, still steadfastly on the whole, grow on in their Baptismal grace; with their falls, the giddiness and forgetfulness of childhood, yet never interposing any such grievous sin, as should check the influx of that life in them. Supported by prayer, strengthened by Confirmation, admitted into closer communion in the Holy Eucharist, they are, line by line, and feature by feature, unobserved, insensibly, because unceasingly, 'changed', the Apostle says, 'into the same image, from glory to glory, as by the Lord, the Spirit'. These need no marked change, because the change we all need is ever going on, unmarked, within them. And many more might these blessed cases be, would parents but more bring home to their memory the blessings pledged in Baptism; that their children have been redeemed out of the evil world, and need not be conformed to it; that they have been received under the protection of the saving Name, and may dwell there in safety 'under the shadow of the Almighty'; that weak, frail, wayward, self-willed, as, through the unsubdued remains of their old nature, they appear and are, they have still lodged within them a hidden strength, mightier than the world and Satan and the powers of darkness, even His strength Who 'hath overcome the world', and trampled upon Satan; that He can and will triumph in these His young soldiers, if they are taught even now to fight; that He, by His childhood, has sanctified their childish age; that out of the mouths of such as them He hath perfected praise; that of such as these is the kingdom of heaven.

E. B. Pusey, *Parochial Sermons*, Parker, 1864, vol. 3, pages 21–2

Pusey wrote a fuller exposition of the subject of baptism in a Tract, asserting baptismal regeneration but, in typical Tractarian manner, holding it as a mystery and an article of faith rather than something that can be philosophically defined.

The doctrine, then, of Baptismal Regeneration (rightly understood) may have a very important station in GOD's scheme of salvation, although many of us may not understand its relation to the rest of that dispensation, and those who do not believe it, *cannot* understand it. For this is the method of GOD's teaching throughout; 'first believe and then you shall understand'. And this may be said, in Christian warning, against those hard words, in which Christians sometimes allow themselves; as, 'the deadening doctrine of Baptismal Regeneration'; language which can only serve to darken the truth to those who use it, and which is by so much the more dangerous, since all Christians believe that Regeneration *sometimes* accompanies Baptism. Since also Baptismal Regeneration was the doctrine of the Universal Church of CHRIST in its holiest ages, and our own reformers (to whom, on other points, men are wont to appeal as having been highly gifted with GOD'S HOLY SPIRIT) retained this doctrine, it would seem to require but little modesty in a private Christian, not to feel so confident in his own judgement, as to denounce, in terms so unmeasured, what may after all be the teaching of GOD; 'lest haply he be found to fight against GOD'.

[...]The difficulty of explaining Baptismal Regeneration is twofold;

First, from its being a mystery; secondly, from men being in these days inclined to lower that mystery. Thus one should prefer speaking of it, with our Catechism, as that whereby we were made 'members of CHRIST'; but then, when people explain 'members of CHRIST' to be 'members of CHRIST'S Church', and that, to mean 'members of His visible Church, or of the society of men called Christians', a description in itself the highest and most glorious, and the source of every other blessing, is made equivalent to 'a mere outward admission into a mere outward assemblage of men'. In either case, however, man is the author of his own difficulties; in the one, by lowering the fullness of Scripture truth; in the other, by carnally inquiring into the mode of the Divine working. For a mystery presents no difficulty to belief; it becomes difficult only when we ask about the mode of its being. Nicodemus asked, 'How can these things be?' and most of our questions about Baptismal Regeneration are Nicodemus-questions. We know it in its author, God; in its instrument, Baptism; in its end, salvation, union with CHRIST, sonship to GOD, 'resurrection from the dead, and the life of the world to come'. We only know it not, where it does not concern us to know it, in the mode of its operation. But this is just what man would know, and so he passes over all those glorious privileges, and stops at the threshold to ask how it can be? He would fain know *how* an unconscious infant can be born of GOD? *how* it can spiritually live? *wherein* this spiritual life consists? *how* Baptism can be the same to the infant and to the adult convert? and if it be not in its visible, and immediate, and tangible effects, *how* it can be the same at all? Yet Scripture makes no difference; the gift is the same, although it vary in its application; to the infant it is the remission of original guilt, to the adult of his actual sins also; but to both by their being made members of CHRIST, and thereby partakers of His 'wisdom and righteousness, sanctification and redemption'; by being made branches of the True Vine, and so, as long as they abide in Him, receiving from Him, each according to their capacities, and necessities, and willingness, nourishment and life; but if they abide not in Him, they are cast forth like a branch, and withered. We can then, after all, find no better exposition than that incidentally given in our Catechism – 'my Baptism, wherein I was made a member of CHRIST, the child of GOD, and an inheritor of the kingdom of heaven'; and with this statement we may well be content, as it expresses most our union with our Redeemer, the fountain of our gifts, and the ground of our hopes. One may then define Regeneration to be, 'that act whereby GOD takes us out of our relation to Adam, and makes us actual members of His Son, and so

His sons, as being members of His Ever-blessed Son; and if sons, then heirs of GOD through CHRIST' (Gal. iv. 7). This is our new birth, an actual birth of GOD, of water, and the Spirit, as we were actually born of our natural parents; herein then also are we justified, or both accounted and made righteous, since we are made members of Him who is Alone Righteous; freed from past sin, whether original or actual; have a new principle of life imparted to us, since having been made members of CHRIST, we have a portion of His life, or of Him who is our Life; herein we have also the hope of the resurrection and of immortality, because we have been made partakers of His resurrection, have risen again with Him. (Col. ii. 12.)

The view, then, here held of Baptism, following the ancient Church and our own, is, that we be engrafted into CHRIST, and thereby receive a principle of life, afterwards to be developed and enlarged by the fuller influxes of His grace; so that neither is Baptism looked upon as an infusion of grace distinct from the incorporation into CHRIST, nor is that incorporation conceived of as separate from its attendant blessings.

He developed baptismal doctrine into an argument for need of a sacramental life for continuing support in grace, as against the teaching of a subjective assurance of justification.

While we bear in mind the continued gifts of His goodness, in the life which He upholds; the fatness of the olive-tree, which He imparts; the membership of the family, which He continues; the stream, or the light, which He pours within us; still there is eminently one date, from which all these present blessings are derived, differing from them in so far as it is one, the sun-rising, the engrafting, the adoption, the birth; one act, transitory as an act, although abiding in its effects. Now this is precisely the mode of speaking which Scripture uses in making mention of our Christian privileges. When it speaks to individuals, it uniformly refers them back to that act, from which their present privileges were derived; it speaks of the gifts, as having been conferred in the past, though they are continued on to the present to such as have not forfeited them. But this is not the way in which the school of Calvin, having unlearned the value of the Sacraments, would speak. To them, Justification must of necessity be simply present; it cannot have any date, except in the opinion of such as hold that every real Christian must be able to assign the precise moment of his conversion; and these are now comparatively few. For since they reject justification *through* the Sacrament of Baptism, and hold it to

be simply the result of the act of faith apprehending CHRIST, laying hold of His merits, and applying them to itself, *this* justification
must necessarily consist in a number of repeated acts, each separately
wrought in the soul by the agency of the HOLY SPIRIT, but none
differing in kind from another, so that the one should be the cause,
the rest the result. Justification then must be to them continually and
simply present; not as the result of any thing past, but as consequent
upon the present act of casting themselves on the Redeemer's merits;
they have been, they trust, and are, justified; but their present justification is the result, they think, *simply* of their present faith; and so
at each former time their then act of reliance on His merits was the
means of their justification, it was *then* to them the present source of
justification; and, in like manner, in such as persevere, to the end.

E. B. Pusey, Tract 67, 'Scriptural Views of Holy Baptism',
pages 4, 22–4, 156–7

*For Newman also, the new life of Christians in Christ came through
baptism.*

This wonderful change from darkness to light, through the entrance
of the Spirit into the soul, is called Regeneration, or the New Birth;
a blessing which, before Christ's coming, not even Prophets and
righteous men possessed, but which is now conveyed to all men
freely through the Sacrament of Baptism. By nature we are children
of wrath; the heart is sold under sin, possessed by evil spirits; and
inherits death as its eternal portion. But by the coming of the Holy
Ghost, all guilt and pollution are burned away as by fire, the devil
is driven forth, sin, original and actual, is forgiven, and the whole
man is consecrated to God. And this is the reason why He is called
'the earnest' of that Saviour who died for us, and will one day give
us the fullness of His own presence in heaven. Hence, too, He is our
'seal unto the day of redemption'; for as the potter moulds the clay,
so He impresses the Divine image on us members of the household of
God. And His work may truly be called Regeneration; for though the
original nature of the soul is not destroyed, yet its past transgressions
are pardoned once and for ever, and its source of evil staunched and
gradually dried up by the pervading health and purity which has set
up its abode in it.

J. H. Newman, *Parochial and Plain Sermons* (1834), Rivington,
1877, vol. 2, page 223

Robert Wilberforce also taught the doctrine of baptismal regeneration.

Renovation must have its root in Regeneration. There must be a gift antecedent to our efforts. This gift is that first union with Christ, whereon all communication with Him depends. Out of this beginning arises the whole system of the Christian life. And this heavenly impulse is expressly declared in Scripture to be extended to us in Baptism. 'As many of you as have been baptized into Christ', says St. Paul, 'have put on Christ'. For 'by one spirit are we all baptized into one Body'. And in Baptism, as the Apostle asserts twice over, that death to the old nature takes place, whereby the new creation in Christ is commenced. 'We are buried with Him by Baptism into death', 'wherein also ye are risen with Him'. So that St. Peter says, that 'Baptism doth also now save us'. For Our Lord Himself had taught that in this ordinance lies the beginning of the spiritual life: 'except a man be born of water and of the Spirit, he cannot enter into the kingdom of God': a passage whereof Hooker reminds us, 'that of all the ancients, there is not one to be named, that ever did otherwise either expound or allege the place than as implying external Baptism'.

Since the statements of Scripture on this subject are so precise, how comes it then that any persons should have dissented from this universal opinion of Our Lord's first disciples? The grounds of men's objection appear to be two. First, an attachment to the idea introduced, or at least systematised by Calvin that grace is not given to any except those who will finally be saved; and secondly, the assertion that no visible results attend on Baptism. The difficulties which these considerations involve, induce men to refer to such passages of Scripture, as express the full effect and ultimate consequence of regeneration, i.e. victory over sin, and final perseverance; and they infer that no gift has really been bestowed in Baptism, unless these ultimate consequences are discerned to be its effect. They deny in effect that a seed has been sown, where fruit is not brought forth. They deny that there can be dead branches in the Christian vine. And the language in which Scripture and the Church speak of something as actually done in Baptism, they consider to be merely a charitable hope that something will be done hereafter – a hope which, in the majority of instances, they say is not borne out by the result. Now, the passages of Scripture which they cite, have in themselves no tendency to show that in Baptism occurs no real work: for they only speak of this work as one, the completion whereof is the extinction of sin; and which must therefore spread itself through man's whole life. But all that is asserted of Baptism is that since it is our first means of union with the manhood of Christ, the basis of our spiritual growth must be laid in it. 'Baptism doth challenge to itself but the inchoation [*incomplete state*] of those graces, the consummation whereof dependeth on mysteries ensuing'. The denial therefore that in Baptism, as rightly and worthily participated, there is any real change made in the recipient of the ordinance – the assertion, that the benefits ascribed to it are merely figurative, contingent, occasional – that they are spoken of prospectively as something to be hereafter attained, and not positively as something actually possessed – all this does not follow from any scriptural authority; the grounds for supposing it are men's antecedent difficulties.

> Robert Wilberforce, *The Doctrine of the Incarnation of Our Lord*
> *Jesus Christ in its Relation to Mankind and to the Church*
> (1848), John Murray, 3rd edn, 1850, pages 435–8

Keble saw baptism as a new creation of each child, an image of the primal Creation.

> Who may the wondrous birth declare
> Of Earth and Heaven so vast and fair?
> Yet whensoe'er to Love's pure spring
> A helpless Little One they bring,
> Those wonders o'er again we see
>   In saving mystery.
>
> All in the unregenerate child
> Is void and formless, dark and wild,
> Till the life-giving holy Dove
> Upon the waters gently move,
> And power impart, soft brooding there,
>   Celestial fruit to bear. [...]
>
> Thee, awful image of the All-good,
> That one atoning day renew'd
> For the whole world: the fontal wave
> To each apart the glory gave,
> Washing us clean, that we might hide
>   In His love-pierced side.

Thus in each day of toil we read
Tokens of joy to Saints decreed.
What if the day of holy rest
The sleep foreshew of infant blest
Borne for the Font, the seal new given,
    Perchance to wake in Heaven?

J. Keble, 'Holy Baptism: New Creation' (1846),
Lyra Innocentium, Methuen, 1903

5

Appeal to Authority

To prove the catholicity of the Church of England, it was necessary to demonstrate its faithful relationship to the sources of authority. Scripture, tradition and reason were the bases which earlier Anglican apologists had claimed to maintain and which the Tractarians affirmed. They gave particular attention to the power of tradition, the element which they believed to be the least honoured in the contemporary Church. The Bible contained all that was needed for salvation, but it was to be understood after the judgement of the Church, not by individual interpretation; the Bible and reason were not the sole guides to truth. The Bible was the revelation of God's word, but not the sole source of Christian doctrine.

Hawkins, Provost of Oriel College, had used the phrase, 'The Church to teach, the Bible to prove' in a sermon on Tradition in 1818. This idea was taken up by Newman, who did not see eye to eye with Hawkins in all respects, but had learned much from him.

Surely the sacred volume was never intended, and is not adapted to *teach us* our creed; however certain it is that we can prove our creed from it, when it has once been taught us, and in spite of individual producible exceptions to the general rule. From the very first, that rule has been, as a matter of fact, for the Church to teach the truth, and then appeal to Scripture in vindication of its own teaching. And from the first, it has been the error of heretics to neglect the information provided for them, and to attempt of themselves a work to which they are unable, the eliciting a systematic doctrine from the scattered notices of the truth which Scripture contains. Such men act, in the solemn concerns of religion, the part of the self-sufficient natural philosopher, who should obstinately reject Newton's theory of gravitation, and endeavour, with talents inadequate to the task, to strike out some theory of motion by himself. The insufficiency of the mere private study of Holy Scripture for arriving at the exact and entire truth which it really contains, is shown by the fact, that creeds and teachers have ever been divinely provided, and by the discordance of opinions which exists wherever those aids are thrown aside; as well as by the very structure of the Bible itself. And if this be so, it follows that, while enquirers and neophytes used the inspired writings for the purposes of morals and for instruction in the rudiments of the faith, they still might heed the teaching of the Church as a key to the collection of passages which related to the mysteries of the gospel; passages which are obscure from the necessity of combining and receiving them all.

J. H. Newman, *The Arians of the Fourth Century*, Rivington,
1833, pages 55–6

The Bible was divinely inspired, but mediated through human agency.

We may, without irreverence, speak even of the words of inspired Scripture as imperfect and defective; and though they are not subjects for our judgement (God forbid), yet they will for that very reason serve to enforce and explain better what I would say, and how far the objection goes. Inspiration is defective, not in itself, but in consequence of the medium it uses and the beings it addresses. It uses human language, and it addresses man; and neither can man compass, nor can his hundred tongues utter, the mysteries of the spiritual world, and God's dealings in this. This vast and intricate scene of things cannot be generalised or represented through or to the mind of man; and inspiration, in undertaking to do so, necessarily lowers what is divine to raise what is human. What, for instance, is the mention made in Scripture of the laws of God's government, of His providences, counsels, designs, anger, and repentance, but a gracious mode (the more gracious because necessarily imperfect) of making man contemplate what is far beyond him? Who shall give method to what is infinitely complex, and measure to the unfathomable? We are as worms in an abyss of divine works; myriads upon myriads of years would it take, were our hearts ever so religious, and our intellects ever so apprehensive, to receive from without the just impression of those works as they really are, and as experience would convey them to us. Sooner, then, than we should know nothing, Almighty God has condescended to speak to us so far as human thought and language will admit, by approximations, in order to give us practical rules for our own conduct amid His infinite and eternal operations.

J. H. Newman, *Sermons, Chiefly on the Theory of Religious Belief,*
preached before the University of Oxford, 2nd edn, 1844,
pages 264–5

Keble asserted that our reverence for the Bible comes through know-
ledge of faith.

He who knows beforehand that the Personal Word is everywhere in the written Word, could we but discern Him, will feel it an awful thing to open his Bible; fasting, and prayer, and scrupulous self-denial, and all the ways by which the flesh is tamed to the Spirit, will seem to him no more than natural, when he is to sanctify himself, and draw near with Moses, to the darkness where God is. And this so much the more, the more that darkness is mingled with evangelical night; for so much the more he may hope to see of God; and we know Who it is, that has inseparably connected seeing God with purity of Heart.

J. Keble, Tract 89, 'On the Mysticism Attributed to the Early Fathers
of the Church', page 138

The Bible is not subject to every attempt at private judgement.

Scripture is not so distinct in its announcements, as readers are morally or intellectually slow in receiving them. And if anyone thinks that this avowal is derogatory to Scripture, I answer that Scripture was never intended to teach doctrine to the many; and if it was not given with this object, it argues no imperfection in it that it does not fulfil it.

I repeat it; while Scripture is written by inspired men, with one and one only view of doctrine in their hearts and thoughts, even the Truth which was from the beginning, yet being written not to instruct in doctrine, but for those who were already instructed in it, not with direct announcements but with intimations and implications of the faith, the qualifications for rightly apprehending it are so rare and high, that a prudent man, to say nothing of piety, will not risk his salvation on the chance of his having them; but will read it with the aid of those subsidiary guides which have ever been supplied as if to meet our need. I would not deny as an abstract proposition that a Christian may gain the whole truth from the Scriptures, but would maintain that the chances are very seriously against a given individual. I would not deny but rather maintain, that a religious, wise and intellectually gifted man will succeed: but who answers to this description but the collective Church? There, indeed, such qualifications might be supposed to exist; what is wanting in one member being supplied by another, and the contrary errors of individuals eliminated by their combination. The Church Catholic may truly be said almost infallibly to interpret Scripture, though from the possession of past tradition, and amid the divisions of the time present, perhaps at no period in the course of the dispensation has she had the need and the opportunity of interpreting it for herself. Neither would I deny that individuals, whether from height of holiness, clearness of intellectual vision, or the immediate power of the Holy Ghost, have been and are able to penetrate through the sacred text into some portions of the divine system beyond without external help; though, since that help has ever been given, as to the Church, so to the individual, it is difficult to prove that the individual has performed what the Church has never attempted. [...] The Church Catholic, the true prophet of God, alone is able to tell the dream and its interpretation.

> J. H. Newman, *Lectures on the Prophetical Office of the Church Viewed Relatively to Romanism and Popular Protestantism: The Via Media of the Anglican Church* (1835), London: Longmans, Green, 1838, vol. 1, pages 192–3

There is the necessity of Church judgement and the proper use of outward forms.

It may fairly be questioned whether religion does not necessarily imply the belief in such sensible tokens of God's favour as the sacraments are accounted by the Church. Religion is of a personal nature, and implies the acknowledgement of a particular Providence, of a God speaking not merely to the world at large, but to this person or that, to me and not to another. The Sacred Volume is a common possession, and speaks to one man as much and as little as his neighbour. Our nature requires something special; and if we refuse what has been given, we shall be sure to adopt what has not been. We shall set up calves at Dan and Bethel, if we give up the true Temple and the Apostolic Ministry. This we see fulfilled before our eyes in many ways; those who will not receive Baptism as the token of God's election, have recourse to certain supposed experiences of it in their hearts. This is the idolatry of a refined age, in which the superstitions of barbarous times displease from their grossness. Men congratulate themselves on their emancipation from forms and their enlightened worship, when they are but in the straight course to a worse captivity, and are exchanging dependence on the creature for self-sufficiency.

J. H. Newman, *Lectures on Justification*, Rivington, 1838, pages 370–1

Newman took the argument further in claiming that Tradition can override the silence of Scripture.

Let us suppose, *for the sake of argument,* that Episcopacy is in fact not at all mentioned in Scripture: even then it would be our duty to receive it. Why? because the first Christians received it. If we wish to get at the truth, no matter how we get at it, if we get at it. If it be a fact, that the earliest Christian communities were universally episcopal, it is a reason for our maintaining Episcopacy ; and *in proportion* to our conviction, it is incumbent on us to maintain it.

Nor can it be fairly dismissed as a non-essential, or ordinance indifferent and mutable, though formerly existing over Christendom; for *who* made us judges of essentials and non-essentials? *how* do we determine them? In the Jewish law, the slightest transgression of the commandment was followed by the penalty of death; vide Lev. viii. 35; x. 6. Does not its universality imply a necessary connection with Christian doctrine? Consider how such reasonings would carry us through life; how the business of the world depends on punctuality in minutes; how 'great a matter' a mere spark dropped on gunpowder 'kindleth'.

But, it may be urged, that we Protestants believe the *Scriptures* to contain the whole rule of duty. Certainly not; they contain a rule of *faith,* not a rule of *practice*; a rule of *doctrine,* not a rule of *conduct* or *discipline.* Where (e.g.) are we told in Scripture, that gambling is wrong? or again, suicide? Our Article is precise: 'Holy Scripture containeth all things necessary to salvation, so that whatsoever is not read therein, &c. it is not required of any man, that it should be *believed* as an article of *faith*'. Again it says, that the Apocrypha is not to be applied 'to establish any *doctrine*', implying that *this* is the use of the canonical books.

However, let us pass from this argument, which is but founded on a *supposition,* that Episcopacy is not enjoined in Scripture. Suppose we maintain, as we may well maintain, that it *is* enjoined in Scripture. An objector will say, that at all events it is but obscurely contained therein, and cannot be drawn out from it without a great deal of delicate care and skill. Here comes in the operation of that principle of *faith,* in opposition to *criticism,* which was above explained; the principle of being content with a little light, where we cannot obtain sunshine. If it is *probably* pleasing to CHRIST, let us maintain it. Now take a parallel case: e.g. the practice of infant baptism; where is this *enjoined* in Scripture? Nowhere. Why do we observe it? Because the primitive Church observed it, and because the Apostles in Scripture *appear* to have sanctioned it, though this is not altogether certain *from* Scripture. In a difficult case we do as well as we can, and carefully *study* what is most agreeable to our LORD and SAVIOUR. This is how our Church expresses it in the xxviith Article. "The baptism of young children is in any wise to he retained in the Church, as most *agreeable* with the institution of CHRIST'. This is true wariness and Christian caution; very different from that spurious caution which ultra-Protestantism exercises. Let a man only be consistent, and apply the same judgement in the case of Episcopacy: let him consider whether the duty of keeping to Bishops, be not *'most agreeable* with the institution of CHRIST'. If, indeed, he denies this altogether, these remarks do not apply; but they are addressed to waverers, and falsely moderate men, who cannot deny, that the evidence of Scripture is in favour of Churchmen, but say it is not strong enough. They say, that if Almighty GOD had intended an uniformity in Church Government among Christians, he would have spoken more clearly.

Now if they carried on this line of argument consistently, they would not baptize their children. Happily they are inconsistent. It would be more happy still, were they consistent on the other side; and, as they baptize their children, because it is safer to observe than to omit the sacrament, did they also keep to the Church, as the safer side. The received practice, then, of infant baptism seems a final answer to all who quarrel with the Scripture evidence of Episcopacy.

But further still, infant baptism, like Episcopacy, is but a case of *discipline.* What shall we say, when we consider that a case of *doctrine,* necessary doctrine, doctrine the very highest and most sacred, may be produced, where the argument lies as little on the surface of Scripture, where the proof, though *most conclusive,* is as indirect and circuitous as that for Episcopacy: viz. the doctrine of the Trinity? Where is this solemn and comfortable mystery formally stated in Scripture, as we find it in the creeds? Why is it not? Let a man consider whether all the objections which he urges against the Scripture argument for Episcopacy may not be turned against his own belief in the Trinity. It is a happy thing for themselves that men are inconsistent; yet it is miserable to advocate and establish a *principle* which, not in their own case indeed, but in the case of others who learn it of them, leads to Socinianism. This being considered, can we any longer wonder at the awful fact, that the descendants of Calvin, the first Presbyterians, are at the present day in the number of those who have denied the LORD who bought them?

J. H. Newman, Tract 45, 'The Grounds of our Faith', pages 4–6

Newman returned to the argument in a later Tract. After giving examples of silences and contradictions in the Bible, and adducing orthodox doctrines which cannot be directly proved from it he continued:

On the whole then, I ask, on *how many* special or palmary texts do any of the doctrines or rites we hold depend? What doctrines or rites would be left to us, if we demanded the clearest and fullest evidence, before we believed any thing? what would the Gospel consist of? Would there be any revelation at all left? Some all-important doctrines indeed at first sight would remain in the New Testament, such as the divinity of CHRIST, the unity of GOD, and the supremacy of divine grace, and our election in CHRIST, and the resurrection of the body and eternal life or death to the righteous or sinners; but little besides. Shall we give up the divinity of the HOLY GHOST, original sin, the Atonement, the inspiration of the New Testament, united worship, the Sacraments, and infant baptism? Let us do so. Well: I will venture to say that then we shall find difficulties as regards those other doctrines, as the divinity of CHRIST, which I have described as at first remaining; they are only clearer than the others, not so clearly stated as to be secured from specious objections. We shall have difficulties about the *meaning* of the word 'everlasting', as applied to punishment, about the *compatibility* of divine grace with free-will, about the *possibility* of the resurrection of the body, and about the *sense* in which CHRIST is GOD. The mind which rejects a doctrine which has but one text in its favour, on the ground that if it were important, it would have more, may, where a doctrine is mentioned often, always find occasion to wonder that still it is *not* mentioned in this or that particular place, where it might be expected. When it is pressed with such a text as St Thomas's confession, 'My LORD and MY GOD', it will ask, But why does our LORD say but seven days before to St Mary Magdalen, 'I ascend to My Father and your Father, to My

GOD and your GOD'? When, with St Peter's confession, 'LORD, Thou knowest all things, Thou knowest that I love Thee', it will ask, But why does CHRIST say of Himself, that He does not know the last day, only the Father? Indeed, the more arguments there are for a doctrine in Scripture, the more objections will be found against it; so that on the whole, I think, even the Scripture evidence for the divinity of CHRIST, will be found in fact as little to satisfy the captious mind, when fairly engaged to discuss it, as that for infant baptism, great as is the difference in the evidence for the two. And the history of these last centuries bears out this remark.

I conclude, then, that there must be some fault *somewhere* in this specious argument; that it does *not* follow that a doctrine or rite is not divine because it is not clearly stated in Scripture; that there are some wise and unknown reasons for doctrines being as they are, not clearly stated there.

J. H. Newman, Tract 85, 'Lectures on the Scripture Proof of the
Doctrines of the Church', pages 12–13

In his Tract on baptism Pusey took occasion to advance the same argument, warning against private dependence on the Bible alone to the exclusion of Church tradition.

The 'doctrine of Baptism' (Heb. vi. 2.) is declared as explicitly, as incidentally, and as variously as that of our Blessed LORD's Divinity or the saving truth of the Holy Trinity, with which its administration is inseparably blended, the belief in which it very chiefly upholds. For both we have the same uniform testimony of the Church Catholic; in both cases alike, those who have refused to listen to the Church, have failed to find the truth in Holy Scripture; there is then as little reason to be moved, that others do not see what we see, in the one case as in the other; and if any see not the Church's doctrine of Baptism in Scripture, they have no reason thence to conclude that it is not there, because they see it not. The force done to Scripture has not been in any way greater in one case than in the other. They who say that 'water and the Spirit', means 'the Spirit only', or that 'the washing of regeneration' means 'spiritual regeneration' independent of any actual 'washing', however they may commiserate the misguided people, who assail other Catholic truth, have nothing assuredly to allege against them for forced interpretations of Holy Scripture. It was in their own school that those systems of interpretation were learnt.

The object then in producing some other chief passages of Holy

Scripture, wherein Baptism is mentioned or alluded to, is not to prove anything further with respect to that Sacrament, or to increase the evidence for what has been alleged; for our LORD's words, when rightly unfolded, of course contain all; and they who hear not Him, as His Church has from the first transmitted the meaning of His words, will not hear His Disciples. 'The servant is not greater than his Lord' (St. John, xv. 20.) The object will be, not to prove anything, but from the mode in which Baptism is spoken of in Holy Scripture, to illustrate the wide difference between the character of mind which that teaching implies and would foster, and that which modern notions imply and reproduce. Each text is only an item, an indication of a difference existing between modern habits of mind and Scripture-teaching. And this, one would fain hope might startle some who, because they have never seen the Catholic system, or its bearings upon Scripture developed, at present oppose it. It seems to us strange how any errors which we do not share should prevail about Scriptural doctrine. We marvel how the Jewish doctors could have reconciled with the plain letter of the law, their permission to a child to dedicate to GOD what its parent needed; we marvel, how the Romanist can reconcile his inculcation of image-worship, with the same law; in either case men have thus far 'made the word of GOD of none effect through their traditions'; in either case, through traditions not 'delivered to their fathers', but the 'inventions of men'; let those then, who, with respect to Baptism, embrace a tradition, whose origin is but as it were of yesterday, consider earnestly whether they may not be in the like case; whether their traditional exposition of the Gospel, derived from the one or other individual in these 'latter days' may not be as little consonant with the real meaning of Holy Scripture, as those by which the Pharisees justified their abuse of the 'Corban', or the Romanists their image-worship; whether they too may not be 'making the word of GOD of none effect through their traditions'.

E. B. Pusey, Tract 67, 'Scriptural Views of Holy Baptism', pages 66–7

Keble followed the same line; after warning against simplistic dependence on a few biblical texts he gave some cautionary examples. Episcopius was the name assumed by Simon Bischop (1583–1643), a Dutch Arminian theologian who taught a reduced version of the divinity of Christ. John Locke (1612–1704) exalted the supremacy of Reason in religion. Benjamin Hoadley (1676–1761) held that the Eucharist was simply commemorative.

It may be well to notice one more symptom of the unconscious rationalism which men are involved by mistrust of Primitive Tradition.
They dwell on single texts or propositions, enouncing some great
Gospel truth (e.g. the resurrection of our Lord) as if acknowledging
them were equivalent to an acknowledgement of the whole Gospel.
And so, virtually and in reason, it is, but not practically, not in the
faith of men's minds. All geometrical truths may be involved in the
original axioms and definitions, but we do not therefore consider
a person who has learned the two or three first pages of Euclid as
actually assenting to all that is important in geometry. Now we see
what fatal use will be made of this particular method of simplifying
beyond what the Church has sanctioned, by the history of the school
of Episcopius, Locke and Hoadley; they set out with this aphorism,
'that the one point of faith necessary to salvation was simply to believe that Jesus is the Christ, the true Messias'. What was the result?
The first discarded the divinity of our Lord from his list of fundamental truths; the second, apparently, was at least an Arian; the third
denied the grace of the Sacraments. True therefore as it may be in
a certain sense to say, that any one book or any one text of Scripture contains in itself, after a sort, all things necessary to eternal
salvation, it is not a truth which in any way dispenses with the use
of Creeds and Confessions of faith; or of Tradition, if any can be
produced capable of guaranteeing such documents. It is not a truth
which can help us to discern fundamentals. For the question will still
remain, 'which among the many things implied in this comprehensive saying are needful to be really thought of and professed by all?'
and the deeper and more comprehensive the proposition may be, the
more is this difficulty enhanced. The appropriate use of such texts
lies, not in the selection of fundamentals, but in their demonstration. 'Tradition', in this respect, 'teaches; Scripture proves'. And we
ought to be very thankful to the Almighty for leaving us a tradition
so complete as the Creed is, not only for our comfort, but because
we are thereby spared a great and otherwise inevitable temptation to
a kind of irreverence, which, as it is, proves but too inviting to many
of us: the irreverence of dealing rudely with the words of the Most
High, while we are handling them as the materials of a system which
we are to plan out for ourselves, instead of marking them with silent
reverence, as the foundations of a vast Temple, the outline whereof,
so far as we can trace it, has been previously delivered into our hands
by an unerring Architect.

J. Keble, Sermons Academical and Occasional, Parker, 1848,
pages 379–81

Keble further defended Tradition as the deposit of faith.

The fact is clearly demonstrable from Scripture, that as long as the canon of the New Testament was incomplete, the unwritten system served as a test even for the Apostles' own writings. Nothing was to be read, as canonical, except it agreed with the faith delivered once for all to the first generation of the saints. The directions of St Paul on this subject are perfectly clear, and without reserve. 'Though we or an angel from heaven preach any other Gospel unto you than that which we have preached unto you, let him be anathema.'

I do not see how we can be wrong in inferring, from these and similar passages, that the faith once for all delivered to the saints, in other words, Apostolical Tradition, was divinely appointed in the Church as the touchstone of canonical Scripture itself. No writing, however plausible the appearance of its having come from the Apostles, was to be accepted as theirs, if it taught any other doctrine than what they at first delivered: rather both it and its writers were to be anathema.

This use of apostolical tradition may well correct the presumptuous irreverence of disparaging the Fathers under a plea of magnifying Scripture. Here is a tradition so highly honoured by the Almighty Founder and Guide of the Church, as to be made the standard and rule of His own divine Scriptures. The very writings of the Apostles were to be first tried by it, before they could be incorporated into the canon. Thus the Scriptures themselves, as it were, do homage to the tradition of the Apostles; the despisers, therefore, of that tradition take part, inadvertently or profanely, with the despisers of the Scripture itself.

On the other hand, it is no less evident that Scripture, being once ascertained, became in its turn a test for every thing claiming to be of apostolical tradition. But on this part of the subject there is the less occasion to dwell, it being, I suppose, allowed on all hands.

J. Keble, *Sermons Academical and Occasional*, Parker, 1848, pages 193–5

Because it is affirmed that the full tradition of Christianity existed before the Christian Scriptures, and so far independent of them, we are charged with alleging two distinct systems or words of God, the one written, the other unwritten, running as it were parallel to each other quite down to our own time. But this, by the terms of the case, is plainly unwarranted. If a man were to say that the Severn and the Wye rise separately in the same mountain, one higher up than the other, must he therefore maintain that they never meet before they reach the sea? Tradition and Scripture were at first two streams flowing down from the mountain of God, but their waters presently became blended, and it were but a vain and unpractical inquiry, to call upon every one who drinks of them to say, how much of the healing draught came from one source, and how much from the other. On account of those who would poison the stream, it is necessary from time to time to analyse it, and show that it contains no ingredients which were not to be found in one or other of the two Mountains; and in so doing, it becomes incidentally manifest, at least in some measure, what portion each of the two has contributed to the general mass; it is manifest, for example, that all necessary *credenda*, all truths essential to salvation, are contained in the Scripture itself; and is it not equally manifest, that many helps of greatest consequence, nay I will say generally necessary, to the right development and application of Scripture, are mostly if not entirely derivable from Tradition? And is it not a poor kind of reasoning to say, Tradition would have been worthless had we been left to it alone, therefore it cannot be of any value, now that Scripture has been all along at hand, to check, to sustain, to interpret, to rectify it, as the several occasions might require?

J. Keble, *Sermons Academical and Occasional*, Parker, 1848, pages 347–8

Proof that the Church of England retains Apostolic Succession of bishops needed to be supported by proof that episcopacy was an essential mark of the Church.

Episcopacy is not a mere question of forms. Episcopacy, and a due gradation of the ministry, are of as vital importance to the well-being of the Church, as a good staff to the efficiency of the army. And this is putting the question on the very lowest ground; because, looking at Scripture and at Church history, we can prove, that the Episcopal form was that in which the Church was founded by the Apostles, and in which it continued for fifteen hundred years. *The Bishops are the only order of the ministry who have received divine authority to ordain, and therefore without their ordination no minister can prove his right to preach the Gospel, or to administer the sacraments.* Therefore we are bound to maintain the Episcopal form of government, not merely from motives of expediency, but from deference to the universal concurrence of the Church, founded on inspired authority. Even if the form of Episcopacy were indifferent, it would be highly presumptuous and disrespectful to separate from the Church on account of it. But if Episcopacy was, as we believe, of apostolic institution, and essential to the constitution of the Church, what before was a matter of insubordination, is now a clear case of desertion or mutiny.

W. Gresley, *Portrait of an English Churchman*, Rivington, 1840, pages 246–7

The Church rests on the unity and co-operation of all baptized Christians, and the Tractarians were as critical of lukewarm laity as of venial clergy.

Priests and people are bound up in one lot; they both must fall or stand together: neither can judge or accuse the other, for both partake of each other's sins. If the Priests are evil and careless, it is because the people pray not for them; if the people fall away, it is because the Priests have not prayed and watched for them.

Hence there is great consolation in speaking on this subject of the awful terrors of the Priests' responsibility on this Sunday, because in this week the people are in an especial manner called upon to pray for them. The Collect for this week is altogether a prayer for them: the Ember Days of this week we set apart on purpose to fast and pray for them. The awful sound of the Advent Trumpet calls on all men to pray for them; for if others cannot stand in that Judgement, how shall they who have so much more to account for? The love and mercies of Christmas-time tenderly appeal to all men to pray for their Pastors.

We complain of the want of Bishops and Clergy; we complain of their great feebleness, and, of what is worse; we complain of the crippled condition of the Church; of thousands and of tens of thousands daily perishing for lack of knowledge and from the deficiencies of Pastoral energy and care, but they who thus complain do not consider how much of all this remains at their own door; for no doubt the real cause which lies at the bottom of all this is that the people do not pray; do not pray as they are required to do for their own Pastor, and for their own Bishop, and for the Church generally, that the Ministers and Stewards of Christ's mysteries may prepare the way before Him. For how did our Lord Himself meet this great want when He was moved with compassion at the sight? His words were, 'Pray ye the Lord of the Harvest'. He knew of no other way but this, neither shall we find it.

Isaac Williams, Sermon for the Third Sunday in Advent, in *A Series of Sermons on the Epistle and Gospel for each Sunday in the Year and the Holy Days of the Church* (1853), 2nd edn, Rivington, 1855, vol. 1, pages 31–2

Liberalism was a target for traditional Anglicans long before the present century. In a poem of June 1833 titled 'Liberalism' Newman deplored diminutions of faith and doctrine which had crept into the Church of England.

Ye cannot halve the Gospel of God's grace;
Men of presumptuous heart! I know you well.
Ye are of those who plan that we should dwell,
Each in his tranquil home and holy place;
Seeing the Word refines all natures rude,
And tames the stirrings of the multitude.

And ye have caught some echoes of its lore,
As heralded amid the joyous choirs;
Ye mark'd it spoke of peace, chastised desires,
Good-will and mercy, and ye heard no more;
But, as for zeal and quick-eyed sanctity,
And the dread depths of grace, ye pass'd them by.

And so ye halve the Truth; for ye in heart,
At best, are doubters whether it be true,
The theme discarding, as unmeet for you,
Statesmen or Sages. O new-compass'd art
Of the ancient Foe! – but what, if it extends
O'er our own camp, and rules amid our friends?

J. H. Newman, *Verses on Various Occasions*,
Burns, Oates, 1880, page 140

The cult of Reason in the Enlightenment of the eighteenth century continued to cause disquiet. It had to be seen as supporting faith but not creating it.

Now, in attempting to investigate what are the distinct offices of Faith and Reason in religious matters, and the relation of the one to the other, I observe, first, that undeniable though it be, that Reason has a power of analysis and criticism in all opinion and conduct, and that nothing is true or right but what may be justified, and, in a certain sense, proved by it, and undeniable, in consequence, that, unless the doctrines received by Faith are approvable by Reason, they have no claim to be regarded as true, it does not therefore follow that Faith is actually grounded on Reason in the believing mind itself; unless indeed to take a parallel case, a judge can be called the origin, as well as the justifier, of the innocence or truth of those who are brought before him. A judge does not make men honest, but acquits and vindicates them: in like manner Reason need not be the origin of Faith, as Faith exists in the very persons believing, though it does test and verify it. This, then, is one confusion, which must be cleared up in the question – the assumption that Reason must be the inward principle of action in religious inquiries or conduct in the case of this or that individual, because, like a spectator, it acknowledges and concurs in what goes on; the mistake of a critical for a creative power.

This distinction we cannot fail to recognise as true in itself, and applicable to the matter in hand. It is what we all admit at once as regards the principle of Conscience. No one will say that Conscience is against Reason, or that its dictates cannot be thrown into an argumentative form; yet who will, therefore, maintain, that it is not an original principle, but must depend before it acts, upon some previous processes of Reason? Reason analyses the grounds and motives of action: a reason is an analysis, but is not the motive itself. As, then, Conscience is a simple element in our nature, yet its operations admit of being surveyed and scrutinised by Reason; so may Faith be cognisable, and its acts be justified, by Reason, without therefore being, in matter of fact, dependent upon it; and as we reprobate, under the name of Utilitarianism, the substitution of Reason for Conscience, so perchance it is a parallel error to teach that a process of Reason is the *sine qua non* for true religious Faith. When the Gospel is said to require a rational Faith, this need not mean more than that Faith is accordant to right Reason in the abstract, not that it results from it in the particular case.

J. H. Newman, *Sermons, Chiefly on the Theory of Religious Belief,*
preached before the University of Oxford, 2nd edn, 1844,
pages 173–5

However, Newman was concerned that Reason properly under-
stood should not be equated with Rationalism which seemed to lead
to doubt and infidelity. 'Mr Hume' is David Hume (1711–76), the
famous sceptical philosopher.

Rationalism then in fact is a forgetfulness of GOD'S power, disbelief of the existence of a First Cause sufficient to account for any events or facts, however marvellous or extraordinary, and a consequent measuring of the credibility of things, not by the power and other attributes of GOD, but by our own knowledge; a limiting the possible to the actual, and denying the indefinite range of GOD'S operations beyond our means of apprehending them. Mr Hume openly avows this principle, declaring it to be unphilosophical to suppose that Almighty God can do any thing but what we see He does. And though we may not profess it, we too often, it is to be feared, act upon it at the present day. Instead of looking out of ourselves, and trying to catch glimpses of GOD'S workings, from any quarter – throwing ourselves forward upon Him and waiting on Him, we sit at home bringing everything to ourselves enthroning ourselves as the centre of all things, and refusing to believe any thing that does not force itself upon our minds as true. Our private judgement is made every thing to us – is contemplated, recognised, and referred to as the arbiter of all questions, and as independent of every thing external to us. Nothing is considered to have an existence except so far forth as our minds discern it. The notion of half views and partial knowledge, of guesses, surmises, hopes and fears, of truths faintly apprehended and not understood, of isolated facts in the great scheme of providence, in a word, of Mystery, is discarded. Hence a distinction is drawn between what is called Objective and Subjective Truth, and Religion is said to consist in a reception of the latter. By Objective Truth is meant the Religious System considered as existing in itself, external to this or that particular mind: by Subjective, is meant that which each mind receives in particular, and considers to be such. To believe in Objective Truth is to throw ourselves forward upon that which we have but partially mastered or made Subjective; to embrace, maintain and use general propositions which are greater than our own capacity, as if we were contemplating what is real and independent of human judgement. Such a belief seems to the Rationalist superstitious and unmeaning, and he consequently confines faith to the province of Subjective Truth, or to the reception of doctrine, as and so far as it is met and apprehended by the mind, which will be differently in different persons, in the shape of orthodoxy in one, heterodoxy in another; that is, he professes to *believe* in that which he *opines*, and he avoids the apparent extravagance of such an avowal by maintaining that the moral trial involved in faith does not lie in the submission of the reason to external truths partially disclosed, but in that candid pursuit of truth which ensures the eventual adoption of that opinion on the subject, which is best for us, most natural according to the constitution of our minds, and so divinely intended. In short, he owns that faith, viewed with reference to its objects, is never more than an opinion, and is pleasing to GOD, not as an active principle apprehending different doctrines, but as a result and fruit, and therefore an evidence of past diligence, independent inquiry, dispassionateness, and the like. Rationalism takes the words of Scripture as signs of Ideas; Faith, of Things or Realities.

J. H. Newman, Tract 73, 'On the Introduction of Rationalistic
Principles in Religion', pages 3–5

William Palmer (1803–85), Fellow of Worcester College, Oxford, supported the early work of the Tractarians, but became opposed to what he and others regarded as their Romeward tendency. Although unsympathetic to both Roman Catholic and Protestant Dissenters, he showed something of an ecumenical spirit in his assessment of the marks of the true Church, with criteria similar to those later set out in the 'Lambeth Quadrilateral'.

Amidst the existing diversities of religious doctrine, it will be found, that all those Churches which have not arisen from schism or voluntary separation from the universal Church, agree to a very great extent in their belief. In proof of this, it may be observed, that the three creeds, called the Apostles', the Nicene, and the Athanasian, are accepted and approved equally by the Greek or Oriental, the British, and the Roman Churches, as well as by the relics of the foreign reformation. The same doctrines which were universally received in the second century are still so in the nineteenth. All Churches believe, and with one mouth confess, one God, who created the world by his only begotten Son, our Lord Jesus Christ, who being co-eternal with the Father, and of equal glory, and power, and majesty, came down from heaven and became man for our salvation, and in his human nature suffered death on the cross, and ascended into heaven, making an eternal and all-sufficient atonement and intercession for us. All believe that the condition of man by nature is such, that he is unable without the aid of Divine grace to turn to God and become pleasing and acceptable to him; that to sinful man Divine grace is given by the free and unmerited mercy of God; and that he is enabled by the sanctifying influences of the eternal Spirit of God, the third person in the most blessed Trinity, to triumph over the sins and infirmities of his nature, and to become sanctified by faith and the love of God, bringing forth the fruits of obedience. All believe that we shall give an account of our works at the last judgement, when the righteous shall be rewarded with life eternal, and the wicked consigned to everlasting fire. The holy Scriptures of the Old and New Testament are universally acknowledged to be the word of God, given by inspiration of the Holy Ghost. The sacraments instituted by Christ are celebrated amongst all nations; and the same Christian ministry has descended by successive ordinations of bishops from the time of the apostles to the present day. Such is the substantial and real agreement in doctrine which exists between Churches which are in some respects dissentient from each other. Their differences turn chiefly on doctrines and practices not taught by our Lord, but which some men in later ages have imagined to be deducible from revelation, or to be allowable and justifiable. Questions as to the truth and lawfulness of such doctrines and practices divide the Christian Churches; but it will probably be found that no article of the faith, no doctrine clearly and distinctly revealed by our Lord, is denied by any of these Churches.

It may be added, that many even of the sectaries or schismatics, who have voluntarily forsaken the Church still maintain the great mass of Christian doctrine, however destitute they may be of Christian charity.

W. Palmer, *Ecclesiastical History*, Burns, 1841, pages 331–2

6

Pursuit of Holiness

The quest for personal holiness and spiritual growth has been the concern of all the Churches, to be followed in various ways. For Newman and his associates, it was necessary for the individual Christian to make progress through the discipline and sacraments ordained by the Church. Practices like fasting and sacramental confession, which had been largely neglected, were brought back into prominence.

Newman presented the personal challenge with his usual solemnity.

Some one may ask, 'Why is it that holiness is a necessary qualification for our being received into heaven? Why is it that the Bible enjoins on us so strictly to love, fear, and obey God, to be just, honest, meek, pure in heart, forgiving, heavenly-minded, self-denying, humble and resigned? Man is confessedly weak and corrupt; why then is he enjoined to be so religious, so unearthly? Why is he required (in the strong language of Scripture) to become "a new creature"? Since he is by nature what he is, would it not be an act of greater mercy in God to save him altogether without this holiness, which it is so difficult, yet (as it appears) so necessary for him to possess?'

Now we have no right to ask this question. Surely it is quite enough for a sinner to know, that a way has been opened through God's grace for his salvation, without being informed why that way, and not another way, was chosen by Divine Wisdom. Eternal life is 'the gift of God.' Undoubtedly He may prescribe the terms on which He will give it; and if He has determined holiness to be the way of life, it is enough; it is not for us to inquire why He has so determined.

Yet the question may be asked reverently, and with a view to enlarge our insight into our own condition and prospects; and in that case the attempt to answer it will be profitable, if it be made soberly. I proceed, therefore, to state one of the reasons, assigned in Scripture, why present holiness is necessary for future happiness.

To be holy is, in our Church's words, to have 'the true circumcision of the Spirit;' that is, to be separate from sin, to hate the works of the world, the flesh, and the devil; to take pleasure in keeping God's commandments; to do things as He would have us do them; to live habitually as in the sight of the world to come, as if we had broken the ties of this life, and were dead already. Why cannot we be saved without possessing such a frame and temper of mind?

I answer as follows: That, even supposing a man of unholy life were suffered to enter heaven, *he would not be happy there;* so that it would be no mercy to permit him to enter.

> J. H. Newman, *Parochial and Plain Sermons* (1834), Rivington, 1877,
> vol. 1, pages 1–2

Keble saw personal holiness and devotion to duty as a necessary response to attacks on the Church.

We have ill learned the lessons of our Church, if we permit our patriotism to decay, together with the protecting care of the state. 'The powers that be are ordained of God', whether they foster the true Church or no. Submission and order are still duties. They were so in the days of pagan persecution; and the more of loyal and affectionate feeling we endeavour to mingle with our obedience, the better.

After all, the surest way to uphold or restore our endangered Church, will be for each of her anxious children, in his own place and station, to resign himself more thoroughly to his God and Saviour in those duties, public and private, which are not immediately affected by the emergencies of the moment: the daily and hourly duties, I mean, of piety, purity, charity, justice. It will be a consolation understood by every thoughtful Churchman, that let his occupation be, apparently, never so remote from such great interests, it is in his power, by doing all as a Christian, to credit and advance the cause he has most at heart; and what is more, to draw down God's blessing upon it. This ought to be felt, for example, as one motive more to exact punctuality in those duties, personal and official, which the return of an Assize week offers to our practice; one reason more for veracity in witnesses, fairness in pleaders, strict impartiality, self-command, and patience, in those on whom decisions depend; and for an awful sense of God's presence in all. An Apostle once did not disdain to urge good conduct upon his proselytes of lowest condition, upon the ground that, so doing, they would adorn and recommend the doctrine of God our Saviour. Surely, then, it will be no unworthy principle, if any man be more circumspect in his behaviour, more watchful and fearful of himself, more earnest in his petitions for spiritual aid, from a dread of disparaging the holy name of the English Church, in her hour of peril, by his own personal fault or negligence.

As to those who, either by station or temper, feel themselves most deeply interested, they cannot be too careful in reminding themselves, that one chief danger, in times of change and excitement, arises from their tendency to engross the whole mind. Public concerns, ecclesiastical or civil, will prove indeed ruinous to those, who permit them to occupy all their care and thoughts, neglecting or undervaluing ordinary duties, more especially those of a devotional kind.

These cautions being duly observed, I do not see how any person can devote himself too entirely to the cause of the Apostolical Church in these realms.

> J. Keble, 'National Apostasy', in *Sermons Academical and Occasional*,
> 2nd edn, Parker, 1848, pages 145–7

This insistence on the unique importance and responsibility of every individual soul was basic to Tractarian spirituality. God's self-revelation in Christ has created an ideal pattern which it is a personal duty to follow, both in one's own life and in the incalculable influence one may have on others. Newman forcefully propounded the individuality of the soul and therefore of personal responsibility.

Survey some populous town: crowds are pouring through the streets; some on foot, some in carriages; while the shops are full, and the houses too, could we see into them. Every part of it is full of life. Hence we gain a general idea of splendour, magnificence, opulence, and energy. But what is the truth? Why, that every being in that great concourse is his own centre, and all things about him are but shades, but a 'vain shadow', in which he 'walketh and disquieteth himself in vain'. He has his own hopes and fears, desires, judgements, and aims; he is everything to himself, and no one else is really any thing. No one outside of him can really touch him, can touch his soul, his immortality, he must live with himself for ever. He has a depth within him unfathomable, an infinite abyss of existence; and the scene in which he bears part for the moment is but like a gleam of sunshine upon its surface.

Again: when we read history, we meet with accounts of great slaughters and massacres, great pestilences, famines, conflagrations, and so on; and here again we are accustomed in an especial way to regard collections of people as if individual units. We cannot understand that a multitude is a collection of immortal souls.

I say immortal souls: each of those multitudes, not only had while he was upon earth, but *has* a soul, which did in its own time but return to God who gave it, and not perish, and which now lives unto Him. All those millions upon millions of human beings who ever trod the earth and saw the sun successively, are at this very moment in existence all together. This, I think, you will grant we do not duly realise.

J. H. Newman, 'The Individuality of the Soul' (1838), Parochial and
Plain Sermons, Rivington, 1877, vol. 4, pages 82–3

The life of faith must be committed in detail to austerity and the demands of personal discipline.

We are, day by day, and hour by hour, influenced by every thing around us; rising or falling, sinking or recovering, receiving impressions which are to last for ever; taking our colour and mould from everything which passes around us and in us, and not the less because unperceived; each touch, slight, as impressed by an invisible spiritual hand, but, in itself, not the less, rather the more lasting, since what we are yielding ourselves to is, in the end, the finger of God or the touch of Satan. In our rising up or our lying down; our labour or our refreshment; our intercourse with others, or our solitary thoughts; our plans for the future or the duties of the day; our purposes and their fulfilments or their failure, our acting or our suffering, we are receiving moment by moment the hallowed impress of the heavenly hand, conforming our lineaments, one by one, each faculty of our spirit, and this poor earthly tenement of our body itself, to the image of God wherein we were re-created, or we are gradually being dried up and withered by the blasting burning touch of the arch-fiend; each touch is of fire, burning out our proud rebellious flesh, or searing our life; some more miserable falls sink us deeper; some more difficult victories, won by God's help over ourselves, the flesh, the world, and Satan, raise us on the heavenward path; but each sense, at every avenue, each thought, each word, each act, is in its degree doing that endless work; every evil thought, every idle word, and still more, each wilful act, is stamping upon men the mark of the beast; each slightest deed of faith is tracing deeper the seal of God upon their foreheads.

E. B. Pusey, Parochial Sermons, Parker, 1864, vol, 3, page 143

Newman felt deeply the hard and often painful aspects of faith and was not slow in urging others to accept them.

Doubtless many a one there is, who, on hearing doctrines such as I have been insisting on, says in his heart, that religion is thus made gloomy and repulsive; that he would attend to a teacher who spoke in a less severe way; and that in fact Christianity was not intended to be a dark burdensome law, but a religion of cheerfulness and joy. This is what young people think, though they do not express it in this argumentative form. They view a strict life as something offensive and hateful; they turn from the notion of it. And then, as they get older and see more of the world, they learn to defend their opinion, and express it more or less in the way in which I have just put it. They hate and oppose the truth, as it were upon principle; and the more they are told that they have souls, the more resolved they are to live as if they had not souls. But let us take it as a clear point from the first, and not to be disputed, that religion must ever be difficult to those who neglect it. All things that we have to learn are difficult at first, and our duties to God, and to man for His sake, are peculiarly difficult, because they call upon us to take up a new life, and quit the love of this world for the next. It cannot be avoided; we must fear and be in sorrow, before we can rejoice. The Gospel must be a burden before it comforts and brings us peace. No one can have his heart cut away from the natural objects of its love, without pain during the process and throbbings afterwards. This is plain from the nature of the case: and, however true it be, that this or that teacher may be harsh and repulsive, yet he cannot materially alter things. Religion is in itself at first a weariness to the worldly mind, and it requires an effort and a self-denial in everyone who honestly determines to be religious.

J. H. Newman, *Parochial Sermons*, Rivington, 1834–42, vol. 1, page 26

Pusey, strict and austere in his own life, set down advice which most Evangelicals would have accepted, and which was followed by devout Anglo-Catholics. It can be seen in the continual examinations of conscience by Charlotte M. Yonge's characters.

Know thyself. Pray God to show thee thyself. Bear in God's light to see thyself, bared of all outward advantages, what thou thyself hast made thyself, what thou hast been, what thou art. By God's grace, the sight will never again let thee be proud.

Keep ever present with thee the knowledge of thine own infirmity.

Never seek praise, nor speak of any good in thee, except for some good end, nor say what may draw out praise. Yea, rather if it be useful to speak of thine own experience, it is best mostly to hide, in some true way, that it is thine own.

Do not even blame thyself, if it makes others think thee humble. Mistrust thyself in everything, and in the very least things, seek, whenever thou canst remember it, the help of God.

Be afraid of the praise of others. If there be good in thee, own it, at least, in thy heart, to be God's, and think of thy evil and thy sins.

Take patiently any humiliation from others. It is a precious gift of God. 'Humiliation is the way to humility, as patience to peace, reading to knowledge'. If thou endurest not to be humbled, thou canst not be humble.

In all things, humble thyself under the Hand of God. Take all things, through whomsoever they come, from Him.

Do not excuse thyself, if blamed, unless respect or love, or the cause of truth and of God require it. It is more value to thee to detect one grain of fault in thyself, than to show to another that thou deservest not, as it were, a hundredweight of blame.

Be not careful to conceal any ignorance or fault in thee, unless it would hurt another to know that thou hast it.

Do willingly humble offices, humbly.

Give way to all, in all things in which thou mayest.

E. B. Pusey, *Parochial Sermons*, Parker, 1864, vol. 2, page 78

Newman also explained that there was no escape for any individual from the comforts and challenges of divine grace.

God 'beholds' thee individually, whoever thou art. He calls thee by thy name. He sees thee, and understands thee, as He made thee. He knows what is in thee, all thy own peculiar feelings and thoughts, thy dispositions and likings, thy strength and thy weakness. He views thee in thy day of rejoicing and thy day of sorrow. He sympathises in thy hopes and thy temptations. He interests Himself in all thy anxieties and remembrances, all the risings and fallings of thy spirit. He has numbered the very hairs of thy head and the cubits of thy stature. He compasses thee round, and bears thee in His arms; He takes thee up and sets thee down. He notes thy very countenance, whether smiling or in tears, whether healthful or sickly. He looks tenderly upon thy hands and thy feet; He hears thy voice, the beating of thy heart, and thy very breathing. Thou dost not love thyself better than He loves thee. Thou canst not shrink from pain more than He dislikes thy bearing it; and if He puts it on thee, it is as thou wilt put it on thyself, if thou art wise, for a greater good afterwards. Thou art not only His creature (though for the very sparrows He has a care, and pitied the 'much cattle' of Nineveh), thou art man redeemed and sanctified, His adopted son, favoured with a portion of that glory and blessedness which flows from Him everlastingly unto the only-begotten. Thou art chosen to be His, even above thy fellows who live in the east and south. Thou wast one of those for whom Christ offered up His last prayer, and sealed it with His precious blood.

J. H. Newman, *Parochial Sermons*, Rivington, 1834–42, vol. 3, pages 134–5

Too much self-accusation could lead to the 'scruples' in matters in-different which are condemned in the Book of Common Prayer. The danger is shown in the private Journals *of Hurrell Froude, written in 1826, just after becoming a Fellow of Oriel. 'N' is probably New-man; the other blanks have not been identified. The square brackets were added by Froude's editors.*

Nov. 10. Fell quite short of my wishes with respect to the rigour of to-day's fast, though I am quite willing to believe not unpardonably: I tasted nothing till after half-past eight in the evening, and before that had undergone more uncomfortableness, both of body and mind, than any fast has as yet occasioned me, having, I hope, laid a sort of foun-dation, on which I may gradually build up the fit spending of a fast in calling my sins to remembrance. But I made rather a more hearty tea than usual [quite giving up the notion of a fast] in W.'s rooms, and by this weakness have occasioned another slip. For having been treated, as I think, without sufficient respect by the youngest – I allowed my self to be vexed, and to think of how I ought to have set him down all the rest of the evening, instead of receiving it with thankfulness from God as an instrument of humility. Also I will record another error, common indeed with me, and which for that reason I have hitherto overlooked, i.e. speaking severely of another without a cause. I said I thought — an ass, when there was not the least occasion for me to express my sentiments about him. And yet I, so severe on the follies, and so bitter against the slightest injuries I get from others, am now presenting myself before my great Father to ask for mercy on my most foul sins, and forgiveness for the most incessant injuries. 'How shall I be delivered from the body of this death!'

Nov. 11. I have become comfortable again, and cannot help thinking that it is owing, in a great measure, to my having seen that it was not from a deliberate intention to slight me, that young — was pert, and from my interest in the argument with N. having died away. How feeble my mind has become, from my having left it so long uncontrolled. I am conscious that I have merited no respect from my past conduct, and always measure the slights offered me by what I know I deserve, and what I should be forced to put up with: and when external trifles make me uncomfortable, then I think it is repentance. Yet, I cannot but think that the consciousness of my great sinfulness had much to do with my wretchedness yesterday, and that our minds are so contrived that this misery must have something external to fasten on, so that it may not be wearing us down continually. This is the first day I have not been to chapel in Oriel; but I was obliged to stay away out of civility to —. I went to Magdalen instead; and though I could not do all the forms, without obtruding myself on notice, yet it seems to me to have been a very impressive service partly from the difficulty of reading; a subject connected with which I have been making a speculation, which I don't recollect having dated. I have again been talking freely of people, partly out of habit, and partly to have something to say to —. Laughed at —, when uncalled for. Have not been the least abstemious in any of my meals.

Nov 12. Felt great reluctance to sleep on the floor last night, and was nearly arguing myself out of it; was not up till half-past six. — was sitting under me in chapel; and I was actually prevented from giving my mind to a great deal of the early part of the service, by the thought crossing me at each response, that he must be thinking I was become a Don, and was affecting religious out of compliance.

Felt ashamed that my trowsers (*sic*) were dirty whilst I was sitting next —, but resolved not to hide them. This sort of shame [about what] we ourselves esteem matters of indifference, because they do not seem so to other people, brings home to our minds what depravity it proves in us to pay so little attention to what we know is serious. I cannot look on this Sunday with any pleasure. I have been inattentive again at evening chapel, and have made the day too much a holiday in the ordinary sense.

R. H. Froude, *Remains of the late Reverend Richard Hurrell Froude M.A.*, Rivington, 1838, vol. 1, pages 42–4

With so much austerity and self-accusation, it is refreshing to find Newman extolling joy as a Christian virtue. After describing how the Apostles renounced worldly things and accepted the consequences of their faith, he took the Primitive Church as an example for the individual believer as well as a model for the Church of his day.

Here we are brought to a third and last characteristic of the Christianity of the New Testament, which necessarily follows from the other two. If the first disciples so unreservedly gave up the world, and if, secondly, they were so strictly and promptly taken at their word, what do you think would follow, if they were true men and not hypocrites? This; they would rejoice to be so taken. This, then, is the third chief grace of primitive Christianity – joy in all its forms; not only a pure heart, not only a clean hand, but, thirdly, a cheerful countenance. I say joy in all its forms, for in true joyfulness many graces are included; joyful people are loving; joyful people are forgiving; joyful people are munificent. Joy, if it be Christian joy, the refined joy of the mortified and persecuted, makes men peaceful, serene, thankful, gentle, affectionate, sweet-tempered, pleasant, hopeful; it is graceful, tender, touching, winning. All this were the Christians of the New Testament, for they have obtained what they desired. They had desired to sacrifice the kingdom of the world and all its pomps, for the love of Christ, whom they had seen, whom they loved, in whom they believed, in whom they delighted; and when their wish was granted, they could but 'rejoice in that day, and leap for joy, for, behold, their reward was great in heaven', 'blessed were they, thrice blessed, because they in their lifetime had evil things', and their consolation was to come hereafter.

Such, I say, was the joy of the first disciples of Christ, to whom it was granted to suffer shame and to undergo toil for His Name's sake; and such holy, gentle graces were the fruit of this joy, as every part of the Gospels and Epistles shows us.

J. H. Newman, 'The Apostolical Christian', in *Sermons Bearing on Subjects of the Day*, Rivington, 1843, pages 323–4

Pusey enjoined frequent and regular prayer as essential in the life of faith.

Pray morning by morning to be enabled to pray; strive against covetousness, or sensuality, or the cares of this life, which prevent thy thinking upon God; make efforts to win thy soul from the business of this life, if but now and then, for a thought on God; use all the stated means in thy power, and make what thou canst. If thou wakest in the night, pray; when thou wakest in the morning, be thy first thought prayer; bethink thee that the journey is hard for thee, the way slippery, thy feet easily wearied, thy strength small, and haste thee 'to the mountain', the Rock of ages, 'lest thou be consumed'.

And above all, neglect not any thought which God puts into thy heart (as He does oftentimes) to pray. The thought to pray must come from Him; it cannot come from thyself or from the evil one. Pray, wherever thou art, whatever thou art doing; man will not see it, but God will; and thy Father Who seeth in secret Himself shall reward thee openly. The first step on this way of frequent prayer, is the first step on Jacob's ladder, its foot on earth, its top in heaven; look not above, lest thou faint and sink back; nor downwards lest thou turn dizzy; but go on, step by step labouring to make thy prayers more and more continual and fervent, and God shall send His angels to conduct thee, and thy Saviour shall intercede for thee, and the Holy Ghost shall strengthen thee, and thou shalt win thy way step by step, until the cloud of death close round thee, and then thou shalt find that the first step to continual earnest prayer was 'the gate of heaven'.

E. B. Pusey, *Parochial Sermons*, Parker, 1864, vol. 3, page 238

There was some Tractarian anxiety that the Evangelical teaching of justification by faith alone could reduce concern for the importance of individual conduct. Newman declared that faith without works is dead.

The question is, What is faith and how can a man tell that he has faith? Some persons answer at once and without hesitation, that 'to have faith, is to feel oneself to be nothing, and God everything; it is to be convinced of sin, to be conscious one cannot save oneself, and to wish to be saved by Christ our Lord; and that it is moreover to have the love of Him warm in one's heart, and to rejoice in Him, to desire His glory, and to resolve to live to Him and not to the world'. But I will answer, with all due seriousness, as speaking on a serious subject, that this is not faith. Not that it is not necessary (it is very necessary) to be convinced, that we are laden with infirmity and sin, and without health in us, and to look for salvation solely to Christ's blessed sacrifice on the cross; and we may well be thankful if we are thus minded; but that a man may feel all this that I have described, vividly, and still not yet possess one particle of true religious faith.

Why? Because there is an immeasurable distance between feeling right and doing right. A man may have all these good thoughts and emotions, yet (if he has not yet hazarded them to the experiment of practice), he cannot promise himself that he has any sound and permanent principle at all. If he has not yet acted upon them, we have no voucher, barely on account of them to believe that they are any thing but words. Though a man spoke like an angel, I would not believe him, on the mere ground of his speaking. Nay, till he acts upon them, he has not even evidence to himself, that he has true living faith. Dead faith (as St James says), profits no man. Of course; the devils have it. What, on the other hand, is living faith? Do fervent thoughts make faith living? St James tells us otherwise. He tells us works, deeds of obedience, are the life of faith. 'As the body without the spirit is dead, so faith without works is dead also'. So that those who think they really believe, because they have in word and thought surrendered themselves to God, are much too hasty in their judgement. They have done something, indeed, but not at all the most difficult part of their duty, which is to surrender themselves to God in deed and act. They have as yet done nothing to show they will not, after saying 'I go', the next moment 'go not'; nothing to show they will not act the part of the self-deceiving disciple, who said, 'Though I die with Thee, I will not deny Thee'; yet straightway went and denied Christ thrice. As far as we know anything of the matter, justifying faith has no existence independent of its particular definite acts. It may be described to be the temper under which men obey; the humble and earnest desire to please Christ which causes and attends on actual services. He who does one little deed of obedience, whether he denies himself some comfort to relieve the sick and needy, or curbs his temper, or forgives an enemy, or asks forgiveness for an offence committed by him, or resists the clamour or ridicule of the world, such a one (as far as we are given to judge) evinces more true faith than could be shown by the most fluent religious conversation, the most intimate knowledge of Scripture doctrine, or the most remarkable agitation and change of religious sentiments. Yet how many are there who sit still with folded hands, dreaming, doing nothing at all, thinking they have done every thing, or need do nothing, when they merely have had these good thoughts, which will save no one.

J. H. Newman, *Parochial Sermons*, Rivington, 1834–42, vol. 1,
pages 197–9

Isaac Williams also made the call to a life of holy obedience.

Jesus Christ is now, and has been at all times, hiding Himself from us, but at the same time exceedingly desirous to communicate Himself, and that exactly in proportion as we show ourselves worthy He will disclose Himself to us; that if we constrain Him He will come in and abide with us; that unsatisfactory as human knowledge is, and the increase of which is the increase of care, a knowledge which puffeth up; yet that there is a knowledge which humbleth, which is infinite in its nature, and is nothing else than deeper, and higher, and broader views of the mystery which is hid in Christ.

That although Scripture does not set before us any sensible joy or satisfaction to be sought for, as the end of holiness, yet it does this knowledge, which is attainable by nothing else but by making the study of divinity to consist in a divine life.

That with regard to any ways of doing good to the world, it is far too great a work for anything of human device, or any plans that partake of this world to perform; but if in the prescribed path of duty we shall be enabled to obtain this fight, it will from us be communicated to others, but perhaps only in some secret way which is known to God, and which the world esteems foolishness, but a power which is of God, and therefore must overcome the world.

That all the means of grace faithfully cherished will lead us, as it were, step by step, into all these treasures, inexhaustible in their nature, limitless in their duration, and exceeding all conception of man, the blessing of the pure in heart, that they shall see God.

I. Williams, Tract 80, 'On Reserve in Communicating Religious
Knowledge', page 83

Although public fasts were occasionally proclaimed at times of national danger, the practice of private fasting had ceased to be widely observed. Pusey pressed for a return to what Church rules ordained.

To a person but little accustomed to observe any stated Fasts, the directions given by our Church on this subject would probably occasion two very opposite feelings. On the one hand, he would be struck by the practical character and thoughtfulness evinced by some of the regulations; on the other, he would probably feel repelled by the number of days, and the variety of occasions, which the Church has appointed to be hallowed. Most Christians, who really loved their Saviour (unless prevented by the habits of early education), would probably see something appropriate and affectionate in the selection of the Friday for a weekly commemoration of their Saviour's sufferings, and of humiliation for their own sins which caused them; or, at all events, they would feel that there was some thoughtfulness in the direction annexed, that this weekly Fast should not interfere with the Christian joyousness brought back by the Festival of their Lord's Nativity when these should in the cycle of years coincide. Again, if they should fail to appreciate the wisdom of appointing certain days to be kept sacred in memory of the holy men who left all to follow Christ, and consequently should be rather deterred than attracted by observing that many of these days were ushered in by a preceding Fast; still they would hardly fail to be struck by the provision, that this previous Fast should not interfere with the Christian's weekly Festival of his Lord's Resurrection, but that 'if any of these Feast-days should fall upon a Monday, then the Fast-day should be kept on the Saturday, not upon the Sunday next before it'. Again, he must observe that during certain periods of the Church's year, which are times of especial joy to the faithful Christian, those, namely, which follow the Nativity and the Resurrection, these preparatory Fasts are altogether omitted. Some or other of these regulations would probably strike most thoughtful minds as instances of consideration and reflection in those who framed them. The Clergy, more especially, would appreciate, abstractedly at least, the imitation of the Apostolic practice of Fasting, when any are to be ordained to any holy function in the Church; and some probably will feel mournfully, that if the Church were now more uniformly to observe those acts of Fasting and Prayer which were thought needful, before even Paul and Barnabas were separated for God's work, we should have more reasonable grounds to hope that many of our Clergy would be filled with the spirit of Barnabas and Paul.

On the other hand, it is naturally to be expected that one not accustomed to any outward restraint in this matter would feel indisposed to ordinances so detailed; that although he could reconcile to himself the one or the other of these observances which most recommended themselves to his Christian feelings, he would think the whole a burdensome and minute ceremonial, perhaps unbefitting a spiritual worship, and interfering with the liberty wherewith Christ has made him free. This is very natural; for we are by nature averse to restraint, and the abuse of some maxims of Protestantism, such as the 'right of private judgement', has made us yet more so: we are reluctant to yield to an unreasoning authority, and to submit our wills, where our reason has not first been convinced; and the prevailing maxims of the day have strengthened this reluctance; we have been accustomed to do 'every one that which was right in his own eyes', and are jealous of any authority, except that of the direct injunctions of the Bible. In extolling also the spirituality of our religion, we have, I fear, intended covertly to panegyrise our own, and so, almost wilfully withdraw our sight from those more humbling provisions which are adapted to us, as being yet in the flesh in our zeal for the blessed truths of the cross of Christ, and of our sanctification by the Holy Spirit, we have begun insensibly to disparage other truths, which bring us less immediately into intercourse with God, to neglect the means and ordinances, which touch not upon the very centre of our faith.

He expounds at length the various benefits of fasting and concludes:

Regular and stated Fasts formed a part of the Discipline by which, during almost the whole period since the Christian Church has been founded, all her real sons, in every climate, nation, and language, have subdued the flesh to the spirit, and brought both body and mind into a willing obedience to the Law of God. They thought this Discipline necessary as an expression and instrument of repentance, as a memorial of their Saviour, to 'refrain their souls and keep them low', to teach them to 'trust in the Lord', and seek communion with Him. To this system our own Church during all her happier times adhered. The value of this remedy for sin has come to us attested by the experience, and sealed by the blood, of Martyrs; who having learned thus to endure hardships, like good soldiers of Christ, at last resisted to the blood, striving against sin. Shall we, untried, pronounce that to be needless for ourselves which the Glorious Company of the Apostles, the Goodly Fellowship of Prophets, the Noble Army of Martyrs, the Holy Church throughout the world, found needful?

I can hardly anticipate other than one answer. Only let not any one be deterred by the irksomeness, or perplexities, or harassing doubts which every one must find in resuming a neglected portion of duty. It were scarcely a discipline if its practice brought with it an *immediate* reward; and we have besides to pay the penalty of our sloth and diseased habits. 'Patiently to lack what flesh and blood doth desire, and by virtue to forbear what by nature we covet, this no man attaineth unto, but with labour and long practice'. [Hooker, *Laws of Ecclesiastical Polity*, book 5, para 72] And if it be that blessed instrument of holiness which they who have tried it assure us, it will not be without some struggle with our spiritual enemy that we shall recover the ground which we have lost. Only let us persevere, not elated with the first petty victories over ourselves, which may be perhaps conceded to us in order to produce over-confidence and carelessness; nor dejected by the obstacles which a luxurious and scoffing age may oppose; not by the yet greater difficulties from within, in acquiring any uniform or consistent habit. Men, aided by God, have done the like; and for us also, His grace will be sufficient.

E. B. Pusey, Tract 18, 'Thoughts on the Benefits of the System of Fasting
Enjoined by our Church', pages 1–2, 27–8

Pusey had more to say about fasting; the 'sacred poet' is George Herbert.

If this be any one's first Lent, I would give some simple rules, which might smooth some difficulties. Let it be an act of obedience. A sacred Poet of our own says, 'The Scripture bids us fast, the Church says now'. Thus shall we do it more simply, not as any great thing; not as of our own will, but as an act of obedience; so will the remarks of others (if such there be) less disturb us, as knowing that we are doing but little, and that not of our own mind. But little in itself, it is connected with high things, with the very height of Heaven and the depths of Hell; our Blessed Saviour and our sins. We fast *with* our Lord, and our sins. The Church brings us nigh to our Lord, Whose Fast and for the merits of Whose Fasting and Passion we partake of. We have to 'humble our own souls with fasting' for our own sins. Remember we both. Review we our past lives; recall to our remembrance what chief sins we can; confess them habitually and in sorrow, with the use of the Penitential Psalms, and especially that daily medicine of the penitent soul, the fifty-first. Fast we, in token that we are unworthy of God's creatures which we have misused. Take we thankfully weariness or discomfort, as we before sinned through ease and lightness of heart. And thus, owning ourselves unworthy of all, think we on Him, Who, for us, bore all, so shall those precious Sufferings sanctify thy discomfort; the irksomeness shall be gladsome to thee which brings thee nearer to thy Lord.

Then for the mode of fasting, begin gently, it is for the most part the most humble. God leads us in all things step by step. They who begin impetuously, do it mostly over-confidently, and so have often grown weary of hardness which they sought to bear in their own strength.

E. B. Pusey, *Sermons During the Season From Advent
to Whitsuntide*, Parker, 1848, pages 150–1

Pusey returned to the subject in a later Tract, replying to some of the objections made against it. His concluding words pick up the strong Tractarian insistence that the Church of England maintained the tradition and purity of the Primitive Church.

Fasting is Popish. If this means, that it has been preserved amid the errors of Romanism, is not this true of most of the truths of the Gospel? Our charge against the Romanists, generally, is not that they have not preserved the truth, but that, like the Pharisees, 'they have made it of none effect by their traditions'; at least, in great measure, to so many of their members. And does not the objection imply that we have forgotten the peculiar character of our church, which is not a mere Protestant, but a Primitive Church? And if we are to prevail in our approaching conflict with Romanism, or to be (as we seem marked out to be) a means of reclaiming that Church, must we not reconsider the character of our own Church, and take our stand in its principles not in the protestantism of other churches, or of the day?

E. B. Pusey, Tract 66, 'On the Benefits of Fasting Prescribed by our Church', page 16

Sacramental confession to a priest, not regarded by the Reformers as a regular duty, was nevertheless accepted in the Book of Common Prayer, and enjoined for unquiet consciences. Pusey, who asked Keble to be his own confessor, commended the practice in these terms. Later Anglo-Catholic teaching was sometimes more insistent on regular confession for all.

Consciences *are* burdened. There is a provision, on the part of God, in His Church, to relieve them. They wish to be, and to know they are, in a state of grace. God has provided a means, however deeply any have fallen, to replace them in it. They feel that they cannot take off their own burden, loose the chains of their past sins, and set themselves free to serve God. They look for some act out of themselves, if there be one, which shall do this. God has provided it. They want something to sever between past and future, that they may begin anew. By His absolving sentence, God does efface the past. They cannot estimate their own repentance and faith. He has provided physicians of the soul, to relieve and judge for those who 'open their griefs' to them. They wish to know how to overcome besetting temptations; God has provided those, experienced in the sad history of man's sins and sorrows, who can tell them how others, through the grace of God, have overcome them.

Such are the cases to which the Church of which we are members, most directly applies the remedy of private Absolution, cases of heavy sin, or of timorous, scrupulous consciences; and this, either previous to the Holy Communion, or at the hour of death. There is a deep instinctive feeling, by which the soul (unless warped by human systems) does long to lay open any oppressive sin, before it comes into the presence of its judge. Persons, who for a long period of life have carried about them the oppressive consciousness of some past, secret sin, cannot bear it then; those who could not bring themselves to endure the pain and shame of confession in life, still often could not bear the thought of carrying their sin with them, unconfessed, into the very Presence of God.

Our Church explicitly contemplates tender consciences, who need comfort, and peace, and reassurance of the favour of their Heavenly Father. For (blessed be God!) there are those who feel the weight of any slight sin, more than others do 'whole cartloads'; and who do derive comfort and strength from the special application of the power of the keys to their own consciences. The words of our Church are very large; 'a full trust in God's mercy and a quiet conscience', 'if any by this means cannot quiet his own conscience herein, but requireth further comfort and counsel', 'to the avoiding of all scruple and doubtfulness'. What Minister of Christ, then, should take upon himself to drive away 'His lambs' as if persons were to have less of the Ministry of comfort, the less they had offended God? As if any thing ought, in the estimation of the Christian Minister, to be of slight account, which disturbs the peaceful mirror of the soul, wherein it reflects God! The 'benefit of Absolution' then, is intended by our Church, not only for the penitent, who are by it assured of God's acceptance of their repentance, and often by it replaced in a state of grace, but for all who can, through its ministry, approach with lightened, more peaceful hearts to the Holy Communion. Our Church, in leaving her children free, did not mean to stint the use of the gifts entrusted to her, to force all consciences to one level; nor because she does not require Confession, therefore, (as some now would seem to interpret her) by an opposite constraint to that which she laid aside, to *hinder* or withhold them from it.

E. B. Pusey, *Nine Sermons preached before the University of
Oxford*, Parker, 1865, Preface

After the years of the Tracts he returned to the subject in answer to criticisms.

My desire has been simply to exercise, in obedience to the Church, 'the office and work of a Priest, committed unto' me 'by the Imposition of' the Bishop's 'hands', for the relief of those souls who come to me for that end. I, in common with all the Presbyters whom I know, fully believed that the Church gave power to her children, to go to any priest they had confidence in, in order to 'open their griefs' for 'the benefit of absolution'. No doubt was ever raised upon it, until very lately (and then, I am satisfied, wholly without foundation), nor had I even the slightest doubt. I did not apply to your Lordship, simply because I had no doubt which could occasion me to do so. Our Prayer Book places no limitation. It says that it is *requisite* for people to come to Holy Communion with a quiet conscience, and, if they need it, suggests this mode of quieting it. I am not aware that any Divine or Bishop in our Church, since the Reformation, has excepted against any thing, except making confession compulsory. The Divines whose writings on this subject I have observed, seem to me to lay especial stress on 'comfort' as one object of it. They followed herein, doubtless, the language of the Prayer Book, which speaks especially of 'comfort', and of 'quieting the conscience', and of 'avoiding scruple'. They had special regard for tender consciences. When the public discipline of the Church could not be restored, as the reformers wished, and it was taught that all sin might be forgiven (as, doubtless, God does forgive it) on true, loving contrition of heart and confession to God Alone, it was almost natural that 'comfort' should be selected, as being a prominent ground for the use of confession. But, this being so, then it would seem most contrary to the spirit both of the English Church and her leading Divines, to deny the privilege of confession or 'opening the griefs for the benefit of absolution' to any one who for his own peace and well-being earnestly desires it.

E. B. Pusey, *Letter to the Right Hon and Right Rev the Lord Bishop of London*, Parker, 1851, pages 234–6

7

Church and Society

The Oxford Movement began with a defence of Church rights and
privileges against the encroachment of state power. Other issues soon
became dominant, but the Tractarians and their successors never lost
sight of the relationship and tensions between Church and State.
They were not systematic social thinkers, but they had a deep concern for the poor and believed that the Church should lead in meeting
all human needs, material as well as spiritual, and maintaining high
moral standards in social work and relief.

*Even before his famous Assize Sermon, Keble had preached against
the passive acquiescence of church members in political decisions
which were contrary to Christian principles. In 1831, preaching
on 30 January, at that time a day for the State Service of Charles,
King and Martyr, he reminds his hearers of the reaction of the
seventeenth-century Church to the execution of Charles I and
warns against losing the proper appreciation of Church rights and
duties.*

These cautions are the more necessary, on account of a peculiar kind
of Fatalism, which is apt to intrude itself, more especially, on our
political opinions and conduct: by reason, I suppose, of men's acting
together, on such occasions, in large masses: which makes it easier
for each person's imagination to transfer his own guilt to others. But
whatever be the cause, certain it is, that such a tendency does exist;
that many consciences are beguiled by it; and must we not add, that
it has of late been visibly and daily gaining ground? For at what time
ever among Christians was the doctrine so often heard, that 'such
and such evils must be complied with, the "spirit of the times" so
requiring?' On every part of literature and conduct, but especially
in reference to political duties, we hear this observation repeated; it

appears, in fact, to be the sum and substance of some men's practical wisdom; but can it win the calm assent of the conscience? Does it not, in fact, amount to a surrender, I do not say of Christian principle only, but of every thing like moral independence and dignity? Can such casuists have root in themselves? can they endure even for a while, when the times are evil and corrupt? 'It is impossible', they plead, 'but offences will come'; and they proceed as if our Saviour had inferred, 'It matters not by whom the offence cometh'. Let it be enough for the condemnation of such a spirit, that it is the direct contrary of the spirit of martyrdom: and we all know how its promptings are applied to palliate great public crimes.

Thus, in regard of the fatal precedent by which our history was this day stained: we are told over and over again, that the season had come round, in a kind of moral cycle, when there could not but be a revolution: that the King was in some sort fairly punished for not understanding the times better: that it was indeed much to be regretted, but could not be helped, and had better be borne with, in consideration of greater benefits ensuing. It is something, at all events, to have upon record the deliberate protest of the Church of England against these lessons of base accommodation: something, that those who are yet willing to take advice from her Prayer-Book, should find there the good old principles, of plain submission and cheerful obedience, applied to a real and near example, and a condition of society like the present. But it is more, to have the verdict of Scripture herself (for such, undoubtedly, may the history of the Passion falling on this day be considered) in favour of those, who have followed their Saviour in making resignation all their glory. Whether wise or unwise in a worldly sense, the doctrine of the Cross is on their side, and can never, surely, be misapplied, when rehearsed to encourage us in imitating them. Again; could any thing tell more significantly against the too fashionable notion of I know not what fatal necessity, suspending, as it were, men's accountable agency, when they yield to the 'spirit of the times' – could any thing more unsparingly condemn the measuring political right and wrong by mere present visible expediency than the parable selected for the Gospel of the day, our Lord's own expressive rebuke to the Jewish rulers, Caiaphas and the rest? They were deceiving themselves, no doubt, more than they did any one else, with the specious plea of public welfare, and the little worth of one man's blood, set against the safety of the whole nation. There was a voice which spoke home to their consciences, when it represented the husbandmen, saying, 'Come, let us kill the heir, and then the inheritance surely will be ours'. And it is our duty to set out the warning, so long as we see people doing such things, or 'taking pleasure in them that do them'.

J. Keble, 'Danger of Sympathising with Rebellion', in *Sermons Academical and Occasional*, Parker, 1848, pages 121–4

H. J. Rose did not contribute to the Tracts, but he followed up the concern of the Hadleigh Conference by a series of articles attacking the proposed legislation, which would transfer some of the revenue of the Anglican Church in Ireland to support the Roman Catholic Church there.

The people of England have a great matter to determine, in which *right* and *equity* are put out of the question, and the appeal is to *power*. The matter for decision may be very shortly stated. Is it the wish of the people of England to retain a national Church, which shall have *dignity, influence,* and *weight*; or to let worldly politicians strip it of *dignity, influence,* and *weight*, reduce its ministers to pensioned paupers, and give the money, which enables them to promote the cause of religion and charity, to any purposes which the caprice or the cry of the moment may dictate? Is it the wish of the people of England to see the national church plundered of its property – today to promote popery, tomorrow to promote education without religion, the third day to supply the wants of this or that new institution, and the fourth (it is just possible, as experience suggests), to supply the wants, not of bodies but of individuals – to furnish an estate to some illustrious house? [...]

Will the people of England, finally, believe that it can be right that what was given centuries ago (and what has been protected by a thousand national acts) in order that the true faith of Christ crucified might be preserved and spread through the country, and that the poor might have the gospel preached to them as they have, without cost, should be taken away when a papist faction, or an infidel faction, can manage so to hold the scale between two parties that their support must be had at any price – at the price of church robbery, or of taking from the poor that pure and apostolical form of worship which they possess?

To argue that the step which robs the church, and makes the subsistence of the clergy depend at any time on what Parliament, under the sway of the faction of the moment, shall decide to be enough for them, must degrade the clergy, is an argument which would recommend the step to too many – not radicals only, but narrow-minded; short-sighted politicians; and unhappily men of property, of very different views, partly from jealousy of the clergy, partly from cupidity, indulge in feelings as discreditable as they are injurious to themselves. Whether the clergy have, from their property, education and station, more influence than some like, or not, such persons ought yet to have sense enough to know, that all that influence is exerted in favour of order, peace, and of maintaining the present institutions of the country, improving them, indeed, if necessary, but not *overthrowing monarchy, aristocracy, &c*. However, with such men (and they exist in all parties) it is in vain to argue. In looking to this question merely as it will affect society, the appeal must be to a different class. The question is, will the middling and lower classes, to whom as a profession, the church was always open, and to whom it has afforded an honourable road to the attainment of a higher grade in society, of associating freely with the first persons in the land, of permanently raising their families, and promoting that quiet and peaceable mixture of the various orders of society which is desirable in a rational and religious view, will they quietly see the church *put down* by worldly politicians, and the clergy reduced in education, weight, influence, and station – made, in short, what too many wish, the servile tools and dependants of the rich, mere degraded creatures, alike unworthy and unable to preach the gospel?

Let the people of England remember that this great question is to be decided *now* and *for ever*.

H. J. Rose, 'Church Matters', The British Magazine, 1835, vol. 7,
pages 602, 605–6

Preaching in 1835 in the state Service to commemorate the failure of the Gunpowder Plot, Pusey took an even gloomier apocalyptic view of the present and future. The Tractarians sometimes experienced tension between desire to flee from a wicked secular world and recognition of the need to face squarely the relationship between Church and state.

What times are coming upon the earth, we know not, but the general expectation of persons of all characters in all nations is an instinct implanted by God to warn us of a coming storm. Not one nation only, but all; not one class of thinkers, but all; they who fear and they who hope; and who fear and hope things opposite, they who are immersed in their worldly schemes and they who look for some 'coming of God's kingdom'; they, who watch this world's signs and they who watch for the next, alike have their eyes intently fixed on that which is coming, though whether it be the vials of His wrath or the glories of His kingdom or whether the one shall be the herald of the other, none can tell. They who can calculate what is likely, speak of it; they who cannot, *feel* its coming; the spirits of the unseen world seem to be approaching to us, and 'awe comes on us and trembling, which maketh all the bones to shake', 'all nations are shaken'; the sound, which these many years has been heard, and spoken of from this place, has been waxing louder and louder, and spreading wider; there is 'upon the earth distress of nations with perplexity; men's hearts failing them for fear and for looking after those things which are coming upon the earth'. Times of trouble there have been before; but such a time in which everything everywhere tends in one direction, to one mighty struggle of one sort of faith with infidelity, lawlessness with rule, Christ with Antichrist, there seems never to have been till now. The ancient images of Antichrist are growing old, and decaying; and a more fearful Antichristian power, that of popular lawlessness which maketh its will its God, and will own neither God nor man but its own rule seems to be held in, not by the weak threads of human rule which it would snap 'as flax burnt by the fire', but by the Almighty power of God discovering His might in human weakness.

E. B. Pusey, 'Patience and Confidence the Strength of the Church', in
Nine Sermons Preached before the University of Oxford, Parker,
1865, pages 45–7

In the first year of the Movement, Newman claimed that the Church is a polity superior to the secular state.

Strictly speaking, the Christian Church, as being a visible society, is necessarily a political power or party. It may be a party triumphant, or a party under persecution; but a party it always must be, prior in existence to the civil institutions with which it is surrounded, and from its latent divinity formidable and influential, even to the end of time. The grant of permanency was made in the beginning, not to the mere doctrine of the Gospel, but to the Association itself built upon the doctrine in prediction, not only of the indestructibility of Christianity, but of the medium also through which it was to be manifested to the world. Thus the Ecclesiastical Body is a divinely-appointed means, towards realising the great evangelical blessings.

Christians depart from their duty, or become in an offensive sense *political*, not when they act a members of one community, but when they do so for *temporal* ends or in an *illegal* manner, not when they assume the attitude of a party, but when they split into many. If the primitive believers did not interfere with the acts of the civil government, it was merely because they had no civil rights enabling them legally to do so. But where they have rights, the case is different; and the existence of a secular spirit is to be ascertained, not by their using these, but their using them for ends short of those for which they were given. Doubtless in criticising the mode of their exercising them in a particular case, differences of opinion may fairly exist; but the principle itself, the duty of using their civil rights in the service of religion, is clear; and since there is a popular misconception, that Christians, and especially the Clergy, as such, have no concern in temporal affairs, it is expedient to take every opportunity of formally denying the position, and demanding proof of it. In truth, the Church was framed for the express purpose of interfering, or (as irreligious men will say) meddling with the world. It is the plain duty of its members, not only to associate internally, but also to develop that internal union in an external warfare with the spirit of evil, whether in Kings' courts or among the mixed multitude; and, if they can do nothing else, at least they can suffer for the truth, and remind men of it, by inflicting on them the task of persecution.

J. H. Newman, *The Arians of the Fourth Century*, Rivington, 1833, pages 276–8

Newman denounced the materialism and greed of contemporary society, in terms worthy of Carlyle or Kingsley.

Now as to the temper of this country, consider fairly is there any place, any persons, any work, which our countrymen will not concern themselves with, in the way of trade or business? For the sake of gain, do we not put aside all considerations of principle as unreasonable and almost absurd? It is not possible to explain myself on this subject without entering into details too familiar for this sacred place; but try to follow out for yourselves what I suggest in general terms. Is there any speculation in commerce which religion is allowed to interfere with? Whether Jew, Pagan, or Heretic, is to be our associate, does it frighten us ever so little? Do we care what side of a quarrel, civil, political or international, we take, so that we gain by it? Do we not serve in war, do we not become debaters and advocates, do we not form associations and parties, with the supreme object of preserving property, or making it? Do we not support religion for the sake of peace and good order? Do we not measure its importance by its efficacy in securing these objects? Do we not support it only so far as it secures them? Do we not retrench all expenses of maintaining it which are not necessary for securing them? Should we not feel very lukewarm towards the established religion, unless we thought the security of property bound up in its welfare? Should we not easily resign ourselves to its overthrow, could it be proved to us that it endangered the state, involved the prospect of civil disturbances, or embarrassed the Government? Nay, could we not even consent to that overthrow at the price of the reunion, of all parties in the nation, the pacification of turbulent districts, and the establishment of our public credit? Nay, further still, could we not easily persuade ourselves to support Antichrist, I will not say at home, but at least abroad, rather than we should lose one portion of the freights which 'the ships of Tarshish' bring us? If this be the case in any good measure, how vain is it to shelter ourselves, as the manner of some is, under the notion that we are a moral, thoughtful, sober-minded, or religious people?

J. H. Newman, 'Abraham and Lot' (1834), *Parochial and Plain Sermons*, Rivington, 1877, vol. 3, pages 12–14

In a further charge he warned Christians against the danger of becoming conformed to the world.

It cannot be denied that the greater part of the world is *absorbed* in the world; so much so that I am almost afraid to speak of the duty of being active in our worldly business, lest I should seem to give countenance to that miserable devotion to the things of time and sense, that love of bustle and management, that desire of gain, and that aiming at influence and importance, which abound on all sides. Bad as it is to be languid and indifferent in our secular duties, and to account this religion, yet it is far worse to be the slaves of this world, and to have our hearts in the concerns of this world. I do not know any thing more dreadful than a state of mind which is, perhaps, the characteristic of this country, and which the prosperity of this country so miserably fosters. I mean that ambitious spirit, to use a great word, but I know no other word to express my meaning – that low ambition which sets every one on the look-out to succeed and to rise in life, to amass money, to gain power, to depress his rivals, to triumph over his

hitherto superiors, to affect a consequence and a gentility which he
had not before, to affect to have an opinion on high subjects, to pretend to form a judgement upon sacred things, to choose his religion,
to approve and condemn according to his taste, to become a partisan
in extensive measures for the supposed temporal benefit of the community, to indulge the vision of great things which are to come, great
improvements, great wonders: all things vast, all things new – this
most fearfully, earthly and grovelling spirit is likely, alas! to extend
itself more and more among our countrymen – an intense, sleepless,
restless, never-wearied, never-satisfied, pursuit of Mammon in one
shape or other, to the exclusion of all deep, all holy, all calm, all
reverent thoughts. This is the spirit in which, more or less (according
to their different tempers), men do commonly engage in concerns of
this world; and I repeat it, better, far better, were it to retire from the
world altogether than thus to engage in it – better with Elijah to fly to
the desert, than to serve Baal and Ashtoreth in Jerusalem.

> J. H. Newman, 'Doing Glory to God in Pursuits of the World' (1834),
> *Parochial and Plain Sermons*, Rivington, 1877, vol. 8, pages 159–60

*Newman took his thoughts further, to declare that the Church should
be leading in matters of social reform and not treated as an append-
age to the state.*

Now it is plain how very far the mass of men are from taking their
standard of things, or seeking a blessing on what they do, from religion. Instead of raising the world by faith to the level of a regenerate
son of God, they debase themselves to the world and its ordinances.
It is plain, as any one will find who gives himself the trouble to attend
to it, that men in general do not give, or feel, or seek for religious
reasons: for what they do. So little is religion, even the profession of
the world at present that men, who do not feel its claims, dare not
avow their feelings – they dare not recommend measures of whatever sort on religious grounds. If they defend a measure publicly, or
use persuasion in private, they are obliged to conceal or put aside
the motives which one should hope do govern them, and they allege
others, inferior, nay, worldly reasons – reasons draw from policy; or
expedience, or common sense (as it is called), or prudence. If they
neglect to do this, they are despised as ill-judging and unreasonable.
Nay, they are obliged thus to act, else they will not succeed in good
objects, and (what is more to the purpose) else they will be casting

pearls before swine. Can we have clearer proof than this, that the current of things at present, in spite of the boasts of men, is essentially and radically evil – more evil indeed, because of their boasts.

Or again, take any of the plans and systems now in fashion, plans for the well-being of the poor, or of the young, or of the community at large; you will find, so far from their being built on religion, religion is actually in the way, it is an encumbrance. The advocates and promoters of these plans confess that they do not know what to do with religion, their plans work very well but for religion; religion suggests difficulties which cannot be got over. On a subject of this kind, one cannot enter into detail; but those who look about them will recognise what I mean, and, I think, will acknowledge its truth.

And so again in those efforts which are laudably made for the sake of preserving things as they are, and hindering ruin and destruction coming on the country, men are afraid to base themselves on 'the old commandment which ye have heard from the beginning'. They are afraid to kindle their fire from the altar of God; they are afraid to acknowledge her through whom only they gain light and strength and salvation, the Mother of Saints.

J. H. Newman, 'The Church and the World', in *Sermons Bearing on Subjects of the Day*, Rivington, 1843, pages 121–2

F. E. Paget (1806–82), Rector of Elford, Lichfield, was one of the country clergy who supported the Oxford Movement and tried to bring its ideas into their parishes. He wrote a number of short novels which combine Tractarian principles with zeal for social reform. The preface to one of them stresses that the Church and not the state should take the lead in relieving poverty.

The ensuing tale is addressed to the consideration of persons whose lot has been cast in the upper and middle ranks of Society; and it was written in the hope that it may be instrumental in prevailing on some, at least into whose hands it may fall, to think more seriously than they have yet done on the subjects discussed in it.

Those subjects are the responsibilities which rank, property, and education involve; the duties of the higher classes to the lower; the importance of other views and measures of Christian Almsgiving, than those which satisfy, the easy and selfish religion of the present day; the true principles of charity, and the difference between its judicious and injudicious exercise; the amount of luxury, folly, extravagance covetousness, and selfishness existing inevitably, though in an unsuspected form (and in a greater or lesser degree, according to circumstances) among all who adopt the received habits and modes of thought which prevail in modern Society, and lastly, the urgent need of great, immediate, and unshrinking sacrifices and self-denials on the part of us all if we would provide – while yet it is possible – for the spiritual necessities, of our teeming population, if we would stop the flood of iniquity which threatens to overwhelm us, and substitute Christianity, in our so-called Christian country, for the absolute heathenism into which great masses of the manufacturing districts are falling.

As, however, it has seemed impossible in the compass of a single volume, to allude to every form in which the selfishness and hard-heartedness of the present generation show themselves, it has been deemed expedient to keep back some of the darker illustrations of this melancholy and most appalling subject, and to reserve them for the ground-work of another tale, to be published hereafter. [...]

No serious-minded person could look on the state of our manufacturing districts without grave and earnest apprehension. A population, of whom it might almost be said that it was without the pale of the Church's influence, without churches, clergy, schools, or any other of the outward machinery by which the means of grace, and hopes of glory are brought before men's minds, exposed continually to the influence of the emissaries of sedition and infidelity! What *can* be the Fruit of such a state of things, but that a once happy country should be turned into an Aceldama of anarchy and irreligion?

Meanwhile, they who might, if they would, put an end to the evil, by providing the funds for supplying what is needed – the upper and middle classes – do nothing or next to nothing, abridge no luxuries, forego no comforts, but go on 'eating and drinking, marrying and giving in marriage', as if this world were to last for ever; as if those who provided their luxuries and comforts were not their brethren; as if there were no duties to be discharged towards the poor of Christ; as if they will not be called to account hereafter for the waste of every single individual farthing, which, at such a time as the present, might have been offered to God – and was not!

If the country is to be saved at all, it will be saved by something different from either Acts of Parliament, or guinea subscriptions. It will, under God, be saved by the Church's influence, and under her guidance.

F. E. Paget, *The Warden of Berkingholt or Rich and Poor*, Parker, 1843, pages ix–xi

J. W. Bowden expressed similar sentiments in verse.

> GOD of our Israel! by our favoured sires
> Once known, once honoured! And is this the creed
> Hailed, in their children's councils, with the meed
> Of godless acclamation; while the fires
> Burn low on Thy dread Altar, and around
> Th' advancing Gentile treads the hallowed ground?
> Yea, it is thus; and nerveless rulers bear,
> Unholy triumph kindling in their eyes,
> And catch fresh ardour from each maddening cheer
> To urge the spoiler toward his glittering prize.
> Yea, worst of all, not Bethel's priest alone,
> Or Bel's adorer swells the plaudit's tone,
> Thine own apostate worshipper, to Thee,
> Mocking or self-deceived, who bends the knee,
> Dares join the clamour; dares, though sworn to wait,
> A faithful guard, before Thy vineyard's gate,
> Tear down her fence, and bid the forest boar
> Uproot Thy cherished vine on green Ierne's shore.

J. W. Bowden, 'National Degradation', Lyra Apostolica (1836),
Mozley, 1841, pages 193–4

Keble returned to the theme of his Assize Sermon with an exegesis of Isaiah 49.23: 'Kings shall be thy nursing fathers, and their queens thy nursing mothers'.

Is not the common interpretation of these words nearly or exactly such as the following: viz. that the Church, of herself feeble and help-less, and so far like an infant, is committed by Divine Providence to the care of the state, as any child might be to the care of its nurse: consequently, that it depends mainly on state support, and could not well exist, at least could not in any sense flourish, were that sup-port withdrawn, any more than an infant could go on and prosper without the attending care of nurses? From which inevitably a ten-dency follows, to sacrifice more, much more, of ecclesiastical rights to political expediency, than would be sacrificed, if the Church were deemed independent.

Now whether such a tendency, considering all things, be right or wrong, wise or unwise – whether the Church, however naturally, in all Christian lands, allied to the state, were meant to remain independent or no – this is not our present question, but simply, whether the analogy adopted by Isaiah will justify the conclusion which has been so frequently deduced from it: whether we are here really taught by the voice of Inspiration to consider the pillar and ground of the truth as an edifice based in any measure on the will of man, however enlightened and however sincere.

It may perhaps appear, on a nearer consideration of the passage, that the meaning is altogether different: that instead of representing the Church as dependent on the state, the holy Prophet intended to point out the entire submission which the state owes to the Church: that is, in other words, the entire submission which God's ministers in temporal things owe to that great enduring plan, which He has set on foot in a lost world for subduing all things to Himself.

For it is plain on consideration of the context, and indeed it is acknowledged by some of the commentators, that when the Church is told, Kings shall be thy nursing fathers, it is not meant that the Church as an infant is lodged in the arms of the civil power, but that as a mother she lodges her children in its arms. The monarchs and princesses of this world are as foster fathers and foster mothers in the family of our Lord Jesus Christ, and of His Spouse, the Holy Church Universal.

J. Keble, 'Church and State', in *Sermons Academical and Occasional*,
Parker, 1848, pages 151–2

Hurrell Froude also condemned state interference with the Church, referring to specific legislation, which seemed to put the Church in danger.

The joint effect of three recent and important Acts, (1) the Repeal of the Test and Corporation Acts, (2) the Concessions to the Roman Catholics, (3) the late Act for Parliamentary Reform, has most certainly been to efface in at least one branch of our Civil Legislature, that character which, according to our great Authorities, qualified it to be at the same time our Ecclesiastical Legislature, and thus to cancel the conditions on which it has been allowed to interfere in matters spiritual.

This is no subject on which we may lightly dogmatise one way or the other; the interests at stake are too important to be so dealt with. We must come to it in a serious considerate frame of mind, looking steadily to the result of our determination. On the other hand, we must weigh well the responsibility we incur if in our time we allow a *new* system to be established, an *usurpation to* be commenced, affecting an Institution so important as Christ's Holy Catholic and Apostolic Church, without taking pains in the first place to assure ourselves that we are not compromising its safety or even dignity; for even the dignity of the Church is not to be lightly disregarded. On the other hand, we must not conceal from ourselves the hazard of the alternative; the more than possibility that a rejection of Parliamentary interference may lose for us Parliamentary protection. On this important question then, the writer of these pages will not take upon himself to dogmatise; he has his own opinion, but he leaves others to form theirs. Of this, however, he is certain, that we are now commencing a new system of Ecclesiastical Polity, the merits of which are yet to be decided. [...]

The extent to which Parliament has lately pressed its claim to interfere with the internal government of the Church, naturally excites attention in the minds of Churchmen: and many who have been led to canvass the justice of the claim, on what appears to be [its] own merits, have found it difficult to devise any reasonable pretext for [it].

It seems at first sight something short of reasonable that persons, not necessarily interested in the welfare of the Church, should deliberate for its good; and still less so, that they should be allowed to dictate laws to it, without the consent of those who are necessarily interested; and least reasonable of all, when we add the consideration, that many of the persons so dictating, are, as a fact, its avowed enemies, and that their dictates are deeply reprobated by the great body of its attached members. And yet that the Parliament of Great Britain and Ireland are not necessarily interested in the welfare of the Church, indeed that many of its members are our avowed enemies, and that the Church as a body, deeply deplores this interference in its concerns, are, it is supposed, admitted facts. So that persons, who have been led to canvass the question on its own merits, have felt in some degree perplexed at the recognition of a claim apparently so ill according with common sense.

R. H. Froude, 'Remarks on State Interference in Matters Spiritual',
Remains of the Late Reverend Richard Hurrell Froude M.A.,
Rivington, 1838, part 2, vol. 1, pages 185–7 (largely reprinted
from *The British Magazine*, with amendments by
the editors of the *Remains*)

Treating the subject at more length in a Tract, Froude distinguished 'State Protection' from 'State Interference' and considered the benefits and drawbacks of Establishment.

We are very naturally jealous of the attempts that are making to dis-unite, as it is called, Church and State; which in fact means neither more nor less, in the mouths of those who clamour for it, than a general confiscation of Church property, and a repeal of the few remaining laws which make the true Church the Church of England.

This is what Dissenters mean by disuniting Church and State; and we are all naturally anxious to avert a step at once so unjust towards men and sacrilegious towards GOD.

Let us not imagine, however, that every one who apparently joins with us in this anxiety must necessarily have the welfare of the Church at heart. Many people seem to join us at this crisis, and protest loudly in favour of the Union of Church and State, who nevertheless mean by this, something very different from what Dissenters mean, and from what we mean when we are opposing Dissenters. The 'Union of Church and State', which many persons so call, and are so anxious to preserve, is in some points almost as great an evil, as it is confessedly, in other points, a good: and there are almost as many persons who support it for its bad points, as there are who hate it for its good.

To make this plain, I shall endeavour to explain what it is that the Union of Church and State consists in, as now enforced by the law of the land.

It consists in two things, STATE PROTECTION and STATE INTERFERENCE; the former of which, Dissenters wish to over-throw; and the latter of which, governments, of whatever kind, are very anxious to retain, while Churchmen have hitherto been contented to accept both conjointly, without perhaps very exactly calculating how little they gain on the one hand, and how much they sacrifice on the other. This subject is indeed one which, indeed, the confidence hitherto placed by us in the integrity of government, has, perhaps, been much less investigated than any other of equal importance. But recent changes in the constitution have now so entirely altered the mutual relations of the Church and the Legislature, that what has in past times been a becoming, though perhaps misplaced, reliance on authority, would at present be a disgraceful negligence about our most sacred interests.

R. H. Froude, Tract 59, 'Church and State', pages 1–2

The question of Church and state relations which Keble had addressed in his Assize Sermon developed in several aspects of Tractarian thought. William Gresley wrote a novel about the perils of militant Socialism and alienation from the Church in following a secular ideology. At the end, there is repentance and reconciliation, and Gresley concludes the novel with his own comments.

Formerly politicians knew the Church's claim, and acknowledged her position; she was accounted, as in truth she is, the authorised instrument *of God* to teach the people: then, in evil days, came a change over men's minds, and the Church was esteemed the authorised agent of *the state*. This false notion prepared the way for that which now exists; and the Church has come to be considered by men of the world only as *one of many agents* to teach religion and morality; and our most influential statesmen seem labouring to adjust affairs to this new standard. Instead of adhering to the Church, and maintaining her cause with holy and affectionate zeal, as their divine instructress; instead of standing on the broad principle, that the Church is God's appointed instrument for the dissemination of truth, and therefore to be reverently upheld for the sake of truth and charity, they begin to look on her claims as unreasonable, and to consider her as a mere human institution, which may rise or fall according to the caprice of man. Thus are some of our best and ablest statesmen beguiled by the latitudinarian spirit of the age: they who should stand up as the instruments of God to maintain the truth, themselves yield to the popular current; and their pusillanimity and indifference to truth spreading itself over the mass of their admirers and adherents adds fearfully to the urgency of the evil.

That which is at the present time above all things necessary, is to endeavour to establish in men's minds a feeling that *truth is something real and discoverable*. We believe that God has given us a revelation from heaven (for I speak to the latitudinarian, not the infidel); we believe that God's word is truth. Well then, if God has given us a revelation of His will, it is absurd, surely, to suppose that there is no way of ascertaining the true sense of that revelation. The various sects and societies, opposed as they are to each other, cannot all be right; and those which are wrong are the adversaries of God's truth, and therefore to be avoided and discountenanced. Moreover, the truth demands, for its own sake, the support and adherence of understanding men; it demands that we should both live according to it and promulgate it. To disregard it, or to obscure it, or to refuse to aid in its propagation, is a sort of irreverence and ingratitude towards God, of which men will surely have to give account.

William Gresley, *Charles Lever*, Burns, 1841, pages 231–3

*Froude, writing against shortening and omissions in services,
denounced those who oppressed the poor.*

There are persons who wish certain Sunday Lessons removed from
our Service: e.g. some of those selected for Lent – nay, Jeremiah v.
and xxii; and this, on the ground that it is painful to the feelings of
Clergymen to read them.

Waiving other considerations which may be urged against innovation in this matter, may we not allow some weight to the following,
which is drawn from the very argument brought in favour of the
change? Will not the same feeling which keeps men from reading the
account of certain sins and their punishment from the *Bible,* much
more keep them from mentioning them in *the Pulpit?* Is it not necessary that certain sins, which it is distressing to speak of, should
be seriously denounced, as being not the less frequent in commission, because they are disgraceful in language? And if so, is it not
a most considerate provision of the Church to relieve her Ministers
of the pain of using their own words, and to allow them to shelter
their admonitions under the holy and reverend language of Inspired
Scripture?

R. H. Froude, Tract 9, 'On Shortening the Church Services', page 4

*Pusey, preaching at Christmas, urged concern for the poor, arguing
that an incarnational and sacramental faith must be socially aware
and active. The same line was followed by later writers, both Anglo-
Catholics and Broad Church Christian Socialists.*

The Mysteries of Faith must needs be an offence to the wisdom of the
world, but we, who truly believe and meditate on the Mystery of the
Incarnation, shall not stumble at any other mystery, nor wonder that
He chose humble means, the elements of this world, whereby to convey His Presence, when He, the Immortal, Invisible, of the Substance
of the Father, took Flesh of our substance, in the Virgin's womb. His
Glory is invisible still to the 'wise and prudent' of this world, and
'revealed unto babes'.

But if we would see Him in His Sacraments, we must see Him
also, wherever He has declared Himself to be, and especially in His
poor. In them also He is 'with us' still. And so our Church has united
mercy to His poor with the Sacrament of His Body and Blood, and
bade us, ere we approach to receive Him, to remember Him in His

poor, that so, 'loving much' we, who are otherwise unworthy, may be 'much forgiven', we, 'considering' Him in His 'poor and needy' may be permitted to behold Him; and for Him parting with our earthly substance, may be partakers of His Heavenly. Real love to Christ must issue in love to all who are Christ's, and real love to Christ's poor must issue in self-denying acts of love towards them. Casual almsgiving is not Christian charity. Rather, seeing Christ in the poor, the sick, the hungry, the thirsty, the naked, we must, if we can, by ourselves, if not, by others, seek them out, as we would seek Christ, looking for a blessing from it, far greater than any they can gain from our alms. It was promised of old time, as a blessing, 'the poor shall never cease out of the land', and now we know the mercy of this mysterious blessing, for they are the Presence of our Lord. 'The poor', He saith, 'ye have always with you, but Me ye have not always', not in bodily Presence, but in His poor, whom we shall ever have.

The poor of Christ are the Church's special treasure, as the Gospel is their special property, the Church the home of the homeless, the mother of the fatherless. The poor are the wealth, the dowry of the Church; they have a sacred character about them; they bring a blessing with them; for they are what Christ for our sake made Himself. Such as them did He call around Him; such as they, whether by God's outward appointment, or by His Spirit directing men's choice, the 'poor, rich in faith', have been the converters of the world; and we, my brethren, if we are wise, must seek to be like them, to empty ourselves, at least, of our abundance; to empty ourselves, rather, of our self-conceit, our notions of station, our costliness of dress, our jewelry, our luxuries, our self-love, even as He, on this day, emptied Himself of the glory which He had with the Father, the Brightness of His Majesty, the worship of the Hosts of Heaven, and made Himself poor, to make us rich, and to the truly poor He hath promised the Kingdom of Heaven; the hungry He will fill, but those in themselves rich, He will send empty away. Year by year there is more need; the poor are multiplying upon us, and distress on them; gigantic needs require gigantic efforts; in these our towns, our Church is losing its best blessing, that of being the Church of the poor; we know not too often of their existence; our fair houses are like painted sepulchres, hiding, by a goodly outside, from our own sight, the misery, and hunger, and cold, and nakedness, which we love not to look upon, but which will rise in judgement against our nation, if we heed it not. Realise we that they are Christ's, yea, that we approach to Christ in them, feed Him, visit Him, clothe Him, attend on Him, and we shall feel (as Saints, even of the noble of this world have felt) that it is a high honour to us to be admitted to them. Such as can, would gladly devote their lives to them. We all should treat their needs with reverence, not relieving them coldly, and as a form, but humble ourselves in heart before their patient suffering, welcome the intercourse with them, as bringing us nearer unto Christ. In them He comes to us, in them we visit Him; in them we may find Him; He in them and for them intercedes for us with the Father; in them He Who gave them to us, the means and the hearts to relieve them, will receive our gifts; He, before men and Angels, shall acknowledge as done to Him, what for His sake, we did to them.

Oh seek we then, at least for ourselves, one by one, while He may be found, our Lord Who, on this day, sought us, in all ways we can. Seek we Him, in the contemplation of His mysterious mercy; love we to be alone with Him, to leave the world, at intervals at least, to behold Him; seek we Him, in His house, whenever two or three may he gathered there; seek we Him, in the temples of our own hearts, where He has promised to dwell; seek we Him, with reverence and awe, in His Sacraments, where He has promised to give us His Body and Blood; seek we Him humbly, in His poor, as the source of true riches to us; and on this day let us, who hope to receive Him, return to Him more largely the alms to be offered to Him, for His use in His poor. So may we hope, in all things seeking Him, at length to find Him, yea to be found of Him, and in Him, and being found in Him, to be accepted for His mercy's sake, and He for ever be 'God with us' and 'we for ever be with the Lord'; loving Him for His mercy, loving Him that He gave us that love, loving Him with everlasting love, and filled and satisfied with His love, Who emptied Himself, that He might give us of His fullness, became the Son of Man, that we might be sons of God.

E. B. Pusey, *Sermons During the Season From Advent to Whitsuntide*, Parker, 1848, pages 57–60

Newman cautioned that while Christians are to be good citizens, this is not the point and proof of Christian faith.

How mistaken is the notion of the day, that the main undertaking of a Christian Church is to make men good members of society, honest, upright, industrious, and well-conducted; and that it fails of its duty, and has cause of shame unless it succeeds in doing so; and that of two religious communities, that must be the more scriptural in its tenets, of which the members are more decent and orderly: whereas it may easily happen that a corruption of the Gospel, which sacrifices the better fruit, may produce the more abundant, men being not unwilling to compound for neglect of a strict rule by submitting to an easy one. How common is it, at this time, to debate the question, whether the plans of education pursued for the last fifty years have diminished crime or not; whether those who are convicted of offences against the law have for the most part been at school or not! Such inquiries surely are out of place, if Christian education is in question. If the Church set out by engaging to make men good members of the state, they would be very much in place; but if the great object of her Sacraments, preaching, Scriptures, and instructions, is to save the elect of God, to foster into life and rear up into perfection what is really good, not in the sight of man merely, but in the sight of God; not what is useful merely, but what is true and holy; and if to influence those who act on secondary motives require a lowering of the Christian standard, and if an exhibition of the truth makes a man worse unless it makes him better, then she has fulfilled her calling if she has saved the few; and she has done more than her calling, so far as by God's grace she has, consistently with the higher object, restrained, softened, or sobered the many. Much doubtless she will do in this way, but what she does must not be by compromise or unfaithfulness. The Church and the world cannot meet without either the world rising or the Church falling; and the world forsooth pleads necessity, and says it cannot rise to the Church, and deems the Church unreasonable when she will not descend instead.

J. H. Newman, 'The Visible Church for the Sake of the Elect' in
Parochial and Plain Sermons, Rivington, 1877, vol. 4,
pages 160–1

8

Doctrine of Reserve

Although the Tractarians were explicit in their views on matters of doctrine and discipline, they also attached much importance to the idea of Reserve. They feared the effect of extreme Evangelical preaching which taught about the Atonement without emphasising the duty of the individual believer to respond with repentance and obedience. They were also distressed by loose talk about religion, whether it was mocking or too overtly pious. The idea of Reserve did not originate with them, but it became one of their distinctive features, and one which aroused some of the strongest opposition.

Newman introduced the idea of Reserve in the first year of the Tracts, seeing it as a principle of the Primitive Church, one to which his followers would often appeal.

If I allow my belief, that freedom from symbols and articles is abstractedly the highest state of Christian communion, and the peculiar privilege of the primitive Church, it is not from any tenderness towards that proud impatience of control, in which many exult as in a virtue; but first, because technicality and formality are, in their degree, inevitable results of public confessions of faith; and next, because when confessions do not exist, the mysteries of divine truth, instead of being exposed to the gaze of the profane and uninstructed, are kept hidden in the bosom of the Church far more faithfully than is otherwise possible; and reserved by a private teaching, though the channel of her ministers, as rewards in due measure and season, for those who are prepared to profit by them; those, i.e., who are diligently passing through the successive stages of faith and obedience. And thus, while the Church is not committed to declarations which, most true as they are, still are daily wrested by infidels to their ruin; on the other hand, much of that mischievous fanaticism is avoided, which at present abounds from the vanity of men, who think that they can explain the sublime doctrines and exuberant promises of the Gospel, before they have yet learned to know themselves, and to discern the holiness of God, under the preparatory discipline of the Law and of Natural Religion.

J. H. Newman, *The Arians of the Fourth Century*, Rivington, 1833, pages 41–2

He took the argument further a few pages later, more specifically condemning indiscriminate preaching of Atonement theology and quoting a text (Matthew 7.6) which was much used in later defences of Reserve.

Here, I shall but observe, in addition to the remarks already made on the passages in the Epistles to the Corinthians and Hebrews, that no one sanction can be adduced from Scripture, whether of precept or of example, in behalf of the practice of stimulating the affections, (e.g. gratitude or remorse) by means of the doctrine of the atonement, in order to the conversion of the bearers; that, on the contrary, it is its uniform method to connect the gospel with natural religion, and to mark out obedience to the moral law as the ordinary means of attaining to a Christian faith, the higher truths, as well as the Eucharist, which is the visible emblem of them, being reserved as the reward and confirmation of habitual piety; that, in the preaching of the Apostles and Evangelists in the Book of Acts, the sacred mysteries are revealed to individuals in proportion to their actual religious proficiency; the first principles of righteousness, temperance, and judgement to come, are urged upon Felix; while the elders of Ephesus are reminded of the divinity and vicarious sacrifice of Christ, and the presence and power of the Holy Spirit in the Church; lastly, that among those converts, who were made the chief instruments of the first propagation of the gospel, or who are honoured with especial favour in Scripture, none are found who had not been faithful to the light already given them, and distinguished, previous to their conversion, by a strictly conscientious deportment. Such are the divine notices given to those who desire an apostolical rule for dispensing the word of life; and as such, the ancient Fathers received them. They received them as the fulfilment of our Lord's command, not to give that which is holy to dogs, nor to cast pearls before swine; a text cited (e.g.) by Clement and Tertullian, among others, in justification of their cautious distribution of sacred truth. They considered them also as the result of the most truly charitable consideration for those whom they addressed, who were likely to he perplexed, not converted, by the sudden exhibition of the whole evangelical scheme.

J. H. Newman, The Arians of the Fourth Century, Rivington, 1833,
pages 51–2

Isaac Williams began the developed and systematic study of the doctrine of Reserve with Tract 80. His opening words were eirenical but made a declaration that would lead to much controversy.

The object of the present inquiry is to ascertain, whether there is not in God's dealings with mankind a very remarkable holding back of sacred and important truths, as if the knowledge of them were injurious to persons unworthy of them. And if this be the case, it will lead to some important practical reflections. It is not intended to speak of it as a mark of judicial punishment, nor as denoting the anger of the Almighty, nor as connected in any way with intellectual acuteness; but, if I may so speak with reverence, I would say that there appears in God's manifestations of Himself to mankind, in conjunction with an exceeding desire to communicate that knowledge, a tendency to conceal, and throw a veil over it, as if it were injurious to us, unless we were of a certain disposition to receive it.

I. Williams, Tract 80, 'On Reserve in Communicating Religious
Knowledge', page 3

Reserve was also to be exercised in personal devotion and speaking of sacred matters. After discussing the way in which religious truths are often partly concealed in the Bible by figurative and symbolic expressions, he continues.

In addition to such holy reserve, and the suggestions of humility, another circumstance, which tends to produce the effect here described, are the commands of Holy Scripture, which enjoin the concealment of religious actions. Now, considering that actions teach more than words, and living examples more than maxims and admonitions, this immediately removes from the sight of men the most powerful appeals of GOD, and evidences of His presence, for all the most purely religious actions are thus withdrawn from view, done from GOD only, who is in secret, and to Him only, who seeth in secret, they begin and end in Him alone, unknown to the world. These are the signs of GOD's presence among us, and of His withholding, that presence from the gaze of the multitude, as too pure and holy for us to look on, and covering those that seek Him in the shadow of His hand. So that in the lives of those, in whom Christ dwells, there is ever something remarkably analogous to the retiring actions of His own life; and the state of such persons, while on earth, no words can express so emphatically as those of Scripture, their *'life is hid with Christ in God'.*

Now it is much to be observed, that these indications, which are found with good men, and increase with holiness of life, and by which we may learn the mode in which the HOLY SPIRIT is dealing with mankind, are not to be found in religious enthusiasm. I would mean by enthusiasm, a state of the mind when the feelings are strongly moved by religion, but the heart is not adequately purified nor humbled. Such therefore, would be most likely to occur when the passions have been strengthened by an irregular life, and the objects that excited them are casually removed from view, and the importance of religion is in consequence seen and felt. Such a state would partake much of the nature of earthly passion, and would be such as might be called in morals, according to the view taken above, a state of ignorance. GOD is not apprehended, as He is set forth in Scripture, as of infinite holiness, but a fiction of the imagination, as each man feigns the idea of GOD according to his own heart, which was shown visibly in the idols of old, and alluded to in the expression, 'Thou thoughtest wickedly that GOD was such an one as thyself'. In such a case men would have no reserve in expressing that which was not at all rightly apprehended, or feared, or loved. And the cause of this state of heart would be a not keeping the commandments which give this light to the eyes, or the not having kept them, and such transgressions not having been repented of. For this is set before us as the great cure for enthusiasm by St. John. It is the Apostle of Divine Love who seems to have been especially commissioned to warn us against this its counterfeit. Not only in his Epistles, but, in recording the parting consolations of our LORD, no less than eleven times in the course of two chapters does he stop, as it were, to insert these cautions, 'If ye keep my commandments'. So that it would be exactly the case with these, as with those heretics of whom Tertullian speaks as having none of that discipline of secret reserve which the Church maintained. 'All things', he says, 'are with him free, and without restraint'. 'They have no fear of GOD, because GOD is not among them; for where GOD is, there must be the fear of Him'. And yet, of course, the effect of this would be a strong contagious influence, after the usual manner of all earthly passion.

Religion does not, under such circumstances, produce its genuine effect of humbling the natural man. To have a knowledge of GOD, without a knowledge of our own guilt and misery, has (as Pascal mentions) the effect of puffing up. And there is a great deal in religion which the natural man may eagerly take hold of, in order to exalt himself. Here, therefore, there would not be humility drawing back into the shade, as in the former instance; nor would there be that delicacy, or modest reserve in the outward expression of feeling; because there would be rather an aiming after the persuasion, than any really deep and true sense, of religion. On the contrary, a mind in this state by strong expressions would be endeavouring to persuade itself, and to persuade others, in order that, through their opinion, it may again in return persuade itself, of its having that sense. And this would account for that deceit which, as B⟨isho⟩p Butler observes, so often accompanies religious enthusiasm; first of all deceiving itself into a false apprehension, and then, in order to support this, deceiving others; and then others, without this self-delusion, as its end.

The third characteristic in holiness of life is also here wanting; i.e. a self-denying and consistent performance of religious duties in secret. For such obedience would clearly remove it; and, therefore, this would account for another circumstance which characterises religious enthusiasm, and that is unsettledness and inconsistency, a state of ever learning, and never coming to the knowledge of the truth; which, of course, arises from not seeking for it by obedience, which, we are told, is a sure way of arriving at it. The actions it does perform are rather the extraordinary, than the ordinary actions of religion, so as to lose that reserve before mentioned; and, for the same reason, it delights in actions of a purely religious character, more than in those, in which the religious motive is concealed in the actions of daily life.

I. Williams, Tract 80, 'On Reserve in Communicating Religious Knowledge', pages 55–7

Williams developed the argument which, probably more than anything in the Tracts, lost Evangelical support.

We now proceed to the consideration of a subject most important – the prevailing notion that it is necessary to bring forward the Atonement *explicitly* and *prominently* on all occasions. It is evidently quite opposed to what we consider the teaching of Scripture, nor do we find any sanction for it in the Gospels. *If* the Epistles of St. Paul *appear* to favour it, it is only at first sight. The singular characteristic of St. Paul, as shown in all his Epistles and speeches, seems to have been a going out of himself to enter into the feelings and put himself in the circumstances of others. This will account for the occasions on which he brings forward this doctrine; as in the Epistles to the Romans and Galatians. In both of these cases, the prejudices which closed up their ears against the reception of the truth were such as were essentially opposed to the Atonement. So much in the writings of St. Paul does the HOLY SPIRIT adapt His teaching to the wants of each, as our LORD did in His Incarnation, a principle which is opposed to this opinion.

There is another point which might seem to countenance it, that Paul speaks of himself as at all times preaching 'CHRIST crucified'; and it being said by Origen that CHRIST crucified was the first doctrine taught, and that of our LORD's divinity the last men came to know. But this, in fact, so far from contradicting, strongly confirms the view here taken; it will be evident. On a little attention, that when St Paul thus speaks, it is not the Atonement and Divinity of our LORD which he brings forward, although it is implied in that saying. The whole of St. Paul's life and actions, after his conversion, and the whole of his teaching, as appears from the Epistles, may be said to have been nothing else but a setting forth of CHRIST crucified, as the one great principle which absorbed all his heart, and actuated all his conduct. It was the wood cast into the waters which entirely changed them into its own nature, and impregnated them with itself. This is intimated by expressions of this kind which are of continual occurrence, such as, 'GOD forbid that I should glory save in the Cross of Our LORD JESUS CHRIST'; 'I was determined not to know any thing among you but CHRIST crucified'; 'But we preach CHRIST crucified'. Now these words of course imply 'the Atonement' as a life-giving principle contained in them; but it is a great mistake to suppose that they contain nothing more, or that, by preaching the Atonement, we are preaching what St Paul meant by CHRIST crucified. It may be seen by an attention to the context in all the passages where these expressions occur, that it is a very different view, and in fact, the opposite to the modern notion, which St. Paul always intends by it. It is the necessity of our being crucified to the world, it is our humiliation together with Him, mortification of the flesh being made conformable to His sufferings and His death. It was a doctrine which was 'foolishness to the wise and an offence to the Jew', on account of the abasement of the natural man which it implied. Whereas, the notion now prevailing is attractive to the world, in the naked way in which it is put forth, so as rather to dimin-

ish, than increase, a sense of responsibility and consequent humiliation. The doctrine of the Atonement is conveyed in the expression
of CHRIST crucified, as used by St. Paul, but it is by teaching, at the
same time, the necessity of our mortification, which is repugnant to
opinions now received. It is expressing, in other words, our Saviour's
declaration, 'he that cometh after Me must take up his cross daily
and follow Me'. They both imply that we cannot approach GOD
without a sacrifice – a sacrifice on the part of human nature in union
with that of our SAVIOUR. Both of which seem to be taught in the
legal sacrifices.

I. Williams, Tract 80, 'On Reserve in Communicating Religious
Knowledge', pages 73–4

*Although the leading Tractarians were notable preachers, they dis-
trusted a cult of the sermon as the principal source of Christian
faith and practice. Williams returned to the attack in a later Tract
with the same title. His reference to 'self-created teachers' strikes
at the nonconformist ministry, seen as being outside the Apostolic
Succession.*

There is another important point in which the modern system is opposed to Scripture in breaking the spirit of reserve, *viz,* in attaching
so great a value to preaching as to disparage Prayer and Sacraments
in comparison. According to this the Church of GOD would be the
House of Preaching; but Scripture calls it the House of Prayer. But
with regard to the subject of preaching altogether, it is, in the present
day, taken for granted, that eloquence in speech is the most powerful means of promoting religion in the world. But if this be the case,
it occurs to one as remarkable, that there is no intimation of this in
Scripture: perhaps no single expression can be found in any part of it
that implies it; there is no recommendation of rhetoric in precept, or
example, or prophecy. There is no instance of it; no part of Scripture
itself appears in this shape, as the remains of what was delivered
with powerful eloquence. Many parts of it consist of poetry, none
of oratory; and it is remarkable that the former partakes more of
this reserve, the latter less so. It speaks of instruction, 'precept upon
precept, line upon line, here a little and there a little', but never of
powerful appeals of speech. The great teacher of the Gentiles, in
whom we would most of all have expected to find it, was 'weak in
bodily presence, and in speech contemptible'; and rendered so, it is
supposed, by 'a thorn in the flesh'. Whereas, it would be thought by

many now, that the great requisites for a successful minister are a powerful bodily presence and eloquent speech. Indeed, St Paul says, that the effect of words of men's wisdom would be to render the Cross of CHRIST of none effect. It is, moreover, observable, that in Scripture all the words denoting a minister of the Gospel throw us back on the commission. Such, for instance, is the word 'Apostle', or 'the Sent', which title is repeated with a remarkable frequency and emphasis, and united, in one instance, with the awful and high expression, 'As my FATHER hath sent me, even so send I you'. And the word 'preaching' as now used, has a meaning attached to it derived from modern notions, which we shall not find in Scripture. 'A preacher', indeed, properly conveys the same idea as 'Apostle', and really signifies the same thing – 'a herald'; for, of course, all the office of a herald depends on him that sent him, not so much on himself, or his mode of delivering his message. All other words, in like manner adopted in the Church, speak the same; they all designate him as one *ministering or serving* at GOD's altar, not as one whose first object is to be useful to men; such, for instance, are the appellations of *diaconus sacerdos*. It is curious that our word 'minister', implying also the same, comes to be commonly used in the other sense, being applied, like that of preacher, to self-created teachers. Thus do men's opinions invest sacred appellations with new meanings, according to the change in their own views.

If people in general were now asked what was the most powerful means of advancing the cause of religion in the world, we should be told that it was eloquence of speech or preaching: and the excellency of speech we know consists in delivery; that is the first, the second, and the third requisite. Whereas, if we were to judge from Holy Scripture, of what were the best means of promoting Christianity in the world, we should say obedience; and if we were to be asked the second, we should say obedience; and if we were to be asked the third, we should say obedience. And it is evident, that if the spirit of obedience exists, simple and calm statement of truth will go far. Not that we would be thought entirely to depreciate preaching as a mode of doing good: it may be necessary in a weak and languishing state; but it is the characteristic of this system as opposed to that of the Church, and we fear the undue exaltation of an instrument which Scripture, to say the least, has never much recommended.

Isaac Williams, Tract 87, 'On Reserve in Communicating Religious
Knowledge', pages 73–5

Newman preached from the pulpit the message which Williams wrote in a Tract, that there was a hiddeness in Christ, both during and after the Incarnation. Thus irreverence and carelessness towards the Church and her sacraments is an offence against Christ.

If He is still on earth, yet is not visible (which cannot to be denied), it is plain that He keeps Himself still the condition which He chose in the days of His flesh. I mean, He is a hidden Saviour, and may be approached (unless we are careful) without due reverence and fear. I say, wherever He is (for that is a further question), still He is here, and again He is secret; and whatever be the tokens of His Presence, still they must be of a nature to admit of persons doubting where it is; and if they will argue, and be sharpwitted and subtle, they may perplex themselves and others, as the Jews did even in the days of His flesh, till He seems to them nowhere present on earth now. And when they come to think Him far away, of course they *feel* it to be impossible so to insult Him as the Jews did of old; and if nevertheless He *is* here, they *are* perchance approaching and insulting Him, though they so feel. And this was just the case of the Jews, for they too were ignorant what they were doing. It is probable, then, that we can now commit at least as great blasphemy towards Him as the Jews did first, because we are under the dispensation of that Holy Spirit, against whom even more heinous sins *can* be committed; next, because His presence now as little witnesses of itself, or is impressive to the many as His bodily presence formerly.

We see a further reason for this apprehension, when we consider what the tokens of His presence now are; for they will be found to be of a nature easily to lead men into irreverence, unless they be humble and watchful. For instance, the Church is called 'His Body': what His material Body was when He was visible on earth, such is the Church now. It is the instrument of His Divine power; it is that which we must approach to gain good from Him; it is that which by insulting we awaken His anger. Now, what is the Church but, as it were, a body of humiliation, almost provoking insult and profaneness, when men do not live by faith? An earthen vessel, far more so even than His body of flesh, for that was at least pure from all sin and the Church is defiled in all her members. We know that her ministers at best are but imperfect and erring, and of like passions with their brethren; yet of them He has said, speaking not to the Apostles merely but to all the seventy disciples (to whom Christian ministers are in office surely equal), 'He that heareth you, heareth Me, and He

that despiseth you despiseth Me, and he that despiseth Me, despiseth
Him that sent Me'.

Again: He has made the poor, weak, and afflicted, tokens and
instruments of His Presence; and here again, as is plain, the same
temptation meets us to neglect or profane it. What He was, such are
His chosen followers in this world; and as His obscure and defence-
less state led men to insult and ill-treat Him, so the like peculiarities
in the tokens of His Presence, lead men to insult Him now.

J. H. Newman, 'Christ Hidden from the World' (1834), *Parochial and
Plain Sermons*, Rivington, 1877, pages 249–50

*As well as writing two substantial Tracts on the subject, Williams
brought the call for personal reserve into his poetry.*

> Things which abide nearest the fountain spring
> Of our affections, cannot bear the light
> Of common day, but shrink at ruder sight,
> And so decay. Love is a heav'n-born thing,
> To live on earth it needs home-cherishing,
> Secret and shade. There is a subtle blight
> In popular talk, and freer glare of light –.
> Soil'd is the bloom that was on Virtue's wing,
> It cannot be restored. No sooner seen
> Than vanity, with silver fingers cold,
> Watches the door, and lets the spoiler in,
> To rifle all her treasury. She hath sold
> Her diamond arms, and tinsel wears instead,
> Shorn the charmed lock when once the charm is read.

I. Williams, 'Christian Reserve', in *Thoughts in Past Years*,
Parker, 1838, page 94

*Keble also condemned unrestrained verbal preaching of the Atone-
ment. After citing Justin Martyr on the appearances of the sign of the
cross in many different forms as a continual reminder to the faithful,
he continued.*

One would have supposed that at least the piety and good meaning
of such trains of thought might remain unquestioned, by all believers in the Cross of CHRIST, whatever judgement might be formed
on their logical accuracy. Yet, so it is, that on passages of this kind a
charge has been grounded against the Fathers, of directing the 'faith

of their readers to the efficacy of the figure of the Cross, rather than to the Atonement made thereon'. A charge which might perhaps be tenable, could it be proved that the general views and conduct of the same Fathers were such as to contradict their truly believing the Atonement. Just as, if there were any persons, either in ancient or in modern times, who observed no rules of self-denial, we might conclude at once that any trust they had, or taught others to have in 'CHRIST crucified', was in fact a trust in a certain form of words, not in the virtue itself of that blessed sacrifice. What was the Cross, as employed by the Fathers, but a 'Verbum visibile', [visible Word] recalling to the minds of the baptized the very truth which they are thus accused of slighting; and to the heathen themselves conveying so much as this, that the Gospel was essentially a doctrine of the Cross, a doctrine of suffering in adherence to a crucified Redeemer? As an expressive symbol, therefore, or word, the Sign of the Cross was liable to the same abuse with words in general: the self-deceit of man might enable him sometimes to acquiesce in the sign without the thing signified; and such a caution might be occasionally needed, as Wesley is reported to have received from William Law: 'Remember that a man may deceive himself as easily by the phrase, "justification by faith", as by any other combination of syllables'.

But supposing no such practical proof against them, may we not say, that the Fathers' veneration for the Cross is *prima facie* as much a proof of their receiving the doctrine of CHRIST crucified, as any form of words in which they could possibly have expressed themselves? And there was this plain and material reason, for their preferring the visible symbol to any mode of speech, in treatises for general reading; that they did not thereby convey more knowledge, than the rule of the Church allowed, to those who were without, while to every baptized believer they conveyed intimations, deep and solemn in proportion to the depth of his faith.

J. Keble, Tract 89, 'On the Mysticism Attributed to the Early Fathers of the Church', page 31

He too expressed his thoughts on reserve in verse.

> E'en human love will shrink from sight
> Here in the coarse rude earth
> How then should rash intruding glance
> Break in upon her sacred trance
> Who boasts a heavenly birth?

So still and secret is her growth,
Ever the truest heart,
Where deepest strikes her kindly root
For hope or joy, for flower or fruit,
Least knows its happy part.

God only, and good angels look,
Behind the blissful screen –
As when, triumphant o'er His woes,
The Son of God by moonlight rose,
By all but Heaven unseen.

J. Keble, 'Fourth Sunday in Lent', in *The Christian Year*
(1827), Oxford University Press, 1914, page 69

*In his second Tract on the subject, Williams extended his argument
to deplore the general contemporary lack of reverence in religion.*

The fearful extent to which this want of reverence in religion has
gone, is, it is to be feared, very little considered or calculated upon.
The degree to which all sense of the holiness of Churches is lost, is too
evident; the efficacy of the Sacraments, the presence of GOD in them,
and in His appointed ministerial ordinances is, it will be allowed, by
no means duly acknowledged, and, indeed, less and less: men's eyes
being not opened, they do not see with the patriarch, 'how dreadful
is this place', 'the LORD was in this place, and I knew it not'. There
is also another point in which all due fear of GOD's awful presence
is lost, very far beyond what many are aware of, and that is in regard
for the Holy Scripture. Some indeed, who profess to uphold and value
them, in order to do so, depreciate the Apocryphal books, and all
others of less plenary inspiration; as if by so doing, they were exalting the Scriptures. But in fact, they do but lower their own standard
of what is holy; and then lower the Scriptures also to meet it. The
effect also of setting aside the Catholic Church as the interpreter of
Holy Scripture, as if it needed none, is of the same kind; it incal-
culably lowers the reverence for Scripture, by making it subject to
the individual judgement. From these things it follows, that although
the Holy Scriptures are pronounced Divine (for no evil is done, but
under a good name) they are treated as if they were not; as if human
thought could grasp their systems, could limit their meaning, and
say to that boundless ocean in which the Almighty walks, 'Hitherto

shalt Thou come and no further'. If Holy Scripture contains within it the living Word, has a letter that killeth, and a Spirit that giveth life, with far different a temper ought we to regard it: by prayer, as the Fathers say, we should knock at the door, waiting till He that is within open to us; it should be approached as that which has a sort of Sacramental efficacy about it, and therefore a savour of life, and also unto death; in short, as our Saviour was of old, by them who would acknowledge Him as GOD and receive His highest gifts. As the Centurion who sent the elders of the Jews unto Him, not venturing himself to approach; thus, humble faith from the dark corner of these latter days would rather seek to interpret through the Ancient Church than herself to presume. Far otherwise are the Sacred Scriptures now treated in evidences, in sermons, in controversial writings, in religious discourse. Divine words are brought down to the rule, and measure, and level of each man's earthly comprehension. And hence arise our Theological disputings, founded on words of Scripture, first brought down to some low, limited sense, and then thought to clash with and exclude each other. The Ancients, on the contrary, considered the Holy Scriptures like the heavens which were marked out by the lituus [*ritual mystic wand*] of the heathen soothsayer, wherein every thing that was found was considered full of Divine import: and speaking from GOD to man. They took Scriptural words as Divine words, replete with pregnant and extensive meaning. Thus when believing in CHRIST, or confessing CHRIST, is spoken of as Salvation, St Augustine remarks that such words are not to be taken after a low and human interpretation, but imply believing and confessing after a real and substantial manner according to the import of Divine words; and that to believe and confess this, according to truth and the vastness of Scripture, is indeed entering into the greatness of the Christian inheritance, which is signified by believing in CHRIST as GOD, with that corresponding awe and obedience which such a belief requires. With like reverential regard St Chrysostom, when commencing his commentary on St Matthew, likens it to approaching the gates of the heavenly city, and adds, 'Let us not then with noise, or tumult enter in, but with a mystical silence. In this city must all be quiet and stand with soul and ear erect. For the letters not of an earthly king, but of the LORD of angels are on the point of being read'. How many thousands of modern books had been unwritten; how much jealous controversy spared, had this sense of Holy Scripture been among us!

I. Williams, Tract 87, 'On Reserve in Communicating Religious Knowledge', pages 119–20

Newman held that the Christian should follow the pattern of quiet reverence shown by characters in the Bible

As the manner of His coming was new, so was His gift. It was peace, but a new peace, 'not as the world giveth'; not the exultation of the young, light-hearted, and simple, easily created, easily lost; but a serious, sober, lasting comfort, full of reverence, deep in contemplation.

And hence the keener, the more rapturous are the feelings of the Christian, the more ardent his aspirations, the more glorious his visions; so much the graver, the more subdued, the more serene must be his worship and his confession. Who was so intoxicated with Divine love as St John? who so overcharged with the Spirit? yet what language can be calmer than when he says, 'Behold what manner of love the Father hath bestowed upon us, that we should be called the sons of God! ... When He shall appear, we shall be like Him, for we shall see Him as He is'? And who was possessed with a more burning zeal than St. Paul? yet observe his injunction to the spiritually-gifted Corinthians; 'Let all things be done unto edifying; the spirits of the prophets are subject to the prophets; for God is not the author of confusion, but of peace ... Let all things be done decently and in order'. And in like manner, in anticipation of Gospel perfection, we read of the impressive gravity and saintly bearing of Samuel and his prophetic company, when Saul came to Ramah; while Saul's extravagance when he came within the Divine influence, prefigures to us the wayward and unpeaceful behaviour of heretical sects in every age, who, in spite of whatever tokens they may bear of the presence of a good spirit among them, yet, whether they preach or pray, are full of tumult and violence, and cause wild alarm or fierce ecstasy, and even strange affections of body, convulsions and cries, in their converts or hearers.

But if gravity and sobriety were seen even in that time, when the heirs of promise were under age, as children submitted to a school-master, and when holy David 'danced before the Lord with all his might, leaping and dancing before the Lord'; much more is the temper of the Christian Church high and heavenly, noble, majestic, calm, and untroubled.

J. H. Newman, 'Christian Nobleness' in *Sermons Bearing on Subjects of the Day*, Rivington, 1843, pages 160–1

In this matter as in others, Newman could express the austerity which was part of the Tractarian ethos.

If we are in earnest, we shall let nothing lightly pass by which may do us good, nor shall we dare to trifle with such sacred subjects as morality and religious duty. We shall apply all we read to ourselves; and this almost without intending to do so, from the mere sincerity and honesty of our desire to please God. We shall be suspicions of all such good thoughts and wishes, and we shall shrink from all such exhibitions of our principles, as fall short of action. We shall aim at doing right, and so glorifying our Father, and shall exhort and constrain others to do so also; but as for talking on the appropriate subjects of religious meditation, and *trying* to show piety, and to excite corresponding feelings in another, even though our nearest friend, far from doing this, we shall account it a snare and a mischief. Yet this is what many persons consider the highest part of religion, and call it spiritual conversation, the test of a spiritual mind; whereas, putting aside the incipient and occasional hypocrisy, and again the immodesty of it, I call all formal and intentional expression of religious emotions, all studied passionate discourse, *dissipation* – dissipation the same in nature, though different in subject, as what is commonly so called; for it is a drain and a waste of our religious and moral strength, a general weakening of our spiritual powers (as I have already shown); and all for what? For the pleasure of the religious excitement. Who can deny that this religious disorder is a parallel case to that of the sensualist? Nay, precisely the same as theirs, from whom the religionists in question think themselves very far removed, of the fashionable world I mean, who read works of fiction, frequent the public shows, are ever on the watch for novelties, and affect a pride of manners, and a 'mincing' deportment, and are ready with all kinds of good thoughts and keen emotions on all occasions.

> J. H. Newman, 'Dangers of Accomplishments' (1834–42), *Parochial and Plain Sermons*, Rivington, 1879, vol. 2, pages 376–7

Newman's deep sense of the sacred quality of the holy mysteries was expressed in his personal correspondence as well as in his published writings. Sacraments were more effective than sermons in creating a proper spirit of worship. Writing to James Stephen on 16 March 1835, he refers to Bishop Joseph Butler (1692–1752) whose Analogy of Religion *was one of the most influential theological works of his time.*

The peculiarity of Butler is this – that, while on the one hand he is reserved, austere, infrequent in the mention of Christian doctrine, in his writings, yet on the other hand he was very earnest for what he calls a Cheap External Religion, put up a Cross in his private Chapel, and was charged with Popery. I conceive his wonderfully gifted intellect caught the idea which had actually been the rule of the Primitive Church, of teaching the more Sacred Truths ordinarily by rites and ceremonies. No mode of teaching can be imagined so public, constant, impressive, permanent, and at the same time reverential than that which makes the forms of devotion the memorial and declaration of doctrine – reverential because the very posture of the mind in worship is necessarily such. In this way Christians receive the Gospel literally on their knees, and in a temper altogether different from that critical and argumentative spirit which sitting and listening engender. The New Testament forcibly enjoins and countenances this mode of teaching by making certain ordinances, not only significant of Christian doctrines, but even exalting them into Sacraments. This is an important consideration. As the Jewish Law had a shadow of good things to come, so has the Christian Church of the same as already come; and in the latter case this shadow is also made the channel and instrument of the substance. Thus even under our spiritual Dispensation (the ceremonial element) is perpetuated as an essential part of its ministration, and that in a much higher sense than that in which they were a characteristic of Judaism.

The Letters and Diaries of John Henry Newman, ed. T. Gornall,
Clarendon Press, 1981, vol. 5, page 46

After extensive quotation from divines requiring assurance of personal feeling in matters of religious devotion, Newman gave the opposing view.

Poor miserable captives, to whom such doctrine is preached as the Gospel! What! is *this* the liberty wherewith Christ has made us free, and wherein we stand, the home of our own thoughts, the region of our own sensations, the province of self, a monotonous confession of what we are by nature, not what Christ is in us, and a resting at best not on His love towards us, but in our faith towards Him! This is nothing but a specious idolatry; a man thus minded does not simply think of God when he prays to Him, but is observing whether he feels properly or not; does not believe and obey, but thinks it enough to be conscious that he is, as he thinks, warm and spiritual; does not contemplate the grace of the Blessed Eucharist, the Body and Blood of his Saviour Christ, except (O shameful and fearful error!) except as a quality of his own mind.

J. H. Newman, *Lectures on Justification*, Rivington, 1838, page 378

Personal reserve in speaking of religion as natural to the truly devout.

You will observe that neither the blessed Martyr [St Polycarp] who had served Christ so long, nor the ignorant Samaritans, who were beginning to acknowledge Him, stated *what* their reasons were, though they had reasons. And, in truth, it is very difficult to draw out our reasons for our religious convictions, and that on many accounts. It is very painful to a man of devout mind to do so; for it implies, or even involves, a steadfast and almost curious gaze at God's wonder-working presence within and over him, from which he shrinks, as savouring of a high-minded and critical temper. And much more is it painful, not to say impossible, to put these reasons forth in explicit statements, because they are so very personal and private. Yet, as in order to the relief of his own perplexity, a religious man may at times try to ascertain them, so again for the service of others he will try, as best he may, to state them.

J. H. Newman, 'Grounds for Steadfastness in our Religious Profession', in *Sermons Bearing on Subjects of the Day*, Rivington, 1843, pages 393–4

The truly converted understand things which may be dangerous for the unconverted to hear: there was a certain élitism in some Tractarian writing.

What a blessed discovery is it to those who make it, that this world is but vanity and without substance; and that really they are ever in their Saviour's presence. This is a thought which it is scarcely right to enlarge upon in a mixed congregation, where there may be some who have not given their hearts to God; for why should the privileges of the true Christian be disclosed to mankind at large, and sacred subjects, which are his peculiar treasure, be made common to the careless liver? He knows his blessedness, and needs not another to tell it him. He knows in whom he has believed; and in the hour of danger or trouble he knows what is meant by that peace, which Christ did not explain when He gave it to His Apostles, but merely said it was not as the world could give.

J. H. Newman, *Parochial Sermons*, Rivington, 1834–42, pages i, 29

Newman commended set forms of prayer as a safeguard against excessive emotionalism.

Granting there are times when a thankful or a wounded heart bursts through all Forms of prayer, yet these are not frequent. To be excited is not the *ordinary* state of the mind, but the extraordinary, the now and then state. Nay, more than this, it *ought not* to be the common state of the mind; and if we are encouraging within us this excitement, this unceasing rush and alternation of feeling, and think that this, and this only, is being in earnest in religion, we are harming our minds, and (in one sense) I may even say grieving the peaceful Spirit of God, who would silently and tranquilly work His Divine work in our heads. This, then, is an especial *use* of Forms of prayer, *when* we are in earnest, as we ought always to be; viz. to keep us from self-willed earnestness, to still emotion, to calm us, to remind us what and where we are, to lead us to a purer and serener temper, and to that deep unruffled love of God and man, which is really the fulfilling of the law, and the perfection of human nature.

Then, again, as to the usefulness of Forms, if we are *not* in earnest, this also is true or not, as we may take it. For there are degrees of earnestness. Let us recollect, the power of praying, being a habit, must be acquired, like all other habits, by practice. In order at length to pray well, we must begin by praying ill, since ill is all we can do. Is not this plain? Who, in the case of any other work, would wait till he could do it perfectly, before he tried it? The idea is absurd. Yet these who object to Forms of prayer on the ground just mentioned, fall into this strange error. If, indeed, we could pray and praise God like the Angels, we might have no need of Forms of prayer; but Forms are to teach those who pray poorly to pray better. They are helps to our devotion as teaching us what to pray for and how, as St John and our Lord taught their disciples; and doubless even the *best* of us prays *but* poorly, and *needs* the help of them. However, the persons I speak of think that prayer is nothing else but the bursting forth of strong feeling, not the action of a habit, but an emotion, and, therefore, *of course to* such men the very notion of *learning* to pray seems absurd. But this indulgence of emotion is as teaching us what to pray for and how, as St. John and our Lord taught their disciples; and, doubtless, even the *best* of us prays but poorly, and *needs* the help of them. However, the persons I speak of, think that prayer in truth founded on a mistake, as I have already said.

J. H. Newman, *Parochial and Plain Sermons* (1834–42), Rivington, 1879, vol. 1, pages 263–4

Keble found 'sacred mysteries' in nature as well in religion, a Words-worthian thought which accords well with the Tractarian principle of Reserve.

There is, too, another strong tie of kinship which binds these two together, in that each is controlled by a tone of modest and religious reserve.

For, on the one hand, all who carefully try to imitate Nature are forced to observe a certain restraint and reserve; at least this far, that like her, they approach each stage of beauty by a quiet and well-ordered movement, not suddenly or, to use a mathematical phrase, *per saltum* [by a leap] (as do those who have no scruple in appearing boldly in public); and on the other hand, the whole principle of piety, such at least as is wisely governed, is ordered by the rule divinely laid down in Holy Scripture, that those things of highest worth should, for the most part, not be offered to listless and unprepared minds; but only be brought into the light when the eyes of those who gaze upon them have been disciplined and purified. Thus the controlling Power which tempers and orders all things has compelled each, by a kind of decree, not to permit any one to have full fruition of the beauteous form and features of Truth, except his devotion be such as leads him to take zealous pains to search her out. Certainly no one who has been trained in this principle from his earliest years will ever allow himself to expose the sacred mysteries either of Nature or religion to public view without regard to the temper and training of the hearers. He would rather be charged with obscureness than pour forth all truths, secret and open alike, without restraint; he would rather be criticised as wanting in ability than wanting in reserve.

J. Keble, *Lectures on Poetry*, trans. E. K. Francis, Clarendon Press, 1912, pages 481–2

9

Aftermath

The reception of Newman into the Roman Catholic Church in 1845 marked the end of the actual Tractarian years. Pusey found himself at the head of the continuing Movement, a position which he did not desire, although he worked faithfully to continue the work which he and others had begun. Pious and learned, conservative rather than radical, he lacked Newman's charisma and persuasive style of writing and preaching. But his personal holiness and integrity, as well as his early association with the Tracts, made him the natural leader. Of the other men who had begun the Movement, Froude was dead, Newman had gone, and Keble had withdrawn from the centre of activity. Further secessions followed, some after the Gorham Judgement in 1847, when the Judicial Committee of the Privy Council upheld the appeal of a clergyman against Bishop Phillpotts of Exeter who had refused to institute him for being unsound about baptismal regeneration: a blow against a Tractarian principle, and a new example of state interference with Church rights. Those who remained soon came to be known as 'Puseyites' and later as 'Anglo-Catholics', a name which the Tractarians themselves had used. The longer influence of the Movement will be considered in the final chapter. There were matters which followed more immediately, and which in time brought later assessments of the whole Movement.

The development of agitation and positive action for re-ordering church buildings in the next decades has sometimes been linked too closely to the Oxford Movement. Both were partly inspired by the wish to assert the unique status of the Church of England and its continuity from the pre-Reformation Church. Proponents of church restoration were caught up in the current admiration for an idealized medievalism, which found expression also in secular Gothic architecture, the poetry of Tennyson, Morris and others, and the political dreams of Disraeli's 'Young England' group in the Tory party. The Cambridge Camden Society was formed in 1839, with the aim of designing new churches and adapting old ones in a way that would emphasize the sacrament of Holy Communion as the central act of worship, instead of focusing on the pulpit and reading desk. In 1846 it became the Ecclesiological Society, based in London. The leading influence was that of J. M. Neale (1818–66), translator of classical hymns and the founder of one of the early Anglican sisterhoods, the Sisterhood of St Margaret in East Grinstead, Sussex. Neale was influenced by the Oxford Movement, but it would be mistaken to see a 'Cambridge Movement' as a partner and collaborator. Neale was critical of the Tractarians for their apparent indifference to the visual beauty and dignity of worship; his aims and ideals were different from theirs. Nevertheless, the Ecclesiological Society and its sympathizers changed the Church of England as much as did the Tractarians and theirs: the one in the physical structure and visual experience of worship, the other in its expression of doctrine and Church tradition.

Neale frequently gave public expression to his views on church architecture. In his introduction to a translation of the thirteenth-century liturgiologist Durandus, he attacked the prevailing fashion and, after stating his ideals, had praise for the Cambridge Camden Society and a sly dig at Oxford, with special reference to Newman's church at Littlemore.

The Church architect must, we are persuaded, make very great sacrifices: he must forego all lucrative undertakings, if they may not be carried through upon those principles which he believes necessary for every good building; and particularly if the end to be answered, or the wants to be provided for, are in themselves unjustifiable or mischievous. Even in church-building itself, he must see many an unworthy rival preferred to him, who will condescend to pander to the whims and comfort of a Church-committee, will suit his design to any standard of ritualism, which may he suggested by his own ignorance, or others' private judgement, who will consent to defile a building meant for GOD's worship with pues [*pews*] and galleries and prayer-pulpits and commodious vestries. But hard as the trial may be, a Church architect must submit to it, rather than recede from the principles which he knows to be the very foundation of his art.

[...] The writers of the Cambridge Camden Society have carried out the system more fully and consistently than any others. It has evidently grown upon them, during the process of their enquiries: yet in their earliest publications, we trace, though more obscurely, the same thing. Their *Few Words to Church Builders* acknowledged the principle to a far greater length; and the *Eccleciologist* has always acted upon it, even when not expressly referring to it. As a necessary consequence, they were the first who dwelt on the absolute necessity of a distinct and spacious Chancel; the first who recommended, and where they could, insisted on, the reintroduction of the Rood-screen; and the first to condemn the use of western triplets. The position and shape of the Font, the necessity of ornamentation, and some other details, they have, but only in common with others, urged.

The Oxford Architectural Society have never recognised any given principles: and in consequence Littlemore is proposed by them as a model – a church either without, or else all, Chancel: and either way a solecism.

> J. M. Neale, *The Symbolism of Churches and Church Ornaments*,
> Green, 1843, pages xxiii, xxxii–xxxiii

Although their aims were different, some supporters of the Oxford Movement also were also enthusiastic for the reordering of churches. Gresley, already quoted as an admirer of Tractarian principles, made his fictional incumbent relate the changes which he managed to effect in his parish church and sum up the benefits which he believed to have followed.

Perhaps some will ask, What was the use of all this trouble about rearrangement and ornament; this minute attention to sittings and kneelings, poppy-heads, eagles, stained glass, and all the rest of it? It might be sufficient to answer, that it was a worthier temple to God than it had been, and that it afforded His people the opportunity of making offerings, such as, if offered with humble faith, He would be pleased to accept. But if any do not feel the force of this reason, I will give them another, which to my mind would be in itself sufficient. The new arrangements in the church contributed in a great degree to the most important object of *making the people worshippers, and not mere hearers; a congregation, not an audience.* It had the effect of leading their minds to dwell on the fact, that they went to church to worship God, and not merely to hear a sermon or a psalm. Previously to the alteration, the impression conveyed by the interior arrangement was, that the people had met together for the sole purpose of listening to the minister who occupied the great staring rostrum in the middle; the very prayers seemed to be preached to them; the Communion-service was scarcely heard. Now a modest, but sufficient, pulpit was erected close by the pillar of the transept; and the whole space, from the western entrance to the altar, was thrown open, so that the minister appeared to be, as he was, the leader of the people, as they addressed the throne of grace. *I had not lowered preaching; but I had raised prayer.* The preaching was listened to with as much attention as ever, and cost me as much pains. But the people saw that it was not the whole, nor indeed the principal object; that there was something even of higher importance, and more essential value. The consequence was, that the congregation naturally fell into the due proprieties of the service.

W. Gresley, *Bernard Leslie*, Burns, 1842, pages 260–2

The Tractarians were not indifferent to ceremonial, but they were not advanced ritualists; their concern was more for the inner than the outward expression of devotion. As Tractarian sympathizers came to fill parish incumbencies, worship became more ceremonial, combining the ideals of the Oxford Movement with those of the ecclesiologists. Ritualism aroused more open and violent opposition than any other innovation, with rioting and disruption of services in these churches, particularly in London. In 1874 the Public Worship Regulation Act authorised legal sanctions against ritual offences. It resulted in the prosecution, and in some cases imprisonment, of priests who refused to change what they believed to be proper in worship. They took their stand on six points of ceremonial: the eastward position at the altar; unleavened eucharistic bread; the mixed chalice; eucharistic vestments; altar lights; the use of incense.

As with church restoration, some of the Tractarian sympathizers went further than their leaders in this matter. Frederick Oakley (1802–80) followed Newman into the Roman Catholic Church in 1845. He was promoting more advanced, or he would say traditional, ideas while the Tracts were still being issued.

We are for carrying out the symbolical principle in our own Church to the utmost extent which is consistent with the duty of obedience to the Rubric. It is quite certain that the first Reformers had no objection to those points of External Religion which were afterwards made matter of cavil by the Puritans. They made no decisive innovations in these respects, whether as regarded the use of the Cross, the arrangements and decorations of churches, church music, or ecclesiastical vestments. They altered only where changes of doctrine made it necessary; as, for instance, in Edward's Injunctions, it is bidden that lights which had previously burned before images should be confined to the Altar. We shall conclude with a few suggestions bearing upon this subject; in which we wish to speak of what seems desirable, rather than speedily or in all places practicable. The utmost allowance is to be made for scruples grounded upon habit and association. Many of the things of which we are about to speak, we certainly consider important, but we do not wish them attempted, or at least persevered in, at the risk of Christian peace and unity.

The use of the Cross both as a sacramental Sign and as a Memorial to the eyes of the Faithful, so far from being forbidden, is even implied, in our Church. In enjoining the practice of crossing in baptism, she has for ever disengaged herself from the modern view, which esteems the use of this holy Symbol, a superstition. We are no advocates of the Crucifix; at all events in the open way in which it is commonly exhibited abroad. Even pictures of the same solemn Subject strike us as bordering on the irreverent, and should at least be always veiled. And we would not hazard an unqualified objection even against the Crucifix as an object for *very* private contemplation under certain trying circumstances; say, for instance, a surgical operation. But as a general rule sculpture is more objectionable than painting, as it is more exact. The Crucifix, openly exhibited, produces the same sort of uncomfortable feeling with certain Protestant exposures in preaching of the Mystery which it represents. But the mere Cross embodies what no Christian should shrink from contemplating; while, of the awful Mystery therewith connected, it is but suggestive. The language of some of the foreign Reformers concerning this sacred Symbol is too shocking to repeat. Alas! how have the lax notions of mere Protestantism grown up with the dishonour done to the material Cross! Out of sight, they say, out of mind. We hope the time will come, when no English church will want, what many possess already, the Image of the Cross in some place sufficiently conspicuous to assist the devotions of the worshipper. It still surmounts our great metropolitan cathedral, reminding us that our Lord has not yet forsaken us. It still graces our Sovereign's crown, teaching both her and us that we are all subjects of the same Spiritual Kingdom. Let us multiply the same holy, efficacious, Emblem far and wide. There is no saying how many sins its awful Form might scare, how many evils avert.

Frederick Oakley, 'The Church Service', The British Critic, 1840,
pages 270-1

In 1871 the Judicial Committee of the Privy Council ruled that a number of ceremonial practices were illegal in the Church of England. The verdict was given against John Purchas (1823–72), vicar of St James's Church, Brighton, and reversed a previous judgement in his favour by an ecclesiastical court. The decision, which came to be known as the 'Purchas Judgement', was invoked in similar cases. Purchas robustly defended ritual practice as not only being acceptable to the rules of the Book of Common Prayer but as restoring what had been neglected.

Every part of the Church must have a ritual, and as there is but one Catholic Church, so the ritual of every portion thereof will have a family likeness, and be one in spirit though diverse in details. Ritual and Ceremonial are the hieroglyphics of the Catholic religion, a language understanded of the faithful, a kind of parable in action, for as of old when He walked the earth, our blessed Lord, still present in His divine and human nature in the Holy Eucharist on the altars of His Church, still spiritually present at the Common Prayers, does not speak unto us 'without a parable'. But as our Lord's 'visage was marred more than any man, and His form more than the sons of men', so has it fared, at least in His Church in this land, with the aspect of His worship on earth. For the last three hundred years, brief but brilliant periods excepted, our ritual has lost all unity of significance of expression. We have treated 'The Book of Common Prayer and Administration of the Sacraments, and other Rites and Ceremonies of the Church' much as if it were simply a collection of sundry Forms of Prayer, overlooking the fact that besides these there are acts to be done, and functions to be performed. And these have been done infrequently, not to say imperfectly.

The old Puritan idea of Divine Service is confession of sin, prayer to God and intercession for our wants, bodily and spiritual. Another theological school, more perhaps in vogue, looks upon praise as the great element of worship – praise, that is, apart from *Eucharisti,* itself, in one sense, a mighty Act of Praise. Hence one Priest with his form-of-prayer theory affects a bald, chilling, and apparently indevout worship, whilst another lavishes all the splendour of his ritual upon his forms of prayer which are said in choir; and both depress, by defective teaching and a maimed ritual, the distinctive service of Christianity. Matins and Evensong are performed with a severe simplicity by the one, in an ornate manner by the other. Both schools have elements of truth in them, both err after the same manner, viz.

in undue exaltation of the Church's ordinary Office, and in depreciation of the Sacramental system – at least the celebration of the Holy Eucharist is not with them the centre of Christian Worship. Yet surely the Communion Service is something more than a mere form of prayer in the opinion of even the laxest school of theology.

J. Purchas, *The Directorium Anglicanum*, 1858, pages vii–viii

Another major change in the Church of England, springing more directly from the Oxford Movement, was the establishment of Anglican religious orders, at first for women. It was an ideal fostered by Pusey, which gained ideological and practical support to the indignation of the more Protestant-minded. The first sisterhood was a community of four, near Regent's Park, London. Two more were founded in 1848, at Wantage and Devonport, and others followed. The Sisterhoods were opposed by many as vigorously as ritualism, but their work with the sick and poor gradually brought respect.

In March 1839 Pusey wrote to W. F. Hook (1798–1875), Dean of Chichester.

I want very much one or more societies of 'Soeurs de la Charité' formed. I think them desirable (1) in themselves as belonging to and fostering a high tone in the Church, (2) as giving a holy employment to many who yearn for something, (3) as directing zeal, which would otherwise go off in some irregular way, or go over to Rome. The Romanists are making great use of them to entice over our people; and I fear we may lose those whom we can least spare; but this is secondary. I think the other two primary, and that they are calculated to draw a blessing upon the Church in which they are found, as the Fathers always speak of the virgins. It seemed best that at first they should not be so discursive as those of the Romish Church in Ireland, but be employed in hospitals, lunatic asylums, prisons, among the females.

He wrote to A. J. B. Hope in 1848 about the Park Village community. Hope (1820–87) was a Member of Parliament and a great Church benefactor. He provided the money for the building of St Augustine's College, Canterbury and All Saints', Margaret Street, in London.

Lord John Manners and I procured us the rules of the Sisters of Charity at Birmingham. I had some rules by me, used by different bodies in England and on the continent. We took as our basis St Augustine's rule, as extant in an Epistle of his to some 'Sanctimoniales' whom he had brought together; thinking it most in accordance with our Church to take rules from one of the Fathers of the Church. On this we engrafted others; always bearing in mind the character of English churchwomen. When it was done, Dodsworth and myself looked over it, with a view to what the Bishop of London would think, and several little points were altered (language chiefly) on his saying, 'The Bishop would not like that'. This was kept to be shown to the Bishop, whenever trial enough had been made of the institution, for him to be ready to take it up. We could not bring it before him sooner, without asking him to do the very thing which he naturally did not wish to do yet. For if he saw the rules and sanctioned them the Sisterhood would have been at once under his sanction. This we wished, but could not ask for. When we had thus reviewed the rules, we showed them to J. Keble.

H. P. Liddon, Life of Edward Bouverie Pusey, Longmans, Green,
1894, vol. 3, pages 6, 22

Some years later, Pusey asked for communities of clergy and sisterhoods to alleviate social problems.

To yourself, my Lord, the whole Church of England owes a deep debt, for the effort which you have made, and to which you sacrificed, perhaps, what God will reward, health and strength, in doing what in you lay to provide Houses of God for the poor of our Metropolis. But you must feel more acutely what a mass remain, sheep scattered abroad who have no shepherd, whom no man seeketh after. We need not single Clergy only, but bodies of Clergy, if the light of the Gospel is ever to penetrate the dark corners of our great towns, and in its streets and lanes visit those abodes of festering wretchedness, where tens of thousands drag out a dying life to, (but for God's mercy not man's) an undying death, 'without hope and without God in the world'.

These cannot be reached by a few additional Clergy, here and there, nor would additional Churches alone gather them in to worship the God whom they know not. Again, among our female poor, in educating religiously the children, orphans, or destitute, or worse than orphans, those with profligate parents and surrounded by profligacy, educated now for sin and Satan, and with Death for their shepherd; or in guarding that perilous age when those who are educated in national schools leave them, to be sucked in (unless care be taken which now can not) in that foul, black whirlpool, ever eddying around their parents' doors; or in recovering out of its sickening stream, those who haply may, from among that suffering mass, 'filthy garments' taken from them, and be anew washed white in the Blood of the Lamb, to dwell with Him for ever; or in tending the destitute sick, or starving, coming among them, (as the poor, who have not known before what the love of Christ was, have called them), 'as Angels from another world', messengers of health to the body, and preparing their souls to receive gladly the message of the Gospel, and finally to 'depart in peace', their dying beds soothed, gladdened, blessed in the love of Christ, taught not in words only but in deeds by those who love Christ – in these and other ways there is a special office for the ministering care of women, of whom our poet has said so beautifully

> When pain and anguish wring the brow,
> A ministering Angel thou.

Such are the needs ten thousand times ten thousand fold multiplied, in our metropolis. And, on the other side, there are those among the daughters of our educated classes, whose hearts God touches, who are unsatisfied with the nothingness in which their life wears away, who long to pass their days like those holy women whom St. Paul speaks of, who 'laboured much in the Lord', who wish to gain the higher reward for more devoted service, whose hearts often prey upon themselves, because they have no adequate object for their being.

E. B. Pusey, *Letter to the Right Hon and Right Rev the Lord Bishop of London*, Parker, 1851, pages 234–6

In Advent 1857 Neale preached to the Sisters at East Grinstead of the privilege of daily communion.

I sometimes fear, my dearest Sisters, lest we should run the risk of not thinking sufficiently of this our privilege of privileges, the sureness of our Living Bread in this place. I must speak plainly about this. Imagine that, years ago, before you had entered on this life, it had been told you that the time would come when, without leaving your own home, without any kind of fatigue, without any sort of uncertainty, regularly, morning after morning, the Body and Blood of your Lord and your God would be given to you. Would not such a blessing have seemed beyond the reasonable limits of possibility? And yet further; if it had been said, 'Always there must be fearful risk in so frequent reception; but still you shall be warned, still the Priest who gives you your greatest strength shall also know your full weakness; still you shall not be able to eat of that sacrament without his reminding you what manner of persons you ought to be in all holy conversation and godliness?' [...] I cannot but feel that thus to have a Priest who can celebrate for you daily; thus to have a Priest (however unworthy in himself does not matter in the least), whose first and dearest care you are; thus to be urged and persuaded to frequent Confession, is a privilege for which you will one day have to answer. You know, my own Sisters, that the number of those who have equal external means of grace with yourselves in England might be reckoned by tens; and then comes that terrible question: 'What do ye more than others?'

J. M. Neale, *Sermons on Passages of the Prophets*, Hayes, 1877, vol. 1, pages 106–7

Although only few felt called to the religious life, many heard the appeal to a more rigid discipline of daily life and devotion, the growth of personal holiness which the Tractarians had often counselled. Pusey's works on fasting had helped to widen and deepen the concern of the Tracts. In a later sermon he expounded the argument that fasting is a discipline not only for the individual but for the integrity of the whole Church.

By fasting only with Prayer were even Apostles enabled to prevail against some kind of devils; amid fasting were Apostles separated to carry on their warfare against Satan's kingdom: by fasting, as by other suffering, no less than 'by pureness of knowledge, by the Holy Ghost, by love unfeigned, by the word of truth, by the power of God', does St. Paul testify that he approved himself as a minister of God. And what should we dare to say of our Blessed Lord's own fast? Our Church rightly counts it among the merciful mysteries of His Life, as well as the temptation for which it prepared, and beseeches Him 'by Thy fasting and temptation', 'have mercy upon us'. Strange mystery, that it should be fitting that His sinless nature should suffer through fasting, the appointed means to discipline our rebellious appetites, or humble ourselves for their rebellion! Strange, that when God, in Him, so consecrated fasting, man should not think that a privilege which was hallowed in his Master and Redeemer! Strange, that when the spotless Son entered into temptation through fasting, we, sin-stained as we are, impure from our mother's womb, and defiled with our own added transgressions, should think that needless for us whereby the Ever-Blessed Son as Man, was perfected! Strange that when all, Saints and sinners, Patriarchs, Prophets, Apostles, righteous kings, leaders of God's heritage, types of the great Mediator, yea, and that Mediator Himself, employed fasting as acceptable with God, persons in this day should think they might neglect or despise it, as a carnal and unprofitable service! Strange would it indeed be, were there any thing strange in Satan's wiles or man's self-deceit!

And yet, after a few years, my brethren, if God, as we trust, continue to restore our Church as He is now doing, we shall think it strange, that members of a Church who, in her prayers, have besought God to be gracious unto them, as 'turning to Him in weeping, fasting, and praying', should not do that for which they beseech Him to be gracious! – that they should ask Him to give them 'grace to use abstinence,' and not seek to practise it! – that they should plead to their Lord, that He fasted for them forty days and forty nights, and themselves fast not at all, with Him or for themselves. It will seem strange that what nature herself suggests, heathen have practised, Scripture directs, the Church enjoins, whereby Martyrs girded themselves to bear their last witness to their Lord, the whole white-robed army of Saints (until such, as in these later years may, in their ignorance of its use and duty, have been brought through without it), subdued the flesh, deepened their penitence, humbled their souls, winged their prayers, died to the world that they might live to their Lord – members of a Church should acknowledge in words, in practice neglect.

E. B. Pusey, 'Fasting', *Parochial Sermons*, Parker, 1864, vol. 1,
pages 186–7

Still refusing to accept the precise doctrine of Transubstantiation, Pusey reiterated his belief in the Real Presence in the Eucharist, in terms even more definite than those which had brought about his inhibition in 1843.

The outward and visible sign is (our Catechism teaches us) 'a means whereby we receive the inward'. As through the Baptism of water in the name of the Trinity we receive the inward part of Baptism, 'the death unto sin and the new birth unto righteousness', so, through the outward elements of the Lord's Supper, 'the bread and Wine', received as Christ has commanded, we receive the 'inward part', 'the Body and Blood of Christ'. But in order that we may receive them; they must be there, for us to receive them.

This, as it is the first teaching of our childish years, training us to look on, and to long for, what we are to receive thereafter, comes naturally, as the first, immediate instruction, preparatory to the first Communion. We had repeated from our early childhood, that 'the Body and Blood of Christ are verily and indeed taken and received by the faithful in the Lord's Supper'. And now, at the first Communion comes the great reality itself. 'Verily and indeed'; in deed and in truth; really and truly, are 'the Body and Blood of Christ taken and received in the Lord's Supper by the faithful', and so by each one of us, if we are faithful. 'If this be not the Real Presence', I heard in my youth from an old clergyman, 'I know not how it could be expressed'.

The gift, then, in the Sacrament of the Lord's Supper, according to our Catechism, is not only grace, nor even any spiritual union with our Lord wrought by God the Holy Ghost; it is no mere lifting up our souls to Him at the Right Hand of God; but it is His Body and Blood in deed and in truth, received by us, if faithful. And, at present, we are concerned with what it is to the faithful, not what it becomes to the unfaithful.

E. B. Pusey, *The Real Presence of the Body and Blood of our Lord
Jesus Christ the Doctrine of the English Church*, Parker, 1869,
pages 165–6

The later Anglo-Catholics took a strong line on sacramental confession as a duty for all communicants. Vernon Staley (1852–1933) was a member of the Anglican community at Clewer, and a prolific writer of devotional works at the end of the nineteenth century and the beginning of the twentieth.

Contrition leads naturally to confession, or the truthful acknowledgement of sin. Confession is self-accusation, and the acknowledgement to God of wrong doing. God demands confession as a condition of pardon. 'If we confess our sins, He is faithful and just to forgive us our sins.' A willingness to confess is an evidence of contrition. The most searching confession is that made privately before a priest. [...]

The Church of England invites sinners, who cannot otherwise make their peace with God, to open their grief (i.e. to reveal the

sin which causes the grief) before the priest, in order that they may
secure 'the benefit of absolution'. Such confession is called by Bishop
Cosin, *Sacramental Confession,* and is a blessed privilege open to
all who heartily desire it. Our blessed Lord has given to his priests
power and authority to absolve from all sins, and He surely means
them to use this power. But before they can fully do so, it is needful
that those seeking absolution should confess their sins. Thus we may
be quite sure that private confession, as an outcome of real contrition, is a practice well pleasing to our Lord.

We must remember that, strictly speaking, to absolve is not to forgive; God alone forgives. To absolve is to unloose the bonds which
sin has placed upon the soul, and to remove the bar to the receiving
of grace. In raising Lazarus from the dead, our Lord pronounced the
words, 'Loose him, and let him go'. This was the part of the people
towards him whom Christ raised. And so God, who pardons the penitent, bids the priest in absolution to loose him and let him go.

Vernon Staley, The Catholic Religion (1893), Mowbray, 1904,
pages 294–6

*It was not only the divines and theologians who encouraged the
pursuit of personal holiness. Christina Rossetti (1830–94) led the
apparently uneventful life of a Victorian spinster, but wrote poetry
which was deeply emotional and insightful. Some was gently erotic,
some playful, but much of it expressed the devotion of her Anglo-
Catholic Christian faith, as in this sonnet.*

Why should I call Thee Lord, Who art my God?
Why should I call Thee Friend, Who art my Love?
Or King, Who art my very Spouse above?
Or call Thy sceptre on my heart Thy rod?
Lo now Thy banner over me is love,
All heaven flies open to me at Thy nod:
For Thou hast lit Thy flame in me a clod,
Made me a nest for dwelling of Thy Dove.
What wilt Thou call me in our home above,
Who now hast called me friend? how will it be
When Thou for good wine settest forth the best ?
Now Thou dost bid me come and sup with Thee,
Now Thou dost make me lean upon Thy breast:
How will it be with me in time of love?

Christina Rossetti, 'After Communion', Poems, Macmillan, 1904

*Charlotte M. Yonge (1823–1901) was a parishioner and pupil of
Keble at Hursley. He taught her Tractarian principles which she incorporated into her prolific output of novels, with many depictions
of characters striving for holiness though Church discipline and
undergoing crises of conscience. In her tribute to Keble's poetry,
she affirms the principle of Reserve, slightly misquoting the title of
Tracts 80 and 87.*

Reserve, reverent reserve, was ever a characteristic of the teaching
of the school of divines of which the 'Christian Year' was the first
utterance. Those who had gone before them, in their burning zeal
to proclaim the central truth of the Gospel, had obtruded it with
little regard to the season of speaking or the frame of mind of the
hearer; and moreover, there was a habit of testing the sincerity of
personal religion by requiring that its growth should be confidently
proclaimed and discussed with great fulness of detail.

The deep mind, whose volumes of thought and feeling, even when
they required expression, retired from the curious gaze, could not but
shrink from all irreverent display and analysis of either holy things or
private feelings; and 'the Rose-bud' as this poem is called, is his veiled
protest, which found a longer echo and commentary in the Tract for
the Times 'On Reserve in Communicating Sacred Knowledge', where
Isaac Williams shewed how in mercy for the hardened Jew, the full
brightness of the Lord's teaching was withheld from the unbelieving
ear, and reserved for the faithful few.

Charlotte M. Yonge, Musings over 'The Christian Year' and
'Lyra Innocentium', 1871, pages 90–1

*J. H. Shorthouse (1834–1903), a Quaker who became an Anglican,
wrote several novels of which the most successful was* John Inglesant
*(1881). Very popular in its time, it tells of the progress of a young
man in the time of Charles I and the Commonwealth who passes
through many adventures before settling in the Church of England,
which he here eulogizes in terms directly descended from the Oxford Movement. Shorthouse admired the Tractarians but had little
respect for later Puseyites.*

The English Church, as established by the law of England, offers the
supernatural to all who choose to come. It is like the Divine Being
Himself, whose sun shines alike on the evil and on the good. Upon

the altars of the Church the divine presence hovers as surely, to those who believe it, as it does upon the splendid altars of Rome. Thanks to circumstances which the founders of our Church did not contemplate, the way is open; it is barred by no confession, no human priest. Shall we throw this aside? It has been won for us by the death and torture of men like ourselves in bodily frame, infinitely superior to some of us in self-denial and endurance. God knows – those who know my life know too well – that I am not worthy to be named with such men; nevertheless, though we cannot endure as they did – at least do not let us needlessly throw away what they have won. It is not even a question of religious freedom only; it is a question of learning and culture in every form. I am not blind to the peculiar dangers that beset the English Church. I fear that its position, standing, as it does, a mean between two extremes, will engender indifference and sloth; and that its freedom will prevent its preserving a disciplining and organising power, without which any community will suffer grievous damage; nevertheless, as a Church it is unique: if suffered to drop out of existence, nothing like it can ever take its place.

J. H. Shorthouse, *John Inglesant* (1881), Macmillan, 1883,
pages 442–3

Concern for the poor, and criticism of the general condition of society, was another Tractarian legacy. W. J. E. Bennett (1804–86), Vicar of Frome-Selwood, Somerset, where he set up a large outdoor series of the Stations of the Cross, believed that the Movement had brought the Church closer to the poor and disadvantaged. He singled out some Anglo-Catholic churches in London for praise.

Riches and rank exercise a baneful influence on the Church. They kill it with patronage; they lull it into sleep by over-security. The most excellent incumbents of these churches, most dear to the writer of this Paper, *want more poor to back them up*. It is the WORLD and its malign powers, its secret influence, its subtle fascination, its gross prejudice, which is too near, too ever present, too much mixed up with the circumstances overcharging all that is done; whereas at S. Alban's, Holborn, and S. Michael's, Shoreditch, and Christ Church, Clapham, and such like churches, there is no *World*, it is the *poor*, and according to the true sign of the MESSIAH, it is they who receive the chief prize in the fullness of the Church's blessing: for 'To the *poor the Gospel is preached*'.

No more need be said. The time is coming, and coming quickly, when class interests will have more power even than they have at present, when the aristocracy both of wealth and rank in this country will have to consider the aggression of the middle classes, and the middle classes the aggression of the working classes, and all will have to consider how best they may stave off the old revolutionary cry of Equality. The Press, in its ignorance of the working of religion in the human mind, and of the necessity for the working of religion, that there should be a Church whose priesthood are the friends of the poor, cry out against such churches as S. Alban's, describe its ritual observances as 'pernicious nonsense', and would have the people believe that the true type of the Church of England is to be found in the be-cushioned pews of the proprietary chapels of the West End, or the comfortable lounging places of S. George's and S. James's. The World is tolerant of the Church, so long as the latter merely shows herself as the servant, not as the master; so long as the 'Establishment', as such, is uppermost, and not religion; so long as the priest only believes and teaches as the Crown directs for the glory of the state. But if any power is gained in the affection of the people, exclusive of the authority of the state, and the voice of the Church is heard speaking independently from her pulpits and her Altars then the cry of the World is 'Popery' and 'Priestcraft'.

[...] This then is a Summary of some of the great results of the teaching of the *Tracts for the Times*. O ye princes and great ones of the World! O ye writers in newspapers, and speakers in the Houses of Parliament! beware, how ye are offended at the Church, when she moves thus downwards from your high estate to the lower portions of the people. Beware, lest haply ye be found fighting against GOD and against yourselves. Beware, lest by so doing ye be destroying the only safety which one day ye may need, when the cry shall come, 'set your houses in order'. Check us not, therefore. Hinder us not. It would be for your own spiritual advantage if you would follow us yourselves, for there is much for you to learn; but certainly it is for your political advantage, and for that of the poor and the people that you let us alone. You may wonder at the externals of ornamentation which you behold at such a cost. You may despise our care for vestments, music, flowers, lights, or incense, and ridicule the desire which so widely prevails for Ritual Order. But know of a surety, that down below all this are deeper things than your philosophy has ever dreamt of – spirituality of life, holiness of self-denial, fidelity of doctrine, perseverance in good works, and altogether such gifts of the HOLY GHOST as prove the origin of the contest, as well as point steadily to the end, namely, though it may be indeed through much tribulation – the victory of Jesus in His Church over Satan and the World.

W. J. E. Bennett, 'Some results of the Tractarian Movement of 1833', in O. Shipley, ed., *The Church and the World: Essays on Questions of the Day*, Longmans, 1867, vol. 1, pages 24–6

R. W. Dolling (1851–1902) was an Anglo-Catholic priest with a strong sense of political as well as religious mission. He did great work in the deprived area of Landport in Portsmouth. In this extract from a sermon he gives the view of many Anglo-Catholics about the social obligations of the Church.

I feel an interest in politics, and express that interest, first of all, because I am a Christian, and, secondly, because I am an Englishman. There was a day, you know, when in a large measure the Church of God exercised a mighty influence by speaking the truth upon political subjects. If you take, for instance, the Old Testament, you will find that in the Book of Psalms, which are, I suppose, the part of the Old Testament most read by modern Christians, the chief idea which underlies large parts of that wonderful collection is the right of the poor to be heard alike by God and man in all their needs and necessities, and to gain the redress of their wrongs. If you go farther into the Old Testament, and take the lives of God's prophets and their words, you will find that, as a rule, they were essentially political and social reformers, speaking with the authority of the voice of God and under the influence of a power which carried them into the palaces of kings and made their voice heard throughout the land of Israel, and even penetrated into the countries which were brought in contact with their own nation. You find these inspired men of God having one single purpose, and that was to preach of the God of Justice, a purpose the execution of which involved a most vigorous onslaught on every kind of oppression and on every species of wrong.

In fact, I suppose there has never been gathered together in any volume such magnificent statements of the rights of the weak and the helpless as you will find in almost every one of the writings of the prophets of the Old Testament.

Then you must remember that these are but the forerunners of Jesus Christ, that He is in Himself the gatherer up of all that the psalmists sung, of that the prophets foretold, and therefore you may expect to find in Him also the Champion of the weak and oppressed, and something more than that – the One who preached with a voice which is still sounding throughout all the world the royalty of every single man, who revealed to man His Divine origin, and showed not merely God's unceasing care for humanity, but God's desire that by his own actions, by using the powers which He had given him, that man should be lifted up even to the very highest of all ideals, that there should be no altitude of virtue or intelligence that it should not be possible for man to attain to, if he were but true to the power which God had placed in his soul. Looking round on the world, Christ discovered that there were those who had, as it were, absorbed or monopolised these human rights, and rendered well-nigh impossible the development of man, and who had by that very monopoly denied to him the possibility of his attainment to the ideal which God had willed for him. Therefore the voice of Christ, whether it speaks from Galilee or whether it speaks in the courts of the temple, sounds and resounds to-day, and it shall never cease to re-echo as long as the world has Christianity existing in its midst. It bids a man not merely to be free in the sense in which human laws could give freedom – that is, to be free from the bondage or the oppression with which the cruelty of others had bound him – but to be free in a much higher and truer sense, that he may reach the stature which our Lord Himself foresaw for him when He made him in the Divine Image. And if there be in any country in which men live any custom, any privilege of others which denies to men this opportunity, the Christian, be he priest or be he layman, must never cease raising his voice until such restriction is removed, until such privilege has been abolished, and the man is able in the fullness of his Manhood to realise God's eternal Will for him.

C. F. Osborne, *The Life of Father Dolling*, Arnold, 1903, pages 131–2

Judgements on the Movement began even before 1845. An example of mingled praise and blame came from James Garbett (1802–79) in his Bampton Lectures. Although himself no poet, Garbett had defeated Isaac Williams in the election of the Professor of Poetry, a contest fought on polemical rather than literary grounds. After speaking of the situation in the early 1830s, when the power of the state over the Church seemed to be changing from protective to destructive – the theme of Keble's Assize Sermon and other early Tractarian writing – he went on to praise much of what had been done.

It was at this moment and in this combination of circumstances, when men's minds and hearts were in suspense, and prepared to receive obediently any impulse in harmony with their pre-existing feelings, that the impulse really came. There appeared that series of remarkable essays which have been the centre and exciting cause of the most signal religious movement since the first struggle of the Reformation, and the contest which sprung from it; till the adjustment, such as it was, of the claims of Church-order with the ultra-Protestant elements, gave an interval of religious repose.

This is not the place to trace the progress of those writings and other works of the same authors – nor to show how, partly by their intrinsic interest, and not a little by an able management of those facilities for the diffusion of opinions which the present times afford, they gradually spread over the land, and began to exercise, whether for good or evil, an undeniable influence to which no observer of the times could be blind. That their first results were beneficial in many ways, few, I imagine, are disposed to deny. At any rate, they soon became a power, *a real element* in the Church, compelling attention to itself – a centre and rallying point of spiritual influences – a something which had a clear vocation, which it was rapidly fulfilling, in the modification of the existing Church-system.

Now, with all reasonable allowance for that concurrence of circumstances, without which no religious or political movement was ever yet successful, and in the absence of which, no intellect, however powerful, can effectually work, it is impossible for a candid mind to deny to such results adequate causes in the writings themselves – rare qualities and powers in the minds which wrought them out. In a word, if we regard the whole phenomenon with a philosophical eye, it must be confessed, whatever judgement may be formed of their ultimate tendency, that so wide an influence could never have been exerted, or the approbation, however qualified, of wise and good men have been obtained, unless they had successfully struck some deep chord – had hit on some real wants of the period – and brought out distinctly into light certain substantive principles which, before their appearance, had required an adequate exponent, and had found none.

J. Garbett, *Christ as Prophet, Priest and King*, 1842, vol. 2, pages 461–2

More measured responses came later, after the dust had settled and there were new controversies about ritualism and scepticism. R. W. Church (1815–90), later Dean of St Paul's, was one of Newman's closest younger associates and as Junior Proctor vetoed the condemnation of Tract 90. His history of the Movement was for many years regarded as the chief authority. In his conclusion he recorded the apparent failure and the subsequent developments after Newman's secession.

It was not an encouraging position. The old enthusiastic sanguineness had been effectually quenched. Their Liberal critics and their Liberal friends have hardly yet ceased to remind them how sorry a figure they cut in the eyes of men of the world, and in the eyes of men of bold and effective thinking. The 'poor Puseyites' are spoken of in tones half of pity and half of sneer. Their part seemed played out. There seemed nothing more to make them of importance. They had not succeeded in Catholicising the English Church, they had not even shaken it by a wide secession. Henceforth they were only marked men. All that could be said for them was, that at the worst, they did not lose heart. They had not forgotten the lessons of their earlier time.

It is not my purpose to pursue farther the course of the movement. All the world knows that it was not, in fact, killed or even much arrested by the shock of 1845. But after 1845, its field was at least as much out of Oxford as in it. As long as Mr Newman remained, Oxford was necessarily its centre, necessarily, even after he had seemed to withdraw from it. When he left his place vacant, the direction of it was not removed from Oxford, but it was largely shared by men in London and the country. It ceased to be strongly and prominently Academical. No one indeed held such a position as Dr Pusey's and Mr Keble's; but though Dr Pusey continued to be a great power at Oxford, he now became every day a much greater power outside of it; while Mr Keble was now less than ever an Academic, and became more and more closely connected with men out of Oxford, his friends in London and his neighbours at Hursley and Winchester. The cause which Mr Newman had given up in despair was found to be deeply interesting in ever new parts of the country: and it passed gradually into the hands of new leaders more widely acquainted with English society. [...] Those times were the link between what we are now, so changed in many ways, and the original impulse given at Oxford; but to those times I am as much of an outsider as most of the foremost in them were outsiders to Oxford in the earlier days. Those times are almost more important than the history of the movement; for, besides vindicating it they carried on its work to achievements and successes which, even in the most sanguine days of 'Tractarianism', had not presented themselves to men's minds, much less to their hopes.

R. W. Church, *The Oxford Movement: Twelve Years 1833–1845* (1891),
Macmillan, 1909, pages 406–8

Others looked back on the Movement with less enthusiasm. J. W. Burgon (1813–88), Dean of Chichester, was typical of the old High Churchmen for whom it was a step too far. He praised the Tractarians for their scholarship and revival of earlier teaching, but took a poor view of the rest, especially their neglect of close Bible study.

It is a memorable fact that throughout this period (1830 to 1850) *Holy Scripture itself* experienced marked neglect. No commentary in the vernacular tongue was so much as attempted. The Romish controversy was revived; but nowhere (that I can discover) was the impassable barrier between England and Rome explained with the vigour, the clearness, the fearlessness which characterised the writings of our elder Divines. The *sufficiency* of our Baptismal and Communion Offices was by no one loyally maintained. On the contrary. There is a tone of discontent – an *undutiful* disposition to find fault – almost everywhere discernible. The Editors of the later 'Tracts' did not perceive that by the course they were pursuing, (intending nothing less), they were bringing discredit on Catholic antiquity generally; sowing distrust and suspicion in a thousand quarters; paving the way for many a dreary secession to Rome, on the one hand, many a lapse into blank unbelief, on the other. To the partial miscarriage of the Tractarian movement is to be attributed, in no slight degree, that miserable lawlessness on the part of a section of the Clergy, which is among the heaviest calamities of these last days; as well as, in an opposite direction, that ugly recoil which has already disestablished Religion in our ancient Universities, and of which we have not yet nearly seen the end.

The praise and true glory of the religious movement which it is customary to connect with the year 1833, consisted in the mighty impulse which was then given to religious thought and sacred learning *on the ancient lines.* Two publications, known as the 'The Library of the Fathers' and the 'Anglo-Catholic Library' (they are but a part of the literary product of the period), led to the dissemination of a vast amount of the best Church teaching. The publication of new and improved editions of the works of all our greatest Divines largely increased men's acquaintance with the resources of our own Anglican Divinity. The movement, notwithstanding every discouragement and drawback, was to an extraordinary extent over-ruled for permanent good: but, *Why* (we sorrowfully ask ourselves), *why* was it so largely frustrated? and why, to so great an extent, disfigured with evil?

J. W. Burgon, 'Henry James Rose', in *Lives of Twelve Good Men*
(1888), John Murray, 1889, pages 225–6

W. F. Hook (1798–1875), Dean of Chichester, sympathized with the Tractarians but fell out with Pusey over later developments. He defended the continuity and full catholicity of the Church of England but, unlike Froude and Ward, had no doubt that the Reformation was real and necessary.

You see, then – and in these days it is particularly necessary to bear the fact in mind – that ours is the Old Catholic Church of England; a Church which traces its origin to the Apostles and our Lord; a Church which in the dark ages laboured under abuses and corruptions, which were removed under the Episcopates of Archbishop Cranmer and Archbishop Parker. Nothing can be more mistaken than to speak of these great men as the founders of our Church. One only is our founder, and that is Christ. And as well might we say of a man when he has washed his face that he is not the same man as he was before his ablution, as to say of the Church of England that she is a different Church since the Reformation from what she was before.

W. F. Hook, *The Church and its Ordinances*, Bentley, 1876, page 109

William Palmer has previously been quoted as a supporter of the Oxford Movement. His attack on what he saw as Romanizing tendencies was one of the reasons for Ward writing his Ideal of a Christian Church. *In 1843 Palmer wrote the first connected account of the Movement. Forty years later he republished the book with an additional account of his retrospective opinion. It was a sad but judicious reflection by one who had not lost his hostility to Rome, and was opposed to ritualism, but could see that in many ways the Church was better for the Oxford Movement.*

As the smoke cleared away, we could gradually see the extent of the disaster. Newman had fallen, with two or three men his immediate partisans, and some forty or fifty clergymen of bigoted opinions, whose names were not known as men of any eminence. I was curious to know on what motives these new converts joined the Church of Rome. I found on inquiry from those who conversed with them, that the usual motive with them for joining the Church of Rome was not any argument or mental conviction that the Church of Rome was the true Church, or any examination of the controversy, but simply an internal impulse, or inclination to join that Church, which was ascribed to the movement of the Holy Ghost. Of course this at once deprived these secessions of all argumentative weight. They appeared

at once in their true character of enthusiastic and irrational movements of self-will, and only weakened the cause of Rome intellectually,
as demonstrating the absence of intellectual proof, and dependence
upon the merest and wildest assumption, such as any system however
monstrous might be able to produce equally well. [...]

Immediately upon Newman's secession, and the collapse of the
Romanizing party, Pusey threw himself into the breach and published
letters announcing himself as the leader of the Tractarian movement,
and mentioning Newman without any censure, as merely taking
service in another part of the Lord's vineyard. Pusey would never
permit a word of censure against Newman; he adopted his views
except those directly opposed to the Church; but he had sufficient
confidence in the Church of England as a branch of the Universal
Church not to sanction any secession from it. His principle, however,
was as far as possible to conciliate the semi-Romanizing party, by
adoption of its tenets and practices, and by the introduction of tenets
and practices from Rome calculated to meet their tastes. With the
same view he prompted and encouraged translations from Roman
Catholic works of a devout character altered to harmonise with the
Church of England; but it is very difficult to divest Roman Catholic
books of principles which are inconsistent with our own.

I must confess that Pusey's proceedings as the self-constituted
leader of the Tractarian party often caused to me very great uneasiness. I shared in the opinions of Bishop Wilberforce and Dr Hook
on this point. I should have gladly seen Pusey attempt to reform mistakes introduced by Newman, and endeavouring to correct, instead
of seeming to go along with the ultra-Tractarian mistakes. I was also
distressed by his assumption of a leadership of an organised party;
but in the end I became satisfied that the position he occupied was
for the good of the Church. He advocated and allowed of nothing
that was actually wrong, nothing which was not open to considerations of expediency. He had to control a very uncertain party, open
to Newman's influence for some time, a party which was unsettled
in principle and might easily be driven into secession. I believe that
under Divine Providence his work was overruled to the great purpose
of gradually steadying in the faith, and making available for the service of the Church, abilities and energies which if harshly and rudely
treated, and cut off from sympathy (as many sincere Christians desired) would have proved a source of weakness to religion, instead of
a source of strength, and under these impressions I cannot but regard
in Pusey a great benefactor of the Church of England.

I should myself have often been in favour of a sterner and more

direct policy towards all who shared in semi-Romanizing and Ritualistic opinions, and whom Pusey conciliated; but my own opinions
were proved to be faulty by the result; for by mild methods the Church
has been saved from further disruption, and retains all the energies
which a different mode of proceeding might have lost. And I also see
that in proportion as time has proceeded, extreme and indefensible
opinions have been gradually eliminated; that the Church has reaped
the benefit of all which have been left; and that the truth has been
gradually finding its level and assuming the ascendancy – in a word
that the principles of the Church of England have been more carefully
studied and more generally adopted, so that, in the long run, the hope
which I originally entertained that truth would eventually find its
level in England, has been happily verified to a great degree.

W. Palmer *A Narrative of Events Connected with the Publication of
the Tracts for the Times*, Rivington, 1883, pages 239–42

*As well as the views of disenchanted sympathizers, there was bitter
opposition from those who hated the notion of anything 'Catholic',
of whom Walter Walsh, assistant editor of an Evangelical paper*
The English Churchman *was one of the most vehement. His* Secret
History of the Oxford Movement *is almost endearing in its attack
on ritual, auricular confession, sisterhoods, the Society of the Holy
Cross and many other post-Tractarian developments. Some of his
sub-headings are 'Dr Pusey secretly wears hair shirts'; 'Faber kisses
the Pope's foot'; 'A ritualistic Sister whipped most cruelly'; 'Immor-
al Ritualistic Confessors ruin women'. The closing sentence of this
paragraph is strangely ironical when we recall the inception of the
Movement as a dispute with state interference.*

It is hoped that this volume may be the means of proving to many
Churchmen, who have hitherto taken no interest in the Ritualistic
question, that the contest now going on within the Church of England, and which, unhappily, threatens to rend her asunder, is not one
about trifles. There are many men and women who love to hear the
best music sung in our Churches, and wish to have the services con-
ducted with the utmost possible reverence, who do not wish to surrender the priceless privileges of the Reformation, including freedom
from Papal tyranny, in order that their Church, and the Church of
their forefathers, shall, instead of going forward, return to the corruptions of the Dark Ages. It is hoped that this volume may enable many
to see that behind the Ritual, and the outward pomp and grandeur of

Ritualistic services, are the unscriptural doctrines which that Ritual is designed to teach, and which our forefathers found unendurable. All loyal Churchmen, by whatever name they call themselves, should unite in ejecting the lawless from their ranks, after an effort has been made to secure their obedience. Things are rapidly drifting towards a state of Ecclesiastical Anarchy. Indeed, in thousands of parishes, Anarchy already prevails, where Ritualistic priests persist in making their own whims and fancies their supreme law, and in doing only that which is right in their own eyes. I think it was Sydney Smith who said, of the Tractarian clergyman of his own time, that 'He is only for the Bishop, when the Bishop is for him'. It is so still; but with this unfortunate difference – as a rule the Bishop *is* for him. Episcopal smiles and favours are heaped on the secret plotters whose work is described in this volume; and the leaders of the state vie with the Bishops in promoting those who are systematically lawbreakers.

W. Walsh, *The Secret History of the Oxford Movement* (1897),
Swan Sonnenschein, 1899, pages xi–xii

Assessment and Legacy

The direct influence of the Oxford Movement on the next two generations is not difficult to trace. Its lasting effect is more difficult to assess, since it meets with so many other changes in the Church and in society. What can we now see to have been its principal features? How were they developed by those who shared its beliefs but expressed them in different ways and with new emphases to meet the demands of their time?

Although in many minds the words 'Puseyite' and 'Anglo-Catholic' were associated mainly with elaborate ceremonial and 'popish' practices, the first concerns of the Tractarians were not with ritual or forms of service but with the identity of the Church of England. They accepted its Establishment, but opposed any suggestion that it was subordinate to the State, or even linked to it in an equal and unbreakable relationship. They set out to prove its independent power as part of the continuing Catholic Church, changed but not severed by the Reformation. Deeply spiritual and often other-worldly as they were, what roused them initially was political alarm about relations with the State, which seemed to be no longer the defender of the Church but rather its opponent. They did not look for innovation, but for the restoration of what they regarded as eternal but neglected truths.

The sources of appeal by which they tried to prove their point were various. Froude's medievalism, consorting well with the current Romantic view of the Middle Ages and the Gothic, did not engage his associates in the same way. They looked to the early Church; seeking evidence as close as possible to the time of the Apostles. In issuing the *Library of the Fathers* they believed that patristic writings should be so widely known as to counteract what they saw as an excessively Protestant bias in the Church They were as cool as Froude towards the English Reformers, though usually less fervent than he in their condemnation. They were ambivalent towards Richard Hooker, regarded as the nearest thing in Anglicanism to a founding father. Keble produced an edition of Hooker's works and made him something of a proto-Tractarian, playing down his moderate but clear Calvinism. They found strength in the Caroline divines and sacred poets, and idealized the Laudian Church. The *Library of Anglo-Catholic Theology* claimed by its title more than could justifiably be found in some of its chosen writers. Yet they did a good service in reviving works which had helped to shape Anglican thought in its formative years, and devotional literature which has continued to support the faith of many. They were depreciatory, almost scornful, towards the Church of England in the eighteenth and early nineteenth centuries. They magnified examples of the undoubted faults of routine and unenthusiastic worship, place-serving and neglect of parish duties, taking little account of the fidelity of many clergy and the quiet devotion of both clergy and laity. They began a fashion, which lasted for a long time, of discounting much that had happened between the Act of Settlement and the Assize Sermon.

They were seen, and some of them at first saw themselves, as putting new life into the High Church party. Although High Churchmen held many of the Tractarian beliefs, the two were never identical and they drifted further away from each other as the Movement developed and changed. In addition to their doctrinal emphasis, the Tractarians brought a more romantic, and even emotional, spirituality into the experience of being a member of the Church of England. They gave more prominence to the feelings in personal devotion, something generally neglected by those whom they called 'High and Dry'. Their principle of Reserve made them distrust what seemed to them the excessive zeal of some Evangelicals. Their pursuit of holiness existed equally in Evangelical devotion, but they gave it a stronger discipline which linked it more firmly to the sacraments and ordinances of the Church. They did not fear the imagination, provided it was monitored by orthodoxy, and they could write and inspire poetry and fiction, some of which has kept its appeal today. The initiators of the Movement were comparatively young men, who could ride about pressing the Tracts upon bewildered parish clergy. Hurrell Froude, and later W. G. Ward, brought excitement, ebullience and a certain degree of confusion into theological issues.

While in one sense it is right to count the Tractarians among the great Anglican thinkers, it is a judgement which needs to be modified. For the most part, they were not speculative or systematic theologians, although their concerns were theological. What they gave to the Church was discipline and order rather than new light on doctrine, the beauty of holiness rather than the deeper philosophy of religion. Pusey's Tracts on baptism and on the Eucharist are the work of a theologian. The principle of Reserve, particularly as expounded by Isaac Williams, introduced something which had received little previous Anglican notice and which the religious temper of their age needed. Newman's wrestling with problems of authority and development bequeathed a rich legacy to the Church which he left. But for the Movement as a whole, the emphasis was on belief expressed in worship, its moral imperatives, and the reference of all aspects of life to the experienced presence of God. The rule of prayer, *lex orandi*, for them was not only linked to the rule of belief, *lex credendi*, but assayed and guided it.

By the end of the decade following Newman's secession, the Church of England, and all the other Christian Churches, were challenged in ways not envisaged in 1833. This is a familiar part of ecclesiastical history: the quarrel between science and religion, Darwinian evolution seeming to undermine the divine purpose in creation and continuing control of the world. Closer and more threatening to traditional faith, biblical criticism struck at the fundamentalist view of Scripture and in some quarters questioned the divinity of Christ. The speculations published in *Essays and Reviews* in 1860 caused its seven Anglican contributors to be described as 'the seven against Christ'. A new generation arose, heirs of the Tractarians in spirit and carrying on many of their principles, but guiding the Church in a different way. Charles Gore (1853–1932) was a leader in new lines of Church defence. The collection of essays by various writers which he edited under the title *Lux Mundi* in 1889 was more open on biblical criticism and incarnational theology, to a degree which alarmed some of the more conservative successors of the Tractarians, like H. P. Liddon (1829–90), Canon of St Paul's and admiring biographer of Pusey. For the ordinary church member, the continuing effect of the Movement was where the Tractarians themselves had placed it: on public and personal devotion. The ritualist conflicts and persecution described in the previous chapter caused a sensation but did not ultimately halt the gradual change in worship. The Eucharist was celebrated more frequently and attended not only with more ceremonial but with greater reverence and preparation. Priests who were evolving something more advanced from the Tractarian tradition tended to look to Rome for ways of celebrating the English liturgy. The Roman Catholic Church itself was in a baroque and ultramontane phase, which affected not only the public worship of Anglo-Catholics, but also their private devotions. Rosaries, novenas, stricter Lenten mortification, the practice of frequent confession as well as communion were the later expression of a Movement which had begun partly from alarm at the restoration of Roman Catholic civil and religious rights. By the beginning of the twentieth century, there was a division in Anglo-Catholicism between Roman and English liturgical use, ceremonial and vestments; between liberal but firm loyalty to the Book of Common Prayer and the introduction of elements from the Roman Missal and other concessions to what came to be called Anglo-Papalism.

The great years of post-Victorian Anglo-Catholicism were from around 1920 to 1950, with rallies and conferences, learned and popular publications; the support of some leading writers like T. S. Eliot, Charles Williams, Dorothy L. Sayers and Rose Macaulay. Like their Tractarian predecessors, the Anglo-Catholics gave high honour to the principle of episcopacy, but could defy the censures of individual bishops and lead opposition to those suspected of being less than orthodox. Even supporters of the English rite were becoming less satisfied with the Book of Common Prayer, seeking its revision in a more catholic and primitive direction, echoing criticisms already made by Isaac Williams in Tract 86. The proposal for a revision of the Prayer Book fell between Catholic and Protestant demands and was rejected by Parliament in 1927 and 1928, although the '1928 Book', closer to the First Prayer Book of 1549, was widely used by toleration and not authority.

In the 1950s the Parish and People Movement, mainly but not exclusively Anglo-Catholic, worked to make the Eucharist the principal Sunday parish service, more corporate, and with greater lay participation. Influenced especially by *The Shape of the Liturgy* by Gregory Dix (1901–52), they sought not a revision of the Prayer Book but its replacement by a new service book, both modernized and drawing on primitive liturgies. The combination was not always entirely successful, and the *Alternative Service Book (1980)* was replaced by the larger *Common Worship* (2000). The Church of England had become less divided into ecclesiastical parties; the new patterns of worship satisfied almost all, while the Book of Common Prayer, after suffering denigration and marginalizing, maintained its traditional strength and continued to be preferred by many. Of the six points of ceremonial so strongly opposed and defended in the previous century, four are found in most, though not all, churches. The eastward position has been replaced by the westward, with the celebrant facing the congregation, and only incense remains to mark a threshold crossed by the more advanced Anglo-Catholic. The Tractarians themselves were not concerned about the number of candles on the altar or the shape of a chasuble. What they did was to restore such reverence for the meaning of the Eucharist that their successors could feel responsibility for the importance of its outward signs.

These were some of the more visible results of the Oxford Movement, many of them matters which were not of first importance for the Tractarians themselves, although there was a direct line, which other influences had joined. The same was true also of other aspects. Social concern and regard for the poor was developed more firmly by the Broad Church Christian Socialists led by F. D. Maurice and Charles Kingsley in the 1850s. It was partly through work in slum parishes that Anglo-Catholic priests picked up this part of their inheritance: Dolling who is quoted above; Stanton, Lowther, Mackonochie; Stuart Headlam and the Guild of St George. More recent social statements like *Faith in the City* have a complex genealogy, but the voice of the Tractarians still echoes in the expressed connection of faith and conscience, of religious principles and social duties. Missionary work abroad, already active early in the nineteenth century, reached its fullest extent by its end. All the Churches had some input into foreign missions, with the result that many shades of doctrine and worship were taught according to who had got there first. Anglo-Catholicism was the force behind UMCA, the Universities Mission to Central Africa, founded in 1857. Bishop Charles Mackenzie, who led its first expedition, took Keble's *Christian Year* with him on his African journeys. John Coleridge Patteson, first Bishop of Melanesia, who was killed in the mission field in 1871, was in the same tradition and was celebrated in a biography by Charlotte M. Yonge.

From the late twentieth century the divisions between parties in the Church of England became less acute, within the wider growth of ecumenism. New tensions came with the ordination of women to the priesthood, and with disputes between those who appealed to more traditional doctrine and biblical interpretation and a more revisionist 'liberal' theology. New alliances brought Anglo-Catholics and Evangelicals closer together than at any time since the Oxford Movement. The heirs of that Movement would recognize themselves in the Evangelical organization 'Reform' as well as in 'Forward in Faith'. Yet many 'Affirming Catholics', supporters of the ordination of women and a more inclusive morality, would also acknowledge their debt to the Tractarians. The enduring contribution of those who came together in defence of the Church in 1833 is a belief that the Anglican ideal is not merely negative or protesting, or compromising; that zeal and reserve can live in a constructive tension; that both intellect and emotion have their proper place in faith; and that the beauty of holiness can be sought and found in public worship and private devotion.

Sources

W. J. E. Bennett, in O. Shipley, ed., *The Church and the World: Essays on Questions of the Day*, London: Longmans, 1867

J. W. Burgon, *Lives of Twelve Good Men* (1888), London: John Murray, 1889

R. W. Church, *The Oxford Movement: Twelve Years 1833–1845* (1891), London: Macmillan, 1909

R. H. Froude, *Remains of the late Reverend Richard Hurrell Froude M.A.*, London: Rivington, 1838

J. Garbett, *Christ as Prophet, Priest and King*, Oxford: for the author, 1842

W. Gresley, *Bernard Leslie*, London: Burns, 1842

W. Gresley, *Charles Lever*, London: Burns, 1841

W. Gresley, *Portrait of an English Churchman*, London: Rivington, 1840

W. F. Hook, *The Church and its Ordinances*, London: Bentley, 1876

J. Keble, *Lectures on Poetry*, trans. E. K. Francis, Oxford: Clarendon Press, 1912

J. Keble, *Sermons Academical and Occasional*, Oxford: Parker, 1848

J. Keble, *On Eucharistical Adoration*, Oxford: Parker, 1857

J. Keble, *The Christian Year* (1827), Oxford: Oxford University Press, 1914

J. Keble, *Lyra Innocentium* (1846), London: Methuen, 1903

H. P. Liddon, *Life of Edward Bouverie Pusey*, 4 vols, London: Longmans, 1893–97

Lyra Apostolica, Derby: Mozley (1836) 1841

J. M. Neale, *Sermons on Passages of the Prophets*, London: Hayes, 1877

J. M. Neale, *The Symbolism of Churches and Church Ornaments*, Leeds: Green, 1843

J. H. Newman, *The Arians of the Fourth Century*, London: Rivington, 1833

J. H. Newman, *Lectures on Justification*, London: Rivington, 1838

J. H. Newman, *Lectures on the Prophetical Office of the Church Viewed Relatively to Romanism and Popular Protestantism: The Via Media of the Anglican Church*, Oxford, Rivington: Parker, 1837

J. H. Newman, *The Letters and Diaries of John Henry Newman*, ed. T. Gornall, Oxford: Clarendon Press, 1981

J. H. Newman, 'Prospects of the Anglican Church', *British Critic*, April 1839

J. H. Newman, *Parochial Sermons*, London: Rivington, 1834–42

J. H. Newman, *Parochial and Plain Sermons*, London: Rivington (1838) 1877

J. H. Newman, *Sermons Bearing on Subjects of the* Day, London: Rivington, 1843

J. H. Newman, *Sermons, Chiefly on the Theory of Religious Belief, preached before the University of Oxford* (1843), 2nd edn, London: Rivington, 1844

J. H. Newman, *Verses on Various Occasions*, London: Burns Oates, 1880

C. F. Osborne, *The Life of Father Dolling*, London: Arnold, 1903

F. E. Paget, *The Warden of Berkingholt or Rich and Poor*, Oxford: Parker, 1843

William Palmer, *Ecclesiastical History*, London: Burns, 1841

William Palmer, *A Narrative of Events Connected with the Publication of the Tracts for the Times*, London: Rivington, 1883

William Palmer, *Origines Liturgicae* (1832), London: Rivington, 4th edn, 1845

A. P. Perceval, *A Collection of Papers Connected with Theological Movement of 1833*, London: Rivington, 1842

J. Purchas, *The Directorium Anglicanum*, 1858

E. B. Pusey, *Sermons During the Season From Advent to Whitsuntide*, Oxford: Parker, 1848

E. B. Pusey, *The Doctrine of the Real Presence*, Oxford: Parker, 1855

E. B. Pusey, *Letter to the Right Hon and Right Rev the Lord Bishop of London*, Oxford: Parker, 1851

E. B. Pusey, *Parochial Sermons*, Oxford: Parker, 1864

E. B. Pusey, *Nine Sermons preached before the University of Oxford*, Oxford: Parker, 1865

E. B. Pusey, *Tracts for the Times*, London: Rivington, 1833–40

J. H. Shorthouse, *John Inglesant* (1881), London: Macmillan, 1883

Vernon Staley, *The Catholic Religion* (1893), London: Mowbray, 1904

W. Walsh, *The Secret History of the Oxford Movement* (1897), London: Swan Sonnenschein, 1899

W. G. Ward, *The Idea of a Christian Church*, London: Toovey, 1844

Robert Wilberforce, *The Doctrine of the Incarnation of Our Lord Jesus Christ in its Relation to Mankind and to the Church* (1850), London: John Murray, 3rd edn, 1850

I. Williams, *The Baptistery*, Oxford: Parker, 1842

I. Williams, *The Cathedral*, Oxford: Parker, 1839

I. Williams, ed., *Plain Sermons by contributors to the Tracts for the Times*, 1840

I. Williams, *A Series of Sermons on the Epistle and Gospel for each Sunday in the Year and the Holy Days of the Church* (1853), 2nd edn, London: Rivington, 1855

I. Williams, *Thoughts in Past Years*, Oxford: Parker, 1838

Bibliography

Much has been written about the Oxford Movement; this list is selective, not definitive.

A. M. Allchin, *The Silent Rebellion: Anglican Religious Communities 1845–1900*, London: SCM Press, 1958

J. E. Baker, *The Novel and the Oxford Movement*, Princeton: Princeton University Press, 1932

G. Battiscombe, *John Keble: A Study in Limitations*, London: Constable, 1963

J. Bentley, *Ritualism and Politics in Victorian England*, Oxford: Clarendon Press, 1978

Piers Brendon, *Hurrell Froude and the Oxford Movement*, London: Paul Elek, 1974

Yngve Brilioth, *The Anglican Revival*, London: Longmans, Green, 1925

Perry Butler, ed., *Pusey Rediscovered*, London: SPCK, 1983

Owen Chadwick, *The Mind of the Oxford Movement*, London: A & C Black, 1960

Owen Chadwick, *The Spirit of the Oxford Movement: Tractarian Essays*, Cambridge: Cambridge University Press, 1990

Owen Chadwick, *The Victorian Church*, 2 vols, London: A & C Black, 1966–70

Raymond Chapman, *Faith and Revolt: Studies in the Literary Influence of the Oxford Movement*, London: Weidenfeld & Nicolson, 1970

C. S. Dessain, *John Henry Newman*, London: Nelson, 1966

Geoffrey Faber, *Oxford Apostles*, London: Faber and Faber, 1933, 2nd edn 1974

C. B. Faught, *The Oxford Movement: A Thematic History of the Tractarians and their Times*, Pennsylvania: Pennsylvania State University Press, 2003

David Forrester, *Young Doctor Pusey*, London: SPCK, 1989

Sheridan Gilley, *Newman and his Age*, London: Darton, Longman and Todd, 1990

A. Hardelin, *The Tractarian Understanding of the Eucharist*, Uppsala: Almqvist and Wiksell, 1965

E. Jay, *The Evangelical and Oxford Movements*, Cambridge: Cambridge University Press, 1983

O. W. Jones, *Isaac Williams and his Circle*, London: SPCK, 1971

Terence Kenny, *The Political Thought of John Henry Newman*, London: Longmans, 1957

Ian Ker, *John Henry Newman: A Biography*, Oxford: Oxford University Press, 1988

Ian Ker and Alan G. Hill, eds, *Newman after a Hundred Years*, Oxford: Clarendon Press, 1990

B. W. Martin, *John Henry Newman, His Life and Work*, London: Chatto and Windus, 1982

B. W. Martin, *John Keble, Priest, Professor and Poet*, London: Croom Helm, 1976

David Newsome, *The Parting of Friends: A Study of the Wilberforces and the Mannings*, Cambridge, Mass.: Harvard University Press, 1966

P. B. Nockles, *The Oxford Movement in Context*, Cambridge: Cambridge University Press, 1994

M. R. O'Connell, *The Oxford Conspirators: A History of the Oxford Movement*, London: Macmillan, 1969

Herbert Paul, *The Life of Froude*, London: Pitman, 1906

W. G. Peck, *The Social Implications of the Oxford Movement*, New York: Scribners, 1934

W. S. F. Pickering, *Anglo-Catholicism: A Study in Religious Ambiguity*, London: Mowbray, 1989

John Shelton Reed, *Glorious Battle: The Cultural Politics of Victorian Anglo-Catholicism*, Nashville, Tenn.: Vanderbilt University Press, 1996

Geoffrey Rowell, *The Vision Glorious: Themes and Personalities of the Catholic Revival in Anglicanism*, Oxford: Oxford University Press, 1983

J. H. L. Rowlands, *Church, State and Society: The Attitudes of John Keble, Richard Hurrell Froude and John Henry Newman 1837–1845*, Worthing: Churchman Publishing, 1989

S. A. Skinner, *Tractarians and the 'Condition of England': The Social and Political Thought of the Oxford Movement*, Oxford: Clarendon Press, 2004

G. B. Tennyson, *Victorian Devotional Poetry: The Tractarian Mode*, Cambridge, Mass.: Harvard University Press, 1981

Meriel Trevor, *Newman: The Pillar of the Cloud*, London: Macmillan, 1962

Paul Vaiss, ed., *From Oxford to the People: Reconsidering Newman and the Oxford Movement*, Leominster: Gracewing, 1996

J. F. White, *The Cambridge Movement*, Cambridge: Cambridge University Press, 1962

Nigel Yates, *Anglican Ritual in Victorian Britain 1830–1910*, Oxford: Oxford University Press, 1999

Index of Authors